Theories of Sustainable Development

T0384438

While sustainability has become a buzzword in discussions about the environment and development, work on theories of sustainable development has received much less attention. However, theory is vital as understanding the origins and development of the concept is the key to achieving successful implementation of sustainability.

This book offers an interdisciplinary collection of research articles on the theories of sustainable development, drawing on a wide range of subjects including history, politics, governance, complex systems, economics and philosophy. It advocates viewing sustainable development not only as the establishment of a permanent, globally practicable and future-capable mode of life and economics, but as a complex array of problems involving a wide range of social-scientific and humanistic disciplines. This innovative approach means that the book is oriented toward current problems, not toward the established academic boundaries, and it draws out lessons that are relevant for those studying and working in sustainability across the world.

This book will be of great interest to researchers and students of sustainable development and environmental politics, as well as practitioners working with sustainable development in politics, business, administration, and civil society organizations.

Judith C. Enders is a member of the study group "Global Issues" of the German Council on Foreign Relations (DGAP). She was Senior Researcher at the Institute for Advanced Sustainability Studies in Potsdam, Germany, and is now conducting freelance social research.

Moritz Remig is a Researcher at the Institute for Advanced Sustainability Studies in Potsdam, Germany, and a PhD candidate at the University of Kassel, Germany.

Routledge Studies in Sustainable Development

This series uniquely brings together original and cutting-edge research on sustainable development. The books in this series tackle difficult and important issues in sustainable development including: values and ethics; sustainability in higher education; climate compatible development; resilience; capitalism and de-growth; sustainable urban development; gender and participation; and well-being.

Drawing on a wide range of disciplines, the series promotes interdisciplinary research for an international readership. The series was recommended in the *Guardian's* suggested reads on development and the environment.

Institutional and Social Innovation for Sustainable Urban Development
Edited by Harald A. Mieg and Klaus Töpfer

The Sustainable University
Progress and prospects
Edited by Stephen Sterling, Larch Maxey and Heather Luna

Sustainable Development in Amazonia
Paradise in the making
Kei Otsuki

Measuring and Evaluating Sustainability
Ethics in sustainability indexes
Sarah E. Fredericks

Values in Sustainable Development
Edited by Jack Appleton

Climate-Resilient Development
Participatory solutions from developing countries
Edited by Astrid Carrapatoso and Edith Kürzinger

Theatre for Women's Participation in Sustainable Development
Beth Osnes

Theories of Sustainable Development

Edited by Judith C. Enders and
Moritz Remig

Routledge
Taylor & Francis Group

LONDON AND NEW YORK

First published 2015
by Routledge
2 Park Square, Milton Park, Abingdon, Oxfordshire OX14 4RN

and by Routledge
711 Third Avenue, New York, NY 10017

First issued in paperback 2016

Routledge is an imprint of the Taylor & Francis Group, an informa business

British Library Cataloguing-in-Publication Data
A catalogue record for this book is available from the British Library

Library of Congress Cataloging-in-Publication Data
A catalog record has been requested

ISBN 13: 978-0-415-39025-5 (pbk)
ISBN 13: 978-1-138-79636-2 (hbk)

Translated from the German by Phil Hill.

Typeset in Goudy
by Apex CoVantage, LLC

Contents

Foreword

The German-speaking environmental research community is more or less convinced that the concept of sustainability, which is so popular since the Brundtland report (1987) and the UN Conference for Environment and Development
(1992), is rooted in eighteenth-century German forestry. Hans Carl von Carlowitz is seen as the founding father and the spiritus rector of the modern idea
of sustainable development, which says that we have to find the right balance
between resource use and the regeneration of natural capital. No doubt, his book
Sylvicultura oeconomica (1713) should be regarded as one of the key documents
to understand the modern sustainability debate. His imperative was simple, but
convincing: do not harvest more wood (or in general: renewable resources) that
nature can reproduce in a given period of time. But one should not forget that
the background of Carlowitz was not just (sustainable) forestry but also mining and generating state income. Problems of overusing nonrenewable resources
(e.g. mining of coal and ore) and environmental pollution (particulates, sulphur
dioxide, nitrous oxide, carbon dioxide, etc.) were not yet in his focus. How could
they? He was a child of his time.

The mainly quantitative approach ("Don't take more wood than the quantity
that is growing again in a given period!") was not so much concerned about
protecting biodiversity but about assuring the needed flow of wood for mining,
construction and the economy as a whole. Furthermore, the enclosure of forests
and the "crowding out" of herders and their cattle out of the woods was not what
we today understand as "social sustainability." Those people "disturbed" the rational use of resources. I think that Carlowitz and his ideas deserve a special place
in the modern sustainability discourse, but they were definitely not "holistic" in a
sense that they fully integrated ecological, social and economic aspects of human
development. Carlowitz's thinking has its roots in Freiberg, the place of mining
and efficient forestry, and not so much in Weimar, the place of German classicism
and idealism.

By saying that sustainability in its eighteenth-century version is mainly driven
by utilitarian ideas I don't say that it is irrelevant to our present times. But we
should contextualize it and recognize that aspects like nature conservation, biodiversity protection and social coherence are equally important. If we don't go for

an integrated or "holistic" approach there is a real danger that sustainable development sooner or later becomes a technocratic concept that leaves out of consideration the social and cultural dimensions. Sustainability is more than number crunching and defining limits and (emissions) budgets; it is about a shared vision, political strategies, lifestyle changes and new social practices. And, yes, it is about conflicts and problem solving. Sometimes the sustainability debate is too "toothless" and too naïve and ignores that there are vested interests that cannot be convinced only by argument.

Over the last two decades we have almost seen a boom of sustainability research, practice and rhetoric. "Green growth" is almost a new buzzword in economic discussions. Real progress has been made in some areas. I will just mention the protection of the ozone layer or the growth of renewable energies in Europe. But if we are honest to ourselves we have to admit that all this is far from being sufficient. Climate change is not at all tackled in an adequate manner, resource use is increasing permanently, biodiversity is still on the decline, the oceans are overfished, over mined, over polluted, desertification is not under control in many parts of the world, and pollution is exploding in the megacities of the southern hemisphere. And even in the "clean" and rich world of Europe, Northern America, Japan and Australia, old problems turn out to be very persistent and new problems arise: from gas fracking to particulate emissions and smog, from groundwater pollution to overfertilization of agricultural lands by intensive agriculture. And all this after almost three decades of modern sustainability talk. What does this mean? Should we give up and become pessimistic and hopeless? Is sustainability an illusion in the meantime and is the only option we have to go for resilience, to make our societies more robust against environmental problems? Or are there still alternatives?

It is the merit of this book by Judith C. Enders, Moritz Remig and their coauthors to systematically discuss the challenges of global environmental change and structure the various approaches to tackle the problem from a philosophical, scientific, technological, cultural and historical perspective. After having read the book it is no longer possible to discuss sustainability in an arbitrary and vague way as it is so popular today among policy makers. Many of them prefer a "broad" (which in fact means a nonbinding) definition of sustainability. But what we need is a clear definition so that we can measure deadlock, regression and (hopefully) progress not just in quantitative but also in qualitative terms. This book is a must for those who really want to understand where the idea comes from and what it means to us as researchers and politically interested and engaged citizens.

Reinhard Loske, Witten/Herdecke
May 2014

1 Theories of sustainable development

An introduction

Judith C. Enders and Moritz Remig

The term sustainable development has received much attention in many spheres: in scientific discourses, in daily life practices, in international negotiations, in local policy measures, in marketing, in business. While the use of the term "sustainability" has become almost inflationary in both science and society, the work on theories of sustainable development has received much less attention. The aim of this interdisciplinary book is to fill this gap and resume the debate on theories of sustainability. It provides a collection of interdisciplinary research articles: history, politics, governance, complex systems, economics, philosophy and cultural studies are only but some approaches this book builds upon.

Many current trends around the globe are unsustainable. We are losing biodiversity and fertile soils; we are contributing to climate change on larger and larger scales; inequalities within and among generations are rising; poverty remains yet to be overcome. These challenges are interconnected and require a joint effort to give rise to sustainable lifestyle and durable development patterns. Prosperity for all within the limits of the carrying capacity of our planet is what sustainable development aims to achieve.

Sustainable development is also a topic to which scientists contribute. To solve problems of unsustainability, interdisciplinary and transdisciplinary research cooperation is necessary because monodisciplinary approaches often fail to capture the interconnected nature of sustainability and global environmental change. Solutions to the problems of the interconnected environmental, economic, and social spheres cannot be reduced to mere technical engineering, but must include social innovations, institutions, innovative governance mechanisms, and politics.

These interdisciplinary and transdisciplinary approaches necessitate simultaneous bridges between different scientific disciplines, which deal with sustainability as a research topic. Yet, it also requires cooperation between scientist and other societal actors. Since the nature of the problems above is also due to a lack of governance and collective action, a bridge between natural sciences and social sciences is required. Many of these bridges have already been constructed; in this book we contribute to strengthen their pillars.

This movement within the scientific community has contributed to the establishment of sustainability sciences to which we are contributing a social sciences perspective. Some universities have founded faculties of sustainability studies, specific scientific societies with their own journals on sustainable development exist, and courses on sustainability are offered at many universities. Sustainable development as a cross-cutting topic is becoming more and more established.

The book is an academic book. Its scope, however, is not restricted to the scientific community alone. The research book can serve as a textbook for courses on sustainable development and environmental politics. Theorizing sustainable development also has implications for the implementation of sustainability. It is necessary to know the development – both in theory and practice – of a concept like sustainability in order to achieve a successful implementation. Therefore, the book is also of interest to all those engaged with sustainable development in politics, business, administration, and civil society organizations. For all those working on sustainable development, this book underpins the practical work by contributing to theory development.

Overview of the book

Ulrich Grober provides a genealogy of the term "sustainable development," which he traces back to Carl von Carlowitz some 300 years ago. While the idea of sustainable development has emerged in many cultures of the world, the conceptualization of sustainable development as such began with Carlowitz in seventeenth-century Europe. Sustainable development can be understood in its complexity only by ensuring that its history embedded in thought traditions be recalled to consciousness once again. Following the evolution of the concept of "sustainable development" from Carlowitz to the Brundtland Commission, Grober's journey through the concept's history has implications for how to implement sustainability today.

Armin Grunwald treats sustainable development conceptually from a different yet complementary perspective. He proposes strategies to overcome several difficulties on the way to a theory of sustainable development. Due to the specific structure of the term "sustainability," particularly the fact that it is not a genuinely scientific term, but rather ultimately a societal and thus political program, it becomes apparent that what is at issue is not the development of a theory of sustainability analogous to a theory of physics. Of highest importance is the constellation that the relation of theory and practice is, on the one hand, inherent in the very notion of sustainability, and on the other, must itself be elucidated theoretically.

Transdisciplinarity is at the heart of the chapter by Thomas Jahn. He shows that the "disciplining" of sustainability knowledge, which is increasingly being demanded, misses the point. On the contrary, it opens the door to counterproductive misunderstandings. Alternatively he argues, thus, for transdisciplinary research for sustainable development that includes a broader stock of knowledge than disciplinary science. He interprets sustainability as a relational concept that should ensure resilient societies. The transformations towards sustainability must overcome some "wicked" problems, which according to Jahn require the inclusion of nonscientific knowledge: orientation knowledge on the normative level, transformation knowledge on the operative level, and system knowledge on the descriptive level.

The article by Rafael Ziegler and Konrad Ott is a revised and updated version of their article "The quality of sustainability science: A philosophical perspective." In this paper they elaborate on the reasons why sustainable development cannot be treated as a monodisciplinary topic. They argue that sustainability science does not fit standard criteria of the quality of sciences. Normativity, inclusion of nonscientists, urgency, and cooperation of natural and social scientists are four particular features of sustainability science. In transdisciplinary research processes, nonscientists must be understood within this demanding context, instead of including them for the sake of inclusion. The discussion in this article also refers to the foundational controversy of sustainability science: the weak versus strong sustainability debate. Normativity, inclusion of nonscientists, urgency, and cooperation of natural and social scientists suggest a convincing case for strong sustainability.

Felix Ekardt presents a social sciences' perspective on sustainable development including societal change, justice, and governance. The key aspect here is not the natural-scientific, but rather the humanistic aspect. Ekardt views sustainable development, not only as the establishment of a permanent, globally practicable and future-capable mode of life and economics, but rather as a complex array of problems, involving a wide range of social-scientific and humanistic disciplines – law, political science, sociology, economics, theology, psychology, philosophy. The article lays out some of the barriers that make societal transformations towards sustainability difficult. It gives a perspective from ethics inspired by a (re-)interpretation of national constitutions, the EU Charter of fundamental rights, and the European convention on human rights in the light of sustainability. Ekardt also argues for a governance architecture that includes multiple instruments on different scales.

Fred Luks's chapter deals on the one hand with the drivers and pressures of our growth-oriented society opposing efficiency and generosity. On the other hand, he argues against simple and mainstream solutions. This essay is about the questions which, in Luks's view, are central to this effort, or should be: What could an attractive alternative construct to the dominant growth-and-efficiency paradigm look like? What will the future role of resiliency be – that quality which currently seems to be the hottest candidate for sharpening and vitalizing the discourse on "sustainability?" And, last but not least: What is to be done in light of the danger of a certain kind of "populism of simple solutions," which seems to be increasingly in evidence in the sustainability discourse? Generosity and resilience are key concept in this contribution.

Joachim H. Spangenberg picks up the issue of complexity. His paper analyzes complexity gradients of natural and social systems which permit an evaluation of the suitability of various models that represent specific system dynamics. As for systems as complex like nature, society, or the economy, the available models have proven, almost without exception, to be insufficiently complex. An alternative is introduced. For economics in particular, the analysis shows that the complexity of real economies by far exceeds that of neoclassical mental and econometric models. Consequently, the latter are suitable as instruments of analysis only in special cases.

Jürgen Kopfmüller elucidates the tension between a universal model of sustainable development and its contextual applications: The concept of sustainable development has been discussed for more than twenty years as a comprehensive and global approach to development, and attempts have been made to implement it through concrete action. Kopfmüller argues that it emerged as a political reaction to the increasing environmental and development issues during the second half of the twentieth century. Today, there are few who question its position as a development model for science, government, business, and civil society. Nevertheless, there are still significant controversies regarding the concrete definition of its goal orientation, and the implementation of its goals. Based on reflections of human rights and international climate policy, the article shows how sustainability might be operationalized through an appropriate linkage between universal and specific, context-referenced elements.

Sustainability is about the long term and thus involves both intergenerational and intragenerational justice considerations. Jörg Tremmel focuses on a particular challenge concerning the relationship with future generations. During the past decades, generational ethics has become firmly established as a branch of ethics, and there is now extensive literature on such theories. Arguments directed against them are thus in effect aimed at sustainability theory in general, so that theoreticians of sustainability are well advised to address them. Of particular interest are arguments which generally deny any obligation toward the generations to come. Tremmel focuses on the non-identity problem, which has often been viewed as a serious challenge to theories of sustainability and intergenerational justice. He concludes that any government policy only accounts for a miniscule causal factor in a network of billions of other miniscule factors in the determination of who will exist in the future. This effectively refutes the non-identity problem as a theoretical stumbling block for theories of sustainability and intergenerational justice, according to Tremmel.

Michael Weingarten's chapter seeks to formulate the basic conditions under which the issue of sustainability might be transformed from his historic model into a program of development theory. Development can be defined as non-identical reproduction. The implementation of this initially very formal definition can be oriented toward research programs initiated primarily by social geography, as a reconstruction of spatial structuring. The main topic of this paper is to show that ecology as a biological discipline and sustainability science as a science dealing with the relations between nature and culture are based on different kinds of items. These items are not natural kinds existing independent of human purposes and actions, but are cultural kinds constituted by us reflecting the purposes of our actions. His notion of environmental sciences encompasses the society-nature relationships. To constitute the item of sustainability science, it is thus necessary to complement the theory of structuration with a concept of reproduction.

Oliver Parodi argues that (non-)sustainability, the debates and efforts for sustainable development, as well as barriers to their implementation, are highly cultural phenomena. However, this fact has received too little elucidation and reflection in the academic discourse. An increased incorporation of cultural-scientific and cultural-theoretical considerations into the theories and concepts of sustainable development provides a more comprehensive view including issues which have hitherto been too little examined. Hence, cultural perspectives contribute to the societal transformations towards sustainable development.

Hans Diefenbacher concludes the book with ten theses on a research agenda for sustainable development. Among others, Diefenbacher argues for a broader inclusion of courses on sustainable development in education. The issue of sustainability in an interdisciplinary or even transdisciplinary perspective has yet to be adopted into the established curricula.

This call for a broader integration of sustainable development in education curricula is consistent with the aims of this book on Theorizing Sustainable Development. Addressing scholars, teachers, politicians, civil society representatives, and all practitioners of sustainable development, this book contributes to a deepening of our thinking and practice of sustainable development. Other theses concentrate on the research agenda between sufficiency and efficiency issues, on the fatal consequences of the dominance of GDP as a political orientation, and on alternative monitoring and measurement concepts of wealth and well-being.

Outlook

The insights, controversies, and inquiries into theories of sustainable development as portrayed in this book give rise to a series of further questions for a research agenda on sustainable development. The discussion of theories of sustainable development is a first step towards sustainability transitions. How such societal transformations – towards more sustainable lifestyles, more sustainable consumption and production patterns, and towards more social justice – can be implemented is yet worth further research.

The quest for sustainability and for human development within the limits of our planet is a global effort. As this book shows, sustainability rather than a uniform concept is a guiding idea that can be implemented differently depending on the cultural and societal context in different regions of the world. The development of such sustainable development pathways for countries, for regions, and on the global level is a joint effort that must include many stakeholders. For sustainability sciences, this can be achieved, for example, by including non-scientific actors in the research process as some articles here argue.

A major task ahead of us is the transformation towards sustainable development pathways and lifestyles. Both theory and practice of sustainability have to be in accordance with each other. Sustainability sciences can provide us some of the necessary tools, concepts, ideas, and methods to achieve these transformations. Such a societal project cannot be solely a scientific one; it requires the participation and inclusion of citizens. For scientists, this task of transdisciplinary sustainability studies is but one contribution to the public good of living in harmony with nature.

2 The discovery of sustainability

The genealogy of a term

Ulrich Grober

Why concern oneself with the genealogy of a term? Does that amount to more than just a "glass bead game"? Is it not more important to "disassemble" and simplify general concepts, operationalize them, and implement them in practice?

In this case, however, various approaches seem to be necessary. Our word, "sustainability" – in German, "*Nachhaltigkeit*" – has become a key term, a guiding concept in the global vocabulary of the twenty-first century. Since the Earth Summit in Rio in 1992, it has established itself as the center of a whole field of concepts. Around it orbit an array of other terms, which develop, take root, come and go. The status of the key term was once more reaffirmed by the UN Conference on Sustainable Development in June 2012 – the "Rio+20" conference.

Given its meteoric ascent to fame, it would at first glance appear surprising that there is no binding definition for this term, and hardly any awareness of its history. The growing worldwide movement which has adopted this term has rather been operating with a flexible inventory of stipulations which a sustainability strategy should fulfill. The term thus serves as a compass which provides orientation for a journey towards a more sustainable future. This openness is necessary; indeed, it is a strength of the concept. However, it also makes it vulnerable to manipulative misuse. Complaints regarding the "inflationary use," "arbitrariness," or "hollowing out" of the concept have in fact become commonplace.

What is to be done? My proposed path in order to clarify and sharpen the term would proceed by way of its conceptual history, that is the way it has been charged with meaning over a long time. The concept of sustainability is not an invention of our time. It can be understood in its complexity only by recalling its history, and its embedding in long thought traditions. From the many aspects which have already been ascertained and considered in the course of its history, a feeling for how to approach its current and future tasks emerges. A look into the mirror of its historical sources can open up a view upon the term's vital essence.

First reflection

In March 1972, the famous future scenario of the Club of Rome was published under the title *The Limits of Growth*. The passage reads:

We are searching for a model output that represents a world system that is 1. sustainable without sudden and uncontrollable collapse; and 2. capable of satisfying the basic material requirements of all of its people.

(Meadows 1972, p. 158)

As far as I know, the English word "sustainable" appears here for the first time in the modern sense. It refers to a model of the future which is "sustainable," or resilient to "sudden and uncontrollable collapse." At the same time, this model is to ensure the "basic material requirements" of all people on this planet.

What exactly does "sustainable" mean? The second element of the term, "-able," of course means "capable of" or "in a position to" do something. The verb "to sustain," on the other hand, is more complex. The 1961 edition of the *Oxford English Dictionary* dedicates several columns to it, and traces it back to the Middle Ages. Of the various definitions, the fourth gives the meaning that appears most interesting to us: it is "to keep in being," in other words to maintain the existence of something. The next definition is "to cause to continue in a certain state," and the one after that, "to keep or maintain at the proper level or standard," and finally, "to preserve the state of." Thus, sustainable means to be able to "maintain," to "preserve," or to "bear, as a load." It stems from the Latin *sustinere*, which various Latin–English dictionaries render as "support," "sustain," or "hold back."

In sum, "sustainable" in various languages means, and has always meant, structures which can hold up, which can bear a load. That is the essential constant in the structure of this term.

A comparison involving the German word for sustainability, *Nachhaltigkeit*, will show the continuity at the semantical level. The German dictionary *Wörterbuch der deutschen Sprache*, published in Brunswick in 1809 by Joachim Heinrich Campe, presumably contains the first dictionary definition of *nachhaltig*. At the time of Goethe, Campe was anything but unknown. In Berlin, he served as a tutor for the Humboldt family, and he would later translate Daniel Defoe's novel *Robinson Crusoe* into German; he was also a prominent supporter of the French Revolution. His dictionary for the first time contained various derivations of the verb *nachhalten*, which he defined as "to have firmness [*Nachhalt*], continuing still longer, persisting" (Campe 1809, p. 403). The noun *Nachhalt* he in turn defined as "the steadfastness which one retains after or beyond others, and to which one holds on to when everything else does not hold any more." *Nachhaltigkeit*, finally, was "the state, the constitution of a thing which is *nachhaltig*."

What is interesting about this parallel of linguistic events, the seminal German dictionary of 1809 and the pathbreaking report of 1972, is that in both cases, sustainability/*Nachhaltigkeit* appears as the opposite of "collapse."

This is what makes the definition so evidently current in our time, at the beginning of the twenty-first century, which appears paralyzed by fears of the "meltdown" of the financial system, the economic "crash," and the "failure" of entire societies. The concept focuses on what is resilient to collapse. To adopt Karl Polanyi's phrase, it represents the "self-protection of society" against the disruptive forces of the markets. To allow, in cold blood, structures which are not sustainable to collapse, and instead to raise the ante so as to strengthen exist-ing sustainable structures, and implement new ones – that is what appears to be the appropriate strategy that will permit us to emerge from the crisis reinforced. However, that requires that we be able to distinguish precisely between what is sustainable and what is non-sustainable.

My archaeology of the term is designed to strengthen this critical capacity to distinguish, by digging down to uncover the prehistoric levels.

An urtext: The theology of providence

Considerations as to what might provide resilience against the collapse have deep roots in the world's cultures. They always involve "the capacity to foresee and to forestall" (Albert Schweitzer, quoted by Carson 1965, Dedication). I would like first of all to present a thought model that I consider an "urtext" of Euro-pean sustainability thinking: the teaching of *providentia* – or divine providence in Christian theology (see Grober 2012, pp. 38–43). This conception describes the divine ability to think and act into eternity. Prediction leads to a preknowledge of things. That which is foreseen, which corresponds to that which is desired, requires measures to ensure that it comes to be, in other words precaution. This in turn requires action appropriate to the intended goal at any given moment.

The structure of providential action has three bearing elements. The funda-mental one is *conservation*, or, too, *sustentatio*. This means preserving, protecting all things in the manner of their existence as established by creation. It is the continuation of creation, and prevents the falling back into nothingness, the *annihilation* – or the collapse. Here, we already see the polarity outlined above.

Gubernatio refers to the steering and leading processes, the exercise of govern-ment over things. An element of that is *cura*, care and caring, including a caring handling of creation. The signs of divine *gubernatio* are the phenomena which occur according to the laws of nature: the consistency of cosmic motion, the regularity of the sequence of the seasons, the water cycle, and the sequence of generations in the natural realms.

The third element of *providentia* is *concursus*, the flowing together or the inter-action of various effective causes. This involves the relationship between divine effect (*actio externa*), the effects of the forces of nature, and free human actions. Divine action is the *prima causa*, the primal cause. Natural forces and human cooperation (*cooperatio*) are *secundae causae*, secondary causes, but also with lee-way, and with their own effects and side effects. Finally, the teaching of *concursus* also addresses the tricky question of how evil affects the course of things. Divine *gubernatio* switches between the options of permission (*permissio*), prevention (*impeditio*), orientation towards divine goals (*directio*), and limitation (*terminatio*) of evil.

Belief in divine providence began to crumble during the eighteenth century. Even theology abandoned it. But its language continues to have an effect in secu-larized systems of thought. The vocabulary of *providentia* reappears today in the global sustainability discourse. The old key concept of *conservatio* has remained almost entirely unchanged in English and in French. Its meaning of *preserving use* has become the counter-term to "over-exploitation" and "environmental destruction." In 1980, without much ado, the International Union for the Conservation of Nature (IUCN) equated "conservation" with "sustainable development" (see below). International policy think tanks today vehemently discuss "global governance" or "earth-system governance" – the old concept of *gubernatio*, or steering, in new attire. In the triangle of sustainability, what is at issue is the integration of ecology, economy, and social forces, i.e., the *cooperatio* of nature and humankind. That is what was once called *concursus*. And what does *terminatio*, the limitation of evil, tell us? At the Climate Summits, the controversy is about the *limitation* of CO_2 emissions. As we are debating – once again – *the limits to growth*, films and books are proposing ever new images of *annihilatio*, the destruction of the planet – the ultimate collapse. Faith has disappeared – yet the conceptual framework of the trust in divine providence has been adapted.

"The time is out of joint," Shakespeare's Hamlet announced around the year 1600 on the stage of London's Globe Theatre and continued, "O cursed spite, that ever I was born to set it right" (Act 1, Scene 5). Shortly thereafter, in 1637, the phrase "*cogito, ergo sum*" was pronounced in Leiden, the Netherlands: "I think, therefore I am." If the world has come out of joint, and, hence, God, having created the mechanism and brought it into operation, has now vanished from the scene, then the hope for the preservation of creation ultimately rests only on the certainty that one is a thinking subject. "Reason to power!" seemed to Descartes the last way out in a time of all-encompassing crisis.

"Self-preservation" – *conservatio sui* – became the central project of the Enlightenment. The path was to win domination over nature, to take possession of her, to impose order upon her. This was done using the method of rational thought: only to recognize as true that which is evident and provable. To take a thing apart, into as many pieces as necessary, to dissect, to analyze, to measure, to reorder and design them – that was the avenue to be taken, upon which the human could imagine himself to be *maitre et posesseur* – lord and master of nature. This view is certainly engraved in the idea of sustainability. But in the long run it is not sustainable. A pupil and critic of Descartes' – also in Leiden – designed a counter-model: from Spinoza's *Ethic* a highly developed theory of sustainability can be distilled (see Grober 2012, pp. 53–56).

Suum esse conservare – to preserve one's own being; preservation, he said, was the fundamental drive (*conatus*) of the human being – as it was, too, for Descartes. Spinoza, however, formulated a radical counterproposal to Descartes. It undertakes the greatest conceivable upgrading of nature: it pronounces God and nature to be identical: *deus sive natura*: God is nature. Nature is God. Here is the primal cause of all existence, including all thinking. The more we know the single phenomena of nature, the more we know God. Spinoza observed nature from two perspectives: *natura naturata* was the "worked," the created, as it were, the empirical nature. Distinct from it he saw *natura naturans*, the living, active, and productive force working within the *natura naturata*. The distinction is essential. As the *natura naturata*, nature is at the disposal of human will. It is manipulable and reproducible. The vital forces of *natura naturans*, however, are overpowering and non-disposable. They are the fullness of life, the power of life itself.

That topples the claim of the human race to power. The classification of natural phenomena into good and evil, useful and harmful, undeveloped and developed, becomes obsolete, and is replaced by the indivisible web of life. As opposed to Descartes' crowning of humankind as the lord and master over nature, Spinoza insists that *humans, too, are part of nature*. In that respect, he in no way abandons the project of "human self-assertion"; rather, he embeds it in a greater ecological context.

Suum esse conservare, the preservation of one's own being – this basic natural drive is the point of departure for all desire, and hence, too, for economic activity. Since its expulsion from paradise, humankind has been responsible for that, too. This economic securing of human existence can, however, only succeed in harmony with nature.

We do not produce the riches of nature; we find them before us. Our freedom consists of bringing our striving into line with reason, which means with the *order of the entire natural world*. Where that succeeds, we can *be completely at peace, and seek to remain permanently in this peace*.

What does that mean for the design of our common society? Reason demands that we tie the preservation of our own being not only to the preservation of the natural foundations of life, but also to the welfare of others. Spinoza states that it is obvious "that human beings can obtain their necessities of life more easily through mutual aid, and that only with combined forces can they avoid the dangers that threaten them from all sides" (quoted by Grober 2012, p. 55). As opposed to the law of the jungle of free competition, he posits the just distribution of goods, and the *potentia multitudinis*, the democratic power of the many.

Blueprint: Sustained yield forestry

During Descartes' and Spinoza's lifetimes, in seventeenth-century Europe, a looming resource crisis emerged as a key economic and political issue. Like today's discussions around such code words as "peak oil," or "the end of oil," people at that time talked about the looming shortage of wood – the most important resource of the day. *"La France perira faute de bois"* – "France will perish for want of wood" – was a commonplace phrase in Louis XIV's day. The capacity to foresee and exercise precaution focused all over Europe on the management of forests.

The actual creator of the classical concept of *Nachhaltigkeit*, blueprint of the modern concept of sustainability in the eighteenth century, was a Saxon cameralist by the name of Hans Carl von Carlowitz (see Grober 2012, pp. 80–85). His portrait shows a self-assured aristocrat, a Baroque figure. Carlowitz was the director of Saxony's Supreme Office of Mines in Freiberg, a position in which he managed the entire silver-mining operation of the Ore Mountains, one of Europe's leading mining regions. The region around Freiberg had largely been clear-cut, so that the most important resource for smelting silver ore was becoming scarce. The shutdown of the mining operations was, as it were, the writing on the wall. In 1713, Carlowitz published his book *Sylvicultura oeconomica oder Anweisung zur wilden Baumzucht* (Economical silviculture, or instruction on the raising of wild trees).

Criticizing the over-exploitation and devastation of forests, the *Sylvicultura oeconomica* stipulated the rule "that wood should be used with care (pfleglich)." In this context, the word *nachhaltig* appeared for the first time. It differed from the traditional term *pfleglich*, in that it combined the notion of long-term continuity with the notion of spatial stability, and was thus able to more clearly incorporate the idea of rationing resources, in other words, the temporal dimension, or the future capability of the use of natural resources. Carlowitz addressed the question as to

> how such a conservation and cultivation of wood can be arranged, so as to make possible a continuous, steady and *sustaining use [nachhaltende Nutzung]*, as this is an indispensable necessity, without which the country cannot maintain its Being.
>
> (Quoted by Grober 2012, p. 83)

Thus it is here, in its participle form *nachhaltend*, and with reference to the then key resource, wood, that the German word *nachhaltig (sustainable)* first appears in the modern sense. We can see at this point how Carlowitz is literally searching and groping for a new concept. He takes a word from everyday speech, *nachhalten*, places it in a sequence with words of similar meaning – constant, continuous – and then he combines it with a generally understood noun, also from everyday speech, to form "nachhaltende Nutzung" – "sustaining use" – of resources, without which the country in its "esse," its existence, "may not endure," in other words, would collapse. This is, indeed, a prominent place in the book. Of course, Carlowitz provides no definition of the term. Only later would this borrowing from everyday language become a technical concept. It was in this way that scientific language emerged during the early part of the Age of Enlightenment; previously, only Latin had been used for such purposes.

It is surprising to see that the dimensions of sustainability, ecology, economy, and social justice can already be seen clearly outlined in this book, published in 1713. What does Carlowitz say about ecology? That nature is "mild"; it is a "benign nature" – Mater natura, Mother Nature. He speaks of the "miracle of vegetation," of the "life-creating power of the sun," and of the "wonder-worthy nurturing spirit of life" which the soil contains. He connects the "outer form" of the trees with their "inner form," their "signature," and the "constellation of the heavens, below which they green," and with the Matrix, the Mother Earth and her natural effects. Nature, he says, is "indescribably beautiful." How pleasant, for example, "the green color of their leaves may be, cannot be told." One must only, he adds, know how to read the "book of nature" – an ancient metaphor, passed down from antiquity.

The point of departure for Carlowitz's economic thinking was the determination that humanity was no longer in the Garden of Eden. He must therefore come to the aid of vegetation, and "act with it." He must not "act against nature," but rather follow it and manage resources thriftily. In this context, Carlowitz formulated his socio-ethical basic principles: all have a claim to food and sustenance, even the "poor subjects" and the "dear posterity," in other words, future generations.

Carlowitz's word creation indeed enters virgin territory. He adopts a word and fills it with a new specific semantic content. Ever since, throughout all definitions of *Nachhaltigkeit, sustained yield forestry,* and *sustainability,* two core thoughts persist: intergenerational justice and respect for the bearing capacity of the ecosystem. Throughout the entire process of expansion of the scope of its meaning, that is what constitutes the substance and the continuity of the concept. And that continuity began with Carlowitz. The *Sylvicultura oeconomica* contains the commonplace word for the first time in a written source in connection with its notional substance that still applies today. That makes this book a linguistic event of significance.

Carlowitz's term "sustaining use" (1713) gradually established itself as a clearly defined concept for new scientific methods of managing forests. *"Nachhaltigkeit"* appears in a decree by Duchess Anna Amalia of Saxe-Weimar in 1760, and as a fully developed and defined term in the writings of the German foresters around the year 1800 such as Georg Ludwig Hartig in Prussia and Heinrich Cotta in Saxony.

During the nineteenth century, the principle was also adopted in other European countries, and the need to translate *Nachhaltigkeit* into other languages became urgent. It was then that derivations of the Latin word *sustinere* first appeared. In the forestry literature of Switzerland, "nachhaltiger Ertrag" was in 1820 translated into French as "rendement soutenu." That term was also adopted by the founders of the French Forestry Academy in Nancy, most of whom had studied in Germany. In the English-speaking countries, the term "sustained yield forestry" became established due to the influence of German forestry experts in the service of the British colonial administration, such as Dietrich Brandis and Wilhelm Schlich.

A restart: Sustainable development

The Brundtland Report appeared in 1987. It was the concluding report a UN commission chaired by Norwegian Social Democratic Prime Minister Gro Harlem Brundtland. She established the concept of "sustainable development" as a new guiding principle for the UN; it would finally be officially adopted at the Rio Earth Summit five years later. This report begins with the look at the blue planet with these words:

> In the middle of the 20th century, we saw our planet from space for the first time. . . . From space, we see a small and fragile ball dominated not by human activity and edifice but by a pattern of clouds, oceans, greenery, and soils.
>
> (WCED 1987, p. 1)

This recourse to the iconic image of the earth from space, as recorded by the crews of the Apollo spaceships during the manned lunar expeditions between 1968 and 1972, is no coincidence. During those years began the great search movement, the politics of the earth, which has continued to this day, and which will determine our fate during the twenty-first century.

The view from outside inspires a new "great narrative" of a few words: the beauty, the uniqueness, the fragility of the blue planet were its keywords. The modern concept of sustainable development/*Nachhaltigkeit* has emerged from the womb of this view, and this conception. These conceptions, these images, these thought-pictures, are part of the rational, emotional, and spiritual core of the concept of sustainability. They are its matrix. If the Club of Rome report of 1972 still used the word "sustainable" relatively parenthetically, it was soon to take on clearer terminological shape.

Two events in that process are of particular interest: The World Council of Churches, at its 1968 plenary in Uppsala, Sweden, set up an investigative commission on the issue of "the future of man and society in the world of knowledge-based technology" (see Birch 1993, pp. 113–115). In 1974, the Commission met in Bucharest to explore a formula for solutions to the worldwide environmental crisis, which would at the same time address the question of justice. Jorgen Randers, a participant at the conference and a coauthor of the Club of Rome Report, suggested the formulation "ecologically sustainable society." This proposal was accepted: at a plenary meeting in Nairobi a year later, the WCC adopted its new model of a "just, participatory and sustainable society."

Another internationally active civil society organization, the International Union for the Conservation of Nature, at its 1969 plenary meeting in New Delhi voted to draft a new program, a process that then took ten years. What emerged at the end of that period was a "World Conservation Strategy," the product of the joint work of the IUCN, the UNEP and the WWF, which was presented to the global public in a spectacular worldwide PR campaign in February 1980. It demanded particularly a new, ethically responsible manner of dealing with the biosphere and its "living resources," and, connected with that, a struggle against poverty in the countries of the global South. The title of the introduction to the document was: "Living Resource Conservation for Sustainable Development," elucidated under Point 3: "For development to be sustainable it must take account of social and ecological factors, as well as economic ones" (IUCN 1980, Introduction). A few sentences later, the World Conservation Strategy redefines the traditional term "conservation": "Conservation is defined here as: the management of human use of the biosphere so that it may yield the greatest sustainable benefits to present generations while maintaining its potential to meet the needs and aspirations of future generations." A remarkable discovery: the Brundtland formula of 1987 is anticipated almost word for word in this 1980 document. In the same context, the vocabulary of providential theology (*conservatio*) and the terminology of eighteenth-century forestry (sustained yield) reappear while the modern term "sustainable development" appears for the first time.

The Brundtland Commission thus adopted a modified form of the IUCN term "conservation" when defining "sustainable development." In its 1987 report it gave the classic definition of "sustainable development," which has been quoted a million times: "Sustainable development is development that meets the needs of the present without compromising the ability of future generations to meet their own needs" (WCED 1987, p. 43).

The linkage of "sustainable" and "development" is a semantical innovation, although it may contribute to blurring the term. For "development" has been and is often equated with "economic growth," with boosting the gross domestic product; we need only recall the now decades-old distinction between "developed" and "underdeveloped" countries. This implies that the developed countries have provided the only possible path to development. In the Brundtland Report, however, "development" is explained more precisely – and twice – immediately following the definition. First, the key term "needs" is specified as meaning "essential needs," or the satisfaction of basic needs. Development is thus placed in the context of the struggle against poverty, and of north–south justice. In the same breath, the report emphasizes that the current and future bearing capacity of the ecosystem must define the limits of technology and civilization. The permanent bearing capacity of the ecosystems thus becomes the standard for economic activity – not the globalized markets.

Conclusion

Let us return to my initial question: sustainability is a holistic design. Its target is the overall whole. It organically connects the three dimensions: ecology, economy, and social justice. And it connects them so tightly that new patterns of production and consumption become apparent, patterns which are compatible with the bearing capacity of the ecosystems, and which will drastically reduce our ecological footprint. In the prism of sustainability we see a different kind of economy, a lower-resource, more natural, socio-ethically well-founded economy. The UN is currently describing that with the code word "green economy."

We are at a turning point of historic significance. The fossil age is coming to an end. Fossil resources have, in the last 200 years, given us an unbelievably dynamic development. They were deposited in the ground; they only needed to be "tapped." If an oil well ran dry, you just had to drill deeper, or somewhere else. That logic needed no sustainability. And indeed, the traditional vocabulary of ecology and sustainability disappeared into the ivory tower of academic disciplines for 100 years. But fossil resources are not regenerated. The oil price shock of 1972 was an initial warning sign. Today, we speak of "peak oil," the beginning of the end of the fossil age. This game cannot go into overtime. Business-as-usual is no longer possible. We will once again have to depend on renewable resources and renewable energies. Sustainability is no longer the icing on the cake of a fossil-fueled lifestyle, but rather a survival strategy and a new civilizational design. We have the necessary intellectual resources. We have the gentle technologies. And we also have the sensitivity for the values of human rights and human dignity.

Peak oil is a historic opportunity, a moment of kairos, at which a window of opportunity is opening. It is bringing us face-to-face with the challenge to design the Great Transformation in all areas.

Back to my initial question: sustainability is not a word that can be manipulated at will. Nor, however, is it a rigid term, explainable in one or two formulas, to be defined once and then simply implemented. It is not a cookbook with finished recipes, or with instructions to do this or that, and then you're sustainable. It is not a state; it is a process, a model. In other words, it is not a final goal to be achieved at some stage, but rather a compass providing orientation for a journey into an unknown future. It will help us to act on this field that evolution has prepared in such a way that human existence will not end on this planet. Sustainability is a *Suchbewegung*, a quest.

Bibliography

Birch, C. (1993). *Regaining Compassion – For Humanity and Nature*. Kensington, Australia: New South Wales University Press.

Campe, J. H. (1809). *Wörterbuch der deutschen Sprache*. Braunschweig, Germany: Schulbuchhandlung.

Carlowitz, H. C. von ([1713] 2013). *Sylvicultura oeconomica*. München: oekom Verlag.

Carson, R. (1965). *Silent Spring*. London: Penguin Books.

Grober, U. (2012). *Sustainability – A Cultural History*. Totnes, UK: Green Books.

IUCN (International Union for Conservation of Nature and Natural Resources). (1980). *World Conservation Strategy. Living Resource Conservation for Sustainable Development*. Gland, Switzerland: IUCN.

Meadows, D. H., Meadows, D. L., Randers, J. & Behrens, W. W. (1972). *The Limits to Growth. A Report to the Club of Rome's Project on the Predicament of Mankind*. London: Earth Island.

Spinoza, B. de (1988). *The Ethics of Spinoza*. Trans. R.H.M Elwes. New York: Kensington Publishing Corp.

WCED (World Commission on Environment and Development). (1987). *Our Common Future*. (Brundtland-Report). Oxford: Oxford University Press.

3 What kind of theory do we need for sustainable development – and how much of it?

Some thoughts

Armin Grunwald

The issue and an overview

Since its stormy adolescent period of ten to fifteen years ago, the theoretical discussion around sustainability has abated almost entirely. Large numbers of definitions and concepts of sustainable development emerged during that initial period, which, however, eventually yielded to a phase of fatigue. For what was the use of all this theoretical contemplation and debate, when so many urgent practical issues were at hand? The only element of this largely theoretical approach to sustainability that has continued to this day seems to be focused on the issue of how research into sustainable development is to be conceptualized, and where it is to be located in the scientific system: Is a separate "sustainability science" called for (Kates et al. 2002), and to what extent should it be interdisciplinary and, especially, transdisciplinary (Bergmann et al. 2010)? While a debate over such issues may give rise to a theory of sustainability research as part of scientific theory or of scientific research, it will hardly be able to engender a theory of sustainable development, which would, after all, have to address the question of what that means terminologically, normatively, conceptually, and operatively.

What is rather called for in place of a theoretical debate is practice in a wide variety of forms: societal practice, such as that in the processes of the Local Agenda 21, political activities for the preparation of the Rio+20 Summit in 2012, as well as a wide variety of activities, especially at schools and colleges, in the context of the UN Decade on Education for Sustainable Development. Also necessary are comprehensive scientific activities, such as the modeling of ecosystems and human/natural interactions on the environmental effects of anthropogenic activity, or investigation into such possibilities for action as the transformation of energy systems for sustainable development. By and large, no one ever asks, in the context of these activities, what sustainable development "means"; the assumption is that that is a settled question, at least inasmuch as both societal and policy-related practice and the scientific advisory activity which supports that practice can build upon it.

In this situation, the question as to what theory is needed would seem to itself require justification, and also a brief consideration of the role of theory itself. Theories are not ends in themselves, but must rather be viewed *instrumentally*.

They have a function in the process of scientific progress and in the further development of science. Theories are designed to fulfill various tasks, several of which are listed below, with no claim to completeness:

- the establishment of a *uniformity of point of view*, from which the object being observed can be described, and delimited from other objective realms;
- the *abstraction* of concrete singularities of – usually – many single cases into general concepts, with the goal of inductively discovering the common and the general in the particular;
- the goal of the *systematization* of knowledge, e.g. for the purposes of storing it and passing it on, which includes the specification of its conceptual, logical, and methodological consistency; and
- the goal of ensuring that the abstraction and integration allow for new possibilities for the interpretation of specific cases, and new combinations, which could then in turn become the points of departure for research (*fruitfulness*).

Depending on the state of knowledge and its processing, theoretical debates are sometimes urgently required; often, however, they are unnecessary. The fact that virtually no theoretical debate on sustainable development has been carried out during the past ten years is thus not necessarily a problem. Theoretical debates should only be conducted if there is a demonstrable need for them, for example, because of unclear interpretations of empirical results, or of far-reaching scientific controversies which can be diagnosed with their aid.

The initial thesis of this paper is that in the case of sustainability, there certainly is currently a considerable need for theoretical work which must, initially, be elucidated (Section 2). Thereafter, several difficulties on the way to a theory of sustainable development will be identified, and approaches for dealing with them proposed (Section 3). Due to the specific structure of the term "sustainability," particularly the fact that it is not a genuinely scientific term, but rather ultimately a societal/political program, it becomes apparent that what is at issue is not the development of a theory of sustainability analogous to a theory of physics. Rather, the important thing is that the problem of theory and practice inherent in sustainability be itself elucidated theoretically; this can, however, only be touched on here (Section 4).

The need for a theoretical debate[1]

Ever since the Brundtland Commission Report (Hauff 1987), a large number of definitions of sustainable development have been suggested, and numerous concepts developed in the context of practice, some of which have been tested in research and practice (Jörissen et al. 1999). Sustainability concepts are competing with one another scientifically, and to some extent also politically. While the scientific controversies have generally been sparked by fundamental premises, such as the substitutability of natural capital by other forms of capital (Ott/Döring 2004), political assessments have often been oriented toward the presumed implications and effects of the selection of certain sustainability concepts, and their compatibility with political positions. Moreover, it should be noted that the representatives of particular interests often do not refer at all to concrete sustainability concepts, but rather give reason for the suspicion that they are merely engaged in rhetoric, or pushing their particular interests under the cover of the positive-sounding term "sustainability"; the same is also true in the media and among politicians.

The great variety of sustainability concepts and the lack of clarity with regard to the meaning of the term "sustainability," as well as the manner of its translation into practical activity, are a strong argument in favor of the necessity for a theoretical debate. I would like to elucidate this below by reference to an imagined practical situation conceived as a thought experiment. Let us imagine a situation in which a decision-maker is faced with the necessity of making political – or other – decisions with regard to, say, energy supply, mobility related facilities, or waste treatment from the point of view of sustainability. In order to do so, s/he reviews the sustainability literature, only to find a number of sustainability concepts which diverge both in their premises and in their results. Now s/he must decide upon a procedure so as to be able to implement political decisions on the bases of the selected concept.[2] If this decision-maker now turns to the scientific community for advice, in order to obtain information as to the "best" sustainability concepts according to the "state-of-the-art," s/he will receive a large number of different, in some cases even mutually incompatible, responses. What should this decision-maker now do?

In this perspective, sustainability-related decision making becomes a two-stage process: at the first stage, it is necessary to make a decision regarding the concept of sustainability with the aid of which, at the second stage, substantive sustainability assessments can be undertaken and political decisions made. The focus of the present paper is on the first of these two stages. The question is, which criterion K is to provide orientation for the selection decision at the first stage, and what can this criterion K be based upon? This is a decisive point for the evaluation of the practical necessity of theory. For the selection decision between various sustainability concepts could have very considerable practical results with regard to many questions of sustainable development and their policy implementation, even if this is certainly not always the case. Depending on the sustainability concept upon which various policies are based, their implementation could turn out very differently. A comparative assessment of sustainability concepts, and the selection of criteria for determining better/worse, or more suitable/less suitable in the selection-decision process are thus of considerable importance in practice. Upon what can the decision-maker depend in making a choice in the supermarket of sustainability products if s/he wants to do so not on the basis of current political opportunity, pure intuition, or considerations of power politics, but rather on the basis of rational and well-founded discourse?

Allow me to briefly illustrate the danger that might result if such a comparative assessment were arrived at not on the basis of transparent and well-founded criteria, but rather either emotionally "at the gut level," or with a view towards the interests and positions that it is likely to affect. Without clear and well-founded assessment and selection criteria, there will be no possibility, in the case of competing concepts of sustainability, of arriving at an argumentatively legitimated, i.e. a *non-arbitrary* assessment. Instead, one would be accepting the reality of the supposed terminologically arbitrary nature of the notion "sustainable development" – and in fact confirming it. This would then no longer be an academic problem, but rather a *practical* one: since sustainability ultimately aims toward activity in a variety of societal areas, it needs at least a minimum of reliability, convergence, and continuity in its orientation for action. Lacking these, sustainability policy would become "disjointed incrementalism,"[3] an aimless groping around in the dark which could no longer even be described as trial and error, as it would be lacking the theoretical basis for identifying an error as *an error*, and then being able to learn from it.

In order to avoid this, i.e. for ultimately practical reasons, a theory of sustainability is needed. The goal must be to overcome a threatening arbitrariness of perception and assessment, and to replace it with a systematic procedure which would first of all address such a fear of arbitrariness, and second, abstractly overarch the casuistry of multiple cases (see Habermas 1978, p. 331).

Only in this way does the usual scientific process of realization, in which theoretical reflection and the relationship between theory and practice, as well as their interaction, have an undeniable place, become possible in the first place. Hence there is no doubt: what is needed is non-arbitrary, argumentatively secured arguments to permit a "rational assessment and selection" in many issues of divergent sustainability concepts. The argumentative security of the criteria for such an assessment would be the main task of the theory of sustainability. And since there has been no such theory to date, a theoretical debate is now in order.

The path to a theory of sustainable development

Accordingly, a comparative assessment of sustainability concepts will require criteria. These criteria cannot themselves be part of the concepts involved, but rather must come from a "third perspective." The question then arises as to the point of departure for obtaining the criteria for such a comparison (Section 3.1). One possibility in the area of sustainable development could be the internationally concluded and legitimized sustainability agreements, albeit only in terms of a provisional ethic according to Descartes, i.e. as a provisional orientation which is itself subject to criticism – where, indeed, criticism is required (Section 3.2).

The point of departure and the initial issue

The first question concerns the level at which criteria for selection decisions between sustainability concepts can or should be sought. An initial approach might be to seek criteria which come from one of the competing concepts itself – in other words, to identify what concretely such a concept is intended to achieve, setting it apart from other ones. Such an argument would however be circular:

for example, the fact that the theory of strong sustainability (Ott/Döring 2004) would give rise to arguments which would make that concept appear advantageous compared with other concepts not based on the idea of strong sustainability, is hardly surprising – however, due to its circular nature, this argument would prove nothing. The criterion K, which we are seeking, must not favor any one of the concepts from which the selection is to be made *a priori*, i.e. because it originates from that concept.

The second approach might be to place several sustainability concepts next to one another, and to develop criteria which would allow for a well-founded selection out of the structural comparison between competing approaches, or in optical juxtapositions, as has been done in the past (Jörissen et al. 1999; Ott 2006). Although these may in many respects be useful in demonstrating the spectrum of possibilities for understanding and operationalizing sustainability, they are *not sufficient* for addressing the issue of criteria as elucidated in Section 2. For while the synopsis does provide heuristic indications for what must be noted in the context of the comparison, because for example in some respects far-reaching commonalities, and in others far-reaching discrepancies, will emerge, it does nothing to facilitate a selection – except in the unrealistic case where there were only commonalities, which would obviate the need for decision – for the identification of commonalities and discrepancies provides no answers to the question as to which criterion K is to determine the result of a better/worse decision. If anything is to be learned for a selection decision from a synoptic juxtaposition, the normative criteria must previously have been obtained from other sources.

A third approach, which is often used to solve the issue of criteria, is to use binding and legitimate politically established factors as the point of departure. Often, the Brundtland definitions are taken, and it is then claimed that one conceptualization or another corresponds to the spirit of this definition better than do others. Often, the history of the sustainability debate and of its precursors is invoked, with the claim that it is necessary to continue along the path of one's own conceptualization of sustainability as comprehensively as possible; or else such documentation as the Rio Process is taken as the basis (e.g. Kopfmüller et al. 2001). The normative grounds for this argumentation are however also doubtful. Any reference to the Brundtland Commission has a *prima facie* dogmatic tinge: after all, to formally base oneself on the status of an official UN document would additionally require a substantive justification as to why particularly this definition should be determinant. And basing oneself on the history of the sustainability debate is to move in the direction of a naturalistic erroneous conclusion regarding that which should be, derived from an observation of that which is: for the debate to date may be subject to errors, unilateral views, or important omissions which, at more careful consideration, could or should be corrected. Generally, reference to political agreements must be rejected as arbitrary or dogmatic.

A fourth possibility could be to derive the sought-after criterion K from a comprehensive theory of sustainability *per se*, which would have to encompass a theory of human society, including its normal activities and their historical dimensions, a theory of human/natural relationships, a theory of nature, and probably much more. Such a theory – which, if it is to solve the problem of selection, must be recognized in consensus and no longer be the object of scientific controversy – does not of course exist. Presumably, moreover, no such holistic theory is even possible, for epistemological reasons, since it would require the observer to assume an external position which is not attainable. The result of this diagnosis is that the theoretical work on sustainability cannot usefully set as its goal *the* theory of sustainability *per se* which would provide conclusively, once and for all, a theoretical grand overview of sustainable development of humankind. For this reason, it is necessary to seek a new understanding of theory than that which many may assume from the phrase "theory of sustainability" (Section 4).

Thus, the search for a criterion for selection would appear to be stuck in a fundamental crisis, faced either with circularity, infinite regression, or dogmatic establishment,[4] all three of which are fatal for any attempt to arrive at a transparent and justified criterion K for a comparison between sustainability concepts. This diagnosis makes it necessary to reflexively take a step back, as it were, and to try to conceptualize a manner in which a rational comparison between, and selection among, various sustainability concepts might be carried out *procedurally*.

Scientific sustainability concepts – and they alone are the object of our considerations here – have a claim to validity beyond the sphere of subjective opinion or belief.[5] This claim to formulation must be rational in discourse (Habermas 1988), i.e. satisfiable by argument. If therefore decision-makers E must, in order to meet the demands of practice, select one from among a number of sustainability concepts, they would have to get the representatives of the competing concepts together around a table in order to initiate a discourse regarding truth and correctness (Habermas 1973). The discourse would serve as a procedure for checking whether, e.g. the claim of a certain sustainability concept A of being worthy of preference can be argumentatively defended against the competing concept B.

However, the question as to the point of departure of such a discourse, which has caused the above-discussed search for criterion K to fail, at least initially, also crops up here. For a discourse to have any chance of success whatever, an acceptance among the participants of *pre-discursive consensuses* is necessary (Gethmann 1979): "Common deliberation presupposes some common ground; without shared values and understandings discussion quickly degenerates in unending dispute" (Burns/Ueberhorst 1989, p. 91). In fact, agreement is often reached if a common basis exists as a point of departure for attempts at reasoning and justification. Pre-discursive consensuses often extend to a disposition toward settling disagreement and conflict by argument in the first place, to a willingness on the part of the participants to accept better arguments and to call their own previous positions into question, and to a common terminological basis, common quality criteria for arguments, and a recognition of *rules* of communications in accordance with the standards of procedural fairness (Gethmann 1979) (cf. Skorupinski/Ott 2000).

If therefore "pre-discursive" consensus indicates the conditions which must be fulfilled in order for discourse to contain the promise of success *at all* (Gethmann 1979), then "pre-deliberative" consensus refers to the conditions required to permit a *concrete* discourse, i.e. a discourse tied to a certain context, to be carried out

(Grunwald 2004). Pre-deliberative consensuses contain more preconditions than do pre-discursive consensuses, since they encompass, too, substantial aspects of the given understood situation, e.g. certain preliminary understandings regarding substantive orientation. Pre-deliberative consensuses are hence strongly context-related.[6] Building upon a recognized pre-deliberative consensus, a discourse might be carried out in accordance with the usual postulates of fairness and the usual rules, in order to determine which of the competing sustainability concepts had the greatest "argumentative firmness," and could hence be distinguished as "the best" in terms of rational discourse. This would be a *procedural* response to the challenge of a selection decision: only in the discourse itself would the determination emerge as to which criterion K was to determine the worthiness of preference of the concepts.

Certainly, this model is only a thought experiment, and not simple to implement as a real process. Nonetheless, it gives an indication as to how the problem elucidated in Section 2 might be handled transparently and logically. I will elucidate this in the next step, in which the question is: assuming the representatives of various sustainability concepts were to subject themselves to the effort of a discourse, where would the pre-deliberative consensus be, to which all would accede, or to which all would have to be able to accede? Clearly, the latter formulation is itself not free of problems, since what would, after all, be at issue would not be an acceptance which could be assumed or expected of the participants, but rather their actual acceptance.

A provisional arrangement at the beginning of theory

The important thing is, then, to search for nontrivial elements of factually accepted determination in the context of sustainability. The factual acceptance of consensus deserves primacy – it is an example of the primacy of practice.

As a first step, this agreement might be sought at the level of sustainability-as-goal. The following sentence provides an indication: "In terms of its normative status, the idea of sustainability is, too, a collective goal for which it is at the same time a duty to strive" (Ott 2006, p. 66). If sustainability is a "collective goal," then we have here discovered a generally binding and hence consensual foundation. If the idea of sustainability is a goal which can be generally accepted and considered as a pre-deliberative understanding in the context of the discourse regarding the worthiness of preference of sustainability concepts, various different sustainability concepts might be compared with regard to their suitability as contributions toward achieving that goal. This would mean an action-theoretical view of sustainability theories and concepts: these would then be means to an end, and comparative assessments would be possible with regard to suitability of these means relative to the consensually agreed-upon goals, which is a common assessment procedure in instrumental means/end rationality.

Unfortunately things are not that simple. For sustainability as a goal has no substance, since it is difficult to imagine anyone arguing against sustainability without falling into self-contradiction. The establishment of sustainability as a goal may be capable of consensus, but would precisely for that reason be devoid of substance, and would be incapable of yielding any conclusion regarding selection criteria among divergent sustainability concepts. The determination of "sustainability" as a goal is under-determined. Its concretization is, after all, to be provided precisely by means of defining conceptions of sustainable development, such as, for example, the theory of strong sustainability (Ott/Döring 2004). The indeterminate nature at the level of the goal is reduced through concepts acting as the means, but in a different way – and thus the problem of selection remains. Hence the concepts are never only the means, but rather, in their defining ideas regarding the goal of "sustainability," also contain elements which must be considered part of the goal level. Controversies regarding concepts are hence not only disagreements regarding the suitability of means for shared goals, but also conflicts, too, at the level of the goal definition itself.

Therefore, it is necessary to reconstruct – or to construct – a pre-deliberative consensus for sustainability, and to test it for roots in societal practice and human living reality, going substantively beyond the mere determination of the goal of "sustainability." At first glance, that might seem impossible, in view of the heterogeneity and plurality of modern societies, of the multifaceted controversies regarding the term and the unfolding of sustainable development, and of the problems of understanding and of intercultural dialogue.

Nonetheless, a level might be found at which a pre-deliberative consensus could be arrived at, at least in general terms (Grunwald 2009): the level of international understanding on sustainability. The model of sustainable development is recognized worldwide at the policy – or at least at the programmatic – level (Grunwald/Kopfmüller 2006). At the UN Conference on Environment and Development in 1992 in Rio de Janeiro, the international community of nations assumed the binding duty to implement that model in concrete policy at the national and global levels. The corresponding documents, their numerous remaining semantical compromises and imprecisions notwithstanding, do at least constitute a certain level of definition of sustainability (cf. e.g. Kopfmüller et al. 2001).

Central to it are the conditions for the possibilities of the reproduction of human societies, from small-scale communities to the global society. The model of sustainable development makes it possible to concentrate to a precisely defined point the present "we-can't-go-on-like-this" feeling of malaise that arises when considering the reproduction of world society, while at the same time constructively seeking possibilities for taking a new direction, in order to permit the conditions for the possibilities of reproduction to even be fulfilled at all. This combination of a largely shared diagnosis and an equally largely shared view that action is necessary – although the question of how to act remains controversial – shows that in spite of all the conflicts and controversies around sustainable development, there are clear signs that a factually recognized pre-deliberate agreement is emerging.[7] For:

- the diagnosis that humankind is currently on a non-sustainable development path is shared by all the various positions; otherwise, there would be no need to debate about sustainable development

- the agreement to sustainability as a "collective goal" (Ott 2006) as stated by the Brundtland Commission can hence be assumed without any major problem
- sustainability as a "collective goal" has been legitimized "for the time being" by policy decisions at the level of the international community of nations, and by the UN
- there are no known arguments in the field of science or ethics which fundamentally call this consensus into question.

Hence, the policy agreements which are binding under international law can be interpreted as indicators, and as an expression of a globally shared predeliberate consensus on sustainability. If that is the case, this pre-deliberate consensus can be used as a point of departure for discourses on the suitability of divergent concepts of sustainable development.

However, two caveats are in order: first, this pre-deliberate consensus is, precisely because of the political nature of its creation, highly indeterminate in terms of substance. As has often been noted – usually critically, from the scientific community – it contains a large number of semantical compromises, unclear terminology, rhetorical stock phrases, etc. Hence, this pre-deliberate consensus, in the form of the Brundtland Report, the Rio documents and the follow-up agreements, etc., is to a high degree in need of elucidation – and it is precisely in the context of these "elucidations" that the conflicts and controversies arise which – see above – involve not only disagreements over the suitable means, but also conflicts at the level of the goals themselves.

Second, the problem described in Section 3.1 must be considered: the fact that this pre-deliberative consensus has come into being on the basis of knowledge and normative orientations which have, in the course of time, proven to be insufficient or even wrong. What we therefore have is the determination of a position legitimized democratically and under international law, on the basis of incomplete knowledge and situational assessments. For this reason, this "consensus" can only be considered valid "for the time being," as a "provisional ethic." It can and must be constantly reflected upon critically and developed further, which leads to the necessity for taking a look at the relationship between the theory and practice of sustainable development (Section 4).

If the above statements are accurate, the primacy of practice is expressed in that legitimated policy settings can be used as a pre-deliberative consensus in a theoretical (i.e. divorced from the level of action; Habermas 1973) discourse on competing determinations and conceptions of sustainability. By the same token however, the set policy framework may not be established arbitrarily, "decisionistically"; rather, it must be assumed that this framework is itself based on diagnoses, orientations, and determinations which have not come into being devoid of theoretical reference, but rather in the context of rational discourse. For then, we would no longer have the prevailing arbitrary situation of the shift between practical – for example political – positions, but would rather reach a situation in which the state of practice would itself be strengthened by theoretical debate, and could only be changed in such a context. Ultimately, it would be presumed that with all the accepted fallibility, an argumentative struggle will have taken place in which the power of the superior argument is at least one factor. Fallibility, time dependency, and the provisional and incomplete character of knowledge will mean that the establishment of policy, as a methodological beginning and as the basis for a discourse, will always remain provisional, and require criticism and further development, in which theoretical argumentation will play a major role.

Theory and practice

The situation diagnosed above leads to the thesis that what is at issue is not the drafting of a comprehensive theory of sustainability, but rather the creation of a fruitful relationship between practice and theory. What "fruitful" means here must be settled on the basis of a pre-deliberative consensus. Instead of a "theory of sustainability," the selection criteria named, and the determination of criteria required for that, need a theory of the theory-practice relationship of sustainability. This does not mean a theory regarding a practice that is in progress, but rather theoretical instructions which – primarily by means of the mentioned selection decisions between competing sustainability conceptions – have an effect on practice, which must then in turn be theoretically reflected upon. We therefore have a double reflexive relationship between theory and practice, as described by Habermas (1978, p. 17).

This situation is an ideal point of departure for scientific work – not only for empirical, but also for the terminological, conceptual, and hermeneutic theoretical work. The key is, in the process of a scientific discourse of definition, to take the existing and factually shared pre-deliberative consensus, fuzzy and in need of interpretation as it may be, as the basis upon which sustainability can be made operable and – largely – by means of definitional and operationalizing proposals, to push the practice of policy-makers and societal public opinion to continue working on the ever provisional pre-deliberate consensus on sustainability, and to develop further and concretize the existing provisional construct. Ultimately, it is a paradoxical program: we are using the pre-deliberative consensus that can be considered legitimated in the context of the political framework as a point of departure, knowing that it is itself in need of criticism, and that a duty to criticism certainly exists; it is indeed a provisional situation. The results are two different modes of scientific work on sustainability:

1 Building on the "political beginning" which has been achieved, albeit provisionally, the operationalization discourse (cf. Grunwald 2009) has the purpose of drawing practical consequences through rational discourse out of the existing beginning, i.e. to determine indicators and targets, to follow current developments, to evaluate them in accordance with these indicators and goals, and finally to plan and implement measures, etc. At the same time, one should act in this mode "as if" the provisional pre-deliberative consensus arrived at were valid.

2   Parallel to this however, the nature of the provisional beginning as a status which has been reached must continually be called into question, in order to discover weaknesses, and to develop it further theoretically (cf. the justification discourse in Grunwald 2009). In case of success, this would result in convincing the practical sphere, and hence engender the development and definition of the "beginning" of the selection discourse. For example the theory of strong sustainability (Ott/Döring 2004), if it becomes convincing in practice, could lead to a corresponding sharpening of the existing consensus.

These two modes are not mutually independent. The knowledge gained in the context of the operationalization discourse and the implementation of its results can affect the further formulation and direction of the justification discourse, and must therefore be among the factors considered there. What is important is not the theory for a certain practice, but rather the theory-practice relationship and its theoretical reflection. The interaction between theory and practice is decisive.

Possibilities for learning must be provided both in the transfer of sustainability concepts into policy decisions and in the conceptions themselves (Bechmann/ Grunwald 2002). The "engine" of learning consists of the fact that in the framework of the selection decision between competing sustainability concepts A and B (see above), one conception is first of all considered *ex ante* worthy of preference, according to pre-deliberatively agreed-upon criteria. However, this constitutes only a *preliminary* determination, for with this selection, the "probation period" of the concept involved only begins. In the context of practical societal-political implementation, and in fact even during work with the concept, experience will be gained regarding its operability, followed later by the empirically observed results of the measures implemented on its basis. Here, it must be demonstrated convincingly that the evaluations of "worthiness of preference" undertaken *ex ante* are also justified empirically, i.e. *ex post,* and can meet expectations in terms of the achievement of the targets connected with sustainability. The assessment of "worthiness of preference" arrived at *ex ante* is only a check made out to a future in which it is to be cashed.

Interpreted in the context of planning theory, this corresponds to the model of "goal-oriented incrementalism" (Grunwald 2000), in juxtaposition to the "disjointed incrementalism" mentioned at the outset. With regard to technological development, the former has been characterized as follows:

> The resulting dynamic of this approach is that directions and goals of development are certainly apparent, albeit not in the sense of straightforward planning . . . but rather as directions which are themselves changeable. . . . Learning effects are thus not excluded *a priori,* but are rather explicitly integrated as the motivating mechanisms of planning modifications. The integration of learning ability is the *key for the openness of the future*. . . . Due to the fundamentally open-outcome nature of decisions

at the branch-off points of the decision tree involved, the results cannot
be anticipated: there are no shortcuts to the goal-oriented incremental-
planning and decision-making discourse.

(Grunwald 2000, p. 110)

If this analogy formulation is of substance, and the "no-shortcuts" thesis of
planning and decision-making discourse is true, then the above assumption that
there will be no comprehensive "theory of sustainability" from which selection
decisions and sustainability measures can, as it were, be "derived," is supported.
Theoretical work will not spare us the toil of deliberative efforts in the context
of planning and decision-making discourses; at the same time, there is hope that
theoretical reflection can support these deliberations.

Conclusions

Often, sustainability is characterized *as a process*. Although in many respects, this
is merely a phrase (Ott 2006), or an attempt to dodge terminological, conceptual,
or substantive decisions, nonetheless, procedural and process-related elements
are inherent to sustainability, if only because precisely the considerable insecurities regarding future knowledge will prevent us from defining and operationalizing sustainability conclusively once and for all, and then passing the remaining
problems on to the administration as a management task. On the one hand,
determinations are necessary, for otherwise no policy of sustainability could be
implemented; on the other, *openness* toward developments and new knowledge
are also requisite (Bechmann/Grunwald 2002). The primary task of theoretical
work on sustainability is the reflection of the associated theory-practice relationship, in order to achieve a maximum of learning.

The hope that a theory of sustainability might emerge in this manner from
the sustainability-related sciences against which politicians "would be helpless"
(as is the case [a] in Ott 2006, p. 65) is however probably a false one. There will
be no theory of sustainability to be found at the end of the paths outlined here
for practice-connected theoretical work, from which – even if the scientific
community were of one mind – policy decisions might emerge as a reflection
of scientific knowledge. On the one hand, scientifically consensual sustainability conceptions would still be *conditionally* normative. Regarding the decision as to whether the antecedent prerequisites which constitute the applicable
conditions of the theory, and the fulfillment of which could transform the if-
then chains of theoretical work into practical policy, have been fulfilled, the
entire if-then chain ultimately can constitute no more than a *proposal* made
to the continuing political process.[8] On the other hand, the theoretical work
described here does not lead to a theoretical type from which such a result
might even be expected. Instead, theory is here only a medium of reflective
learning, itself a passage on the way to a reflected further development of pre-
deliberate consensuses and theory-practice relationships.

Notes

1 This diagnosis could already be seen in Grunwald (2009). That paper, which addressed a comparison between the Greifswald approach (Ott/Döring 2004) and the integrative concept (Kopfmüller et al. 2001), is, as it were, the forerunner of the present paper with regard to many theses, which will not be identified separately below.

2 This situation is here described in an oversimplified manner. Of course, in a democratic public context (Habermas 1968; Grunwald 2008), the decision-making process requires deliberation, which cannot, however, be elaborated upon here.

3 A construct of planning theory which has been fittingly lampooned in the following: "We do stagger through history like a drunk putting one disjointed incremental foot after another" (Boulding 1964, p. 931) – an absurd concept for sustainable development.

4 This reflects a general problem known in the theory of science as the "Münchhausen trilemma" (Janich et al. 1974; Gethmann 1979; Grunwald 1998), after one of the tall tales of Baron Hieronymus von Münchhausen, who claimed, when stuck in a swamp, to have pulled himself out by the tail of his own wig.

5 "This selection [i.e. the decision-making suggested and discussed in Section 2 - A. G.] should of course not be purely a matter of faith" (Ott/Döring 2004, p. 150).

6 One such example might be a discourse to be carried out regarding the best site for a waste incinerator, in which a substantive agreement would have to have been reached as to the necessity for building the facility in the first place.

7 Of course, that then raises the issue as to who the participants in this discourse, among whom such an agreement is to prevail, are concretely. It should be permitted, in this conceptually oriented paper, to refrain from dwelling upon that question further, and to rather continue with the argumentation as a thought experiment.

8 Anything else would be a form of technocracy (cf. Habermas 1968): scientists would determine the "one best solution," and politicians would have no other choice but to implement it.

Bibliography

Bechmann, G., Grunwald, A. (2002). Experimentelle Politik und die Rolle der Wissenschaft in der Umsetzung von Nachhaltigkeit. In: K.-W. Brand (ed.). *Politik der Nachhaltigkeit. Voraussetzungen, Probleme, Chancen – Eine kritische Diskussion.* Berlin, 113–130.

Bergmann, M., Jahn, T., Knobloch, T., Krohn, W., Pohl, C., Schramm, E. (2010). *Methoden transdisziplinärer Forschung.* Frankfurt/New York.

Boulding, K. (1964). Review of a Strategy of Decision. *American Sociological Review* 29, 921–942.

Burns, T. R., Ueberhorst R. (1989). *Creative Democracy. Systematic Conflict Resolution and Policymaking in a World of High Science and Technology.* New York.

Gethmann, C. F. (1979). *Proto-Logik. Untersuchungen zur formalen Pragmatik von Begründungsdiskursen.* Frankfurt.

Grunwald, A. (1998). Das prädiskursive Einverständnis. Prozedurale Rechtfertigung und Bedeutung für den Begriff der wissenschaftlichen Wahrheit. *Journal of the General Philosophy of Science* 29, 205–223.

Grunwald, A. (2000). *Handeln und Planen.* München.

Grunwald, A. (2004). Spuren des Seins im Sollen. Das lebensweltliche Fundament der Ethik. In: B. Emunds, G. Horntrich, G. Kruip, G. Ulshöfer (eds.). *Vom Sein zum Sollen und zurück. Zum Verhältnis von Faktizität und Normativität.* Frankfurt, 66–86.

Grunwald, A. (2008). *Technik und Politikberatung. Philosophische Perspektiven.* Frankfurt.

Grunwald, A. (2009). Konzepte nachhaltiger Entwicklung vergleichen – Aber wie? Diskursebenen und Vergleichsmaßstäbe. In: T. von Egan-Krieger, J. Schultz, Ph. P. Thapa,

L. Voget (eds.). *Die Greifswalder Theorie starker Nachhaltigkeit. Ausbau, Anwendung und Kritik.* Marburg, 41–64.

Grunwald, A., Kopfmüller, J. (2006). *Nachhaltigkeit.* Frankfurt: Campus.

Habermas, J. (1968). *Technik und Wissenschaft als Ideologie.* Frankfurt.

Habermas, J. (1973). Wahrheitstheorien. In: H. Fahrenbach (ed.). *Wirklichkeit und Reflexion. Walther Schulz zum sechzigsten Geburtstag.* Pfullingen, 211–265.

Habermas, J. (1978). *Theorie und Praxis. Sozialphilosophische Studien.* Frankfurt.

Habermas, J. (1988). *Theorie des kommunikativen Handelns.* Frankfurt, 2 vols.

Hauff, V. (ed.) (1987). *Unsere gemeinsame Zukunft. Der Brundtland-Bericht der Weltkommission für Umwelt und Entwicklung.* Greven.

Janich, P., Kambartel, F., Mittelstraß, J. (1974). *Wissenschaftstheorie als Wissenschaftskritik.* Frankfurt/Main.

Jörissen, J., Kneer, G., Rink, D., Paskalewa, K. (1999). Synopsis on the implementation of the model of sustainable development in conceptual studies and national plans. HGF Project: "Untersuchungen zu einem integrativen Konzept nachhaltiger Entwicklung: Bestandsaufnahme, Problemanalyse, Weiterentwicklung." Final report. Vol. 1. Karlsruhe.

Kates, R. W., Clark, W. C., Corell, R., Hall, J. M., Jaeger, C., Lowe, I. . . . Svedin, U. (2002). *Sustainability Science.* Cambridge.

Kopfmüller, J., Brandl, V., Jörissen, J., Paetau, M., Banse, G., Coenen, R., Grunwald, A. (2001). *Nachhaltige Entwicklung integrativ betrachtet. Konstitutive Elemente, Regeln, Indikatoren.* Berlin.

Ott, K. (2006). "Friendly Fire." Bemerkungen zum integrativen Konzept nachhaltiger Entwicklung. In: J. Kopfmüller (ed.). *Ein Konzept auf dem Prüfstand. Das integrative Nachhaltigkeitskonzept in der Forschungspraxis.* Berlin, 63–82.

Ott, K., Döring, R. (2004). *Theorie und Praxis starker Nachhaltigkeit.* Marburg.

Skorupinski, B., Ott, K. (2000). *Ethik und Technikfolgenabschätzung.* Zürich.

4 Theory of sustainability?

Considerations on a basic understanding of "sustainability science"

Thomas Jahn

Introduction

The year 2012 marked the twentieth anniversary of the Rio Summit, a central event for the sustainability discourse. At the same time – and certainly not by coincidence – German Chancellor Angela Merkel proclaimed that year as Germany's Year of Sustainability Research. The selection of this issue for a new "Scientific Year" is notable for two reasons. First, it shows that the term "sustainability" – once iridescent, today, if not worn out, then at least overused – is still socially acceptable, even though it has so far not proven possible to develop a substantially more precise definition for it than that presented by the Brundtland Commission Report. Moreover, the selection can be considered late recognition of the fact that the problems of sustainable development, no matter how they are conceived or understood, cannot be resolved in the normal course of operations of the scientific community, but that what is rather needed is a specific research approach adequate to the structure and quality of the problems.

In the academic discourse, this insight has for some time become increasingly accepted. The historical stations here are the debates around interdisciplinarity and transdisciplinarity in the early 1970s (Jantsch 1972), around *post-normal science* and *"Mode 1/Mode 2"* at the beginning of the 1990s, and recently, around *sustainability science*. The latter is a handy code word which has in recent years become increasingly popular, as evidenced by the conferences which use it in their titles, and also by such new scientific journals as the ISI-listed Springer journal *Sustainability Science*, or the e-journal *Sustainability: Science, Practice, & Policy* published by ProQuest. But what is the book inside the cover of sustainability science? Is it about a new super- or supra-discipline *sui generis*, or about a new structure or means of orientation of the systems of knowledge production? The literature contains evidence of both perspectives.[1] In the following, I would like to show that the "disciplining" of sustainability knowledge, which is increasingly being demanded, misses the point, and in fact opens the door to counterproductive misunderstandings. In terms of the second perspective above I will then advocate an alternative concept which could better serve science's and society's capacities to deal with problems of sustainable development. This perspective is based on over twenty-five years of theoretical work and research practice at the Institute for Social-Ecological Research (ISOE) in Frankfurt am Main.

Sustainability science as a new discipline?

The concept of sustainability science as a discipline in its own right has been the topic of numerous academic publications in recent years (cf. e.g. Frame & Brown 2008; Kauffman 2009; Kajikawa 2008; Komiyama & Takeuchi 2006; Steinfeld & Mino 2009; Ziegler & Ott 2011). Kajikawa, for example, believes

> that sustainability science as a discipline *in statu nascendi* will develop its own corpus of knowledge and its own specific methodology for handling sustainability issues, and defines "sustainability science [as] a distinct discipline engaged in a transdisciplinary effort arching over existing disciplines."
>
> (2008, p. 216)

This artful, but fundamentally contradictory definition already shows where the key problem lies in the attempt to conceive sustainability science as a discipline in its own right: regardless of whether one accepts a Popperian or a Kuhnian conception of science, the establishment of a discipline is always a process of conclusion or delimitation; a frame is set up within which research questions on the constituent objects of the discipline are to be formulated. Of course, the proponents of sustainability science as a discipline do not deny that their issues are resistant to disciplinary fencing in, and that they "will not do us the favor of defining themselves as disciplines, let alone as areas of specialty," as Mittelstraß has aptly put it (2005, p. 19, English translation by the author). However, that means that no matter how broadly we define the frame today, we will tomorrow face problems which lie beyond its established boundaries – which will by then already have been fixed by tradition. That fact collides with the evidently essential normativity of a possible sustainability science (cf. Baumgärtner et al. 2008; Frame & Brown 2008; Ziegler & Ott 2011): the handling of *urgent* problems for the reestablishment of society's capacity to act and to develop.[2]

What characterizes problems of sustainable development is their context dependency, which is essentially, but of course not exclusively, determined by their *human* dimension. However, it is precisely this context dependency which prevents, or at least limits, the construction of a separate corpus of knowledge, a necessary constituent of any scientific discipline. For knowledge about the sustainability, or lack thereof, of societal development has been recognized to encompass more than merely scientific knowledge; experiential, institutional and traditional knowledge, etc., are at least as important. Hence, to put it in only slightly exaggerated terms, every society, be it at the national, regional or local level, will have to construct its own characteristic corpus of knowledge for dealing with its own specific sustainability problems. Methodological knowledge, on the other hand, is different: even if methods may be context-specific, decontextualization and systematization are possible here, as Bergmann and colleagues (2012) have shown. In the next section, I will come back to the question of the role of methods in determining what a suitable framework for handling problems of sustainable development might be.

Finally, to speak of a science or discipline implies the idea of problem-solving or, in the Kuhnian sense, "puzzle solving." However, as e.g. Farrell (2011) has argued, the engineering concept of problem-solving is misleading in the context of sustainable development.[3] "Wicked problems" (Rittel & Webber 1973) at best lead to "clumsy solutions" (Verweij et al. 2006) – temporary solutions which themselves may then generate problems, and will therefore have to be continually subjected to observation and revision.

Looking back at the pathbreaking work on post-normal science (Funtowicz & Ravetz 1993), Mode 2 (Gibbons et al. 1994) and transdisciplinarity (cf. e.g. Thompson Klein et al. 2001), and at the intensive and productive discourse which emerged from it around new forms of knowledge production in view of increasingly complex problems, the attempt to establish sustainability science as an original discipline would appear at first glance as a curious anachronism. However, it becomes understandable if we take into account the central epistemic interest of a sustainability science which is explicitly stressed in virtually all conceptions: the understanding of the interaction between social and ecological systems, or, to put it more succinctly, between society and nature. I will enter into this aspect in greater detail in the section after the next.

Transdisciplinary sustainability research

Today's super-discipline is tomorrow's sub-discipline. Instead of establishment or canonization, what is needed is a flexible research mode which will do justice to the dynamics, and to the temporal, spatial, social, cultural etc. uniqueness of sustainability issues. That is an approach which can develop along with the systems for which it is drafting transformational perspectives, and of which it is itself a part. Transdisciplinarity is such a research mode.

Shortly after the introduction of the Sustainable Development model or "Leitbild" into societal discourse at the Rio Conference in 1992, the call for new research approaches which would be appropriate to the integrative challenges that it would involve was raised. And it is indeed demonstrable that approaches such as "post-normal science" or Mode 2 have been substantially influenced and moved forward by the sustainability debate. The ensuing discussion around these two approaches, which has in many respects remained controversial to this day, has lent new momentum to the discourse about transdisciplinarity, which goes back to the 1970s. It soon became clear that an essential area of application of this mode of research would be problems of sustainable development (cf. Gibbons et al. 1994; Thompson Klein et al. 2001). This linkage of transdisciplinary with sustainability issues has since then emerged as a consensus in broad sections of the scientific community (Baumgärtner et al. 2008; Boserup 2010; Farley et al. 2010; Frame & Brown 2008; Jahn et al. 2012; Kauffman 2009; Schneidewind 2010; Vandermeulen & Huylenbroeck 2008; Weinstein 2010). However, how can this linkage be conceptualized?

An understanding of sustainability

At the ISOE, we see sustainable development as a normative model for a *criti-cal* science. In this context, criticism as a fundamental attitude means first of all a reference to the major ecological crisis phenomena, such as climate change, loss of biodiversity, land degradation or the overuse of natural resources. We at the ISOE see these aspects as the issue of the successful or failed regulation and transformation of the *societal relations to nature* ("*gesellschaftliche Naturverhält-nisse*"; see also the following section). Second, criticism means to systematically question the production of knowledge and its use by various societal actors in the pursuit of their goals; the mirror image of that is the methodologically guided self-reflexive examination as to how science deals with the tension between its constituent search for the truth on the one hand, and society's continually grow-ing claims upon the utility of its research on the other.

In order for it to be able to function as a model in this sense, we place sustain-able development in the so-called corridor or crash-barrier model which starts from an analysis of non-sustainable processes (Hummel & Keil 2006; Becker & Jahn 1999, pp. 6–8).[4] The point of departure is the analysis of non-sustainable processes, with the definition of non-sustainable states opening a corridor for various paths towards more sustainable development, channeled by ecological, economic and social "crash barriers." Within this corridor of not only possible, but also desirable, developments, it will then be possible to identify and deal with the concrete sustainability problems specific to the problems of daily life, for various periods of activity and at various spatial, temporal and social scales. In this context, our understanding of sustainability can be briefly characterized as follows:

- Sustainability is a relational, not a substantive concept; it refers to processes, or, more precisely, to the preservation of the continuability of processes, and not to a stable "final condition."
- Sustainability as a normative category triggers a specific complex of inte-gration problems: changes in one dimension of sustainability, in accor-dance with the "pillar model," always also trigger dynamics in the other dimensions; however, these are often neither sufficiently understood nor even perceived. Changes can emerge in marginal or general functional conditions of systems, or else as disturbances, often with systemic (posi-tive) feedbacks.
- Sustainability as a critical concept heuristically generates problems and questions as to what needs to be preserved in order for a process to be con-tinuable, or, less normatively formulated, it serves to identify patterns and relationships which may be preserved through changed conditions. Here, the primary scientific challenges lie in the context of sustainable develop-ment, because these patterns and relationships fundamentally refer to inter-actions between nature and society (see Section 4).

The sustainability discourse

A science which makes sustainable development its normative model must refer to the heterogeneous and controversial sustainability discourse in society, and reconstruct it critically. For this purpose, it is important to distinguish the levels which structure that sustainability discourse. They are empirically difficult to keep apart; analytically, however, they can and must be kept separate. They are the *normative*, the *operative* and the *descriptive* levels (cf. Becker & Jahn 1999, pp. 4–6; Becker 2002).

- *The normative level: What should we do?* Every concept of sustainable development contains normative settings for what is societally desirable, and for the scopes of action and of decision-making processes oriented towards that end. These include such examples as: inter- and intra-generational justice, the preservation of the natural foundations of life, or the intelligent regulation of supply systems. At this level of discourse, orientation knowledge is necessary for the evaluation of goals, the distinction between non-desirable and desirable developments and conditions, etc. At issue are moral principles and their interpretations, as well as criteria and indicators for sustainable development in the three inseparably linked sustainability dimensions. At this level, the key question is: How can a process be designed in the course of which a consensus regarding what is desirable will emerge, and which role will scientific knowledge have in that process (keywords: inclusivity, legitimacy and fairness)?
- *The operative level: What can we do?* Sustainability always implies a strong reference to operative, strategic activity, and to concrete, controllable and affordable solutions to specific problems in various fields of activity and sectors of society (with the familiar problems of scale and of generalization). Here, action or transformation knowledge is necessary. The integration of scientific and practical – political, institutional, business, etc. – knowledge and associated questions of knowledge transfer are the priority here. The important thing is useful and practically implementable concepts, i.e. what is feasible, not simply what is desirable.
- *The descriptive level: What is true?* At the descriptive or analytical level, the question is: Which developments are possible at all? That presupposes knowledge about system dynamics (system knowledge), and begins with the analysis of non-sustainable development directions and conditions. The methodologically guided integration of primarily scientific knowledge for a better understanding of complex effective contexts is the main characteristic at this level of discourse.

Transdisciplinarity

We propose *transdisciplinarity* as a research mode for a critical science which would take sustainable development as a normative Leitbild (Jahn 2013). Even if the discourse regarding transdisciplinarity is still heterogeneous, the development of a broadly shared basic understanding can be ascertained (Jahn et al. 2012). The key points of this basic understanding can briefly be outlined as follows: transdisciplinarity is a research practice which processes complex, real-life problems by means of methodological, guided cooperation between disciplines, and between researchers and practical actors, in order to enable common learning processes between the scientific community and society. In that context, integration is a central cognitive challenge for the research process.

At the ISOE, we are working with the general model of transdisciplinarity which we developed several years ago, and have since been testing and refining it in numerous research projects (Jahn 2005; Bergmann et al. 2005; Bunders et al. 2010; Jahn & Keil 2006; Jahn 2008; Jahn et al. 2012; see Figure 4.1). We cannot enter into the details of the model here (for a detailed explanation, see Jahn 2008, pp. 28–32). Its point of departure is the only apparently self-evident assumption that the handling of societal problems requires that they be linked to gaps in scientific knowledge, i.e. with fundamentally scientific problems. This assumption enables the contributions to societal *and* scientific progress to be viewed as the epistemic goal of a single research dynamic. Moreover, this approach links the two fundamental concepts of transdisciplinarity, which are still distinguished in academic discourse: the real-life approach, in which society employs science in order to design practical solutions to concrete problems; and the internal-scientific approach, in which science basically pursues its own fundamental goals – the production of new knowledge, methods, models and theories – albeit with reference to societal problems.

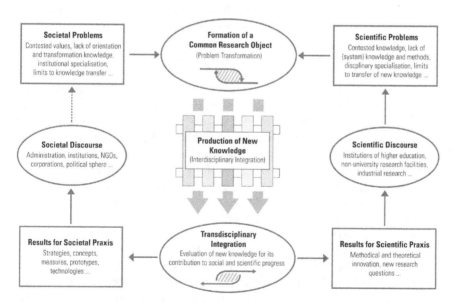

Figure 4.1 Transdisciplinary research process
Source: Jahn, Bergman and Keil (2012).

The conceptual linkage of this understanding of transdisciplinarity with sustainability as a normative Leitbild is possible by means of a simple problem typology. We are adopting it from a scheme developed by the US Committee of Scientists (1999, p. 131). It distinguishes four problem types, according to their strength of consensus regarding knowledge and values. If the forms of knowledge characteristic for the problems of sustainable development are entered into the four fields of this matrix (see Section 3.2), four transdisciplinary research approaches can be distinguished for the purpose of processing the respective problems (Jahn et al. 2012).[5]

1   In cases in which both the knowledge consensus and the value consensus are strong, transformation knowledge is primarily required; in order to generate it, a real-life transdisciplinarity approach will "suffice," for the integration requirements are relatively slight, since the existing knowledge is seen as sufficient to handle a problem, and since the negotiation of orientation knowledge will, thanks to the strong value consensus, be likely to proceed consensually. The participation of actors from the practical sphere is to be recommended in this case (e.g. in phases of product design and assessment), but is not absolutely necessary (standardized social-empirical methods will generally suffice here).
2   If the knowledge consensus is strong, but the value consensus is weak, not only transformation knowledge, but also orientation knowledge, will be needed. As in the first case, for this type of problem, too, a real-life approach is often sufficient. However, integration requirements increase, since conflicts are to be expected in the process of negotiating research goals. The same is true for the evaluation of the relevance of results for societal practice; for this reason, and for reasons of acceptance, the direct participation of practical actors is absolutely necessary, especially for the formulation of problems at the outset of the research process, and also in the integration and evaluation of the results.
3   In the third problem type, knowledge consensus is weak, while value consensus is strong. For this reason, new system knowledge will be needed, together with transformation knowledge. This is the reverse of the first problem type: here, what is needed is rather an internal-scientific approach to transdisciplinarity, and the integration requirements are high, especially for the interdisciplinary production of new scientific knowledge. The participation of practical actors is, as in the first case, advisable, e.g. for the evaluation of the relevance of scientific results to be used to process the original societal problems, albeit not absolutely necessary.
4   In the case of the complex, or "wicked" problems, both the knowledge consensus and the value consensus are weak. Most problems of sustainable development fall into this class; here, specific knowledge in all three categories is necessary. Accordingly, the integration requirements are highest in this case; the real-life and internal-scientific transdisciplinarity approaches combine to form a *single* research dynamic. The participation of practical actors at all phases of the research process is urgent in this case.

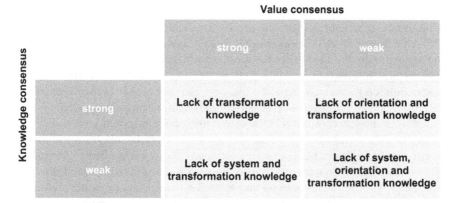

Figure 4.2 Problem typology, according to the strength of knowledge and value consensuses
Source: US Committee of Scientists 1999, p. 131, modified.

Transdisciplinarity is a research practice which continually develops further, together with the cross-disciplinary, historically contingent objects with which it deals. This is true both of its methods and with regard to the forms of participation of practical actors in the research process – i.e. the conceptualization and perception of the interface between science, society and politics – as well as the roles which researchers and stakeholders assume within it. For this reason, the distinctions established above must of course remain broad brush; the empirical richness of transdisciplinary research lies in the spaces between these four types (see Figure 4.2). Thus, transdisciplinarity, unlike a "sustainability science" discipline – however it might be defined – can, as an evolutional research mode, provide the required flexibility of a critical science oriented toward the normative model of "sustainable development."

The epistemic object: Nature–society interactions

The nature–society interactions are, under most conceptions of sustainability science, emphasized as the central object of investigation, or as an essential epistemic interest (cf. Baumgärtner et al. 2008; Kajikawa 2008; Komiyama & Takeuchi 2006; Schellnhuber et al. 2004; Steinfeld & Mino 2009; Weinstein 2010). In view of the growing impact of human activities upon the biosphere, the geosphere, the atmosphere and the hydrosphere, the Nobel prize-winning chemist Paul Crutzen (2002) coined the term *anthropocene* to describe the mutual interdependence between natural and social processes on various spatial and temporal levels. However, understanding these relationships between nature and society demands plenty in the way of preconditions, and raises the question as to how they can become the object of scientific investigation in the first place, i.e. categorized, theoretically considered and scientifically investigated. For it is patterns of relationships which will have to be observed, not isolatable single phenomena.

At the ISOE, we theoretically conceive these dynamic patterns of relation-ships between humans, society and nature as *societal relations to nature* (cf. Becker 2012; Becker et al. 2011; Becker et al. 2006): how are societal and natural ele-ments, structures and processes interconnected through certain practices, insti-tutions and mechanisms, or how are interactive effects between natural and societal processes formed. Analytically, one can distinguish between material/energetic and cultural/symbolic aspects of such relationships. This analytical dis-tinction enables an expression of the materiality of natural conditions, and at the same time their embedding in symbolic orders, interpretive contexts and social constructs. The distinction between nature and society is applied to particular phenomenological contexts, such as transportation and mobility, land use and food, etc.; in other words societal and natural elements and processes are inter-connected in varying areas of activity, and each in a specific manner.

Societal relations to nature are seen as regulated, or at least as regulable and shape-able. The normative view here is that all interactions with nature which are identi-fied as *basal* will have to be designed and regulated in such a manner that societal life processes are intergeneratively continuable, so that societies will not collapse. This presupposes concepts of *successful* regulation, reproduction and development – and thus places the concept of societal relations to nature in the horizon of sustainable development, i.e. in reference to basic needs and the concept of process.

For some time, attempts have been made to view societal relations to nature as systemic contexts, i.e. as *social-ecological systems* (SES) (e.g. Berkes et al. 2003), and to operationalize the analysis of long-term satisfaction of fundamental human needs within that context by means of a model of supply systems (Hum-mel et al. 2011). SESs are concentrated on "hybrid objects" (the intermeshing of material/energetic and cultural/symbolic aspects), and are characterized by com-plexity and adaptability. Conceived as SESs, interactive relationships between nature and society can be researched as a complex of relationships intrinsic to the system. If sustainability problems are reformulated within this concept, the question posed immediately changes: How can these *interlinked* systems – and not merely isolated subsystems – develop sustainably? Criteria can then be developed to determine which system dynamics, in accordance with the above introduced corridor model, could be identified as sustainable, and which not.

A significant task of a transdisciplinary research for sustainable development would first and foremost involve an analysis of the conditions for the preser-vation of the development capability of social-ecological systems under pres-sure to change. The research goal would be the development of options for less non-sustainable regulation of these systems or system complexes – with a focus on sustainable transformations, the preservation of capabilities to develop, and openness for the future.

Conclusions

In this debate over sustainable development, which has been only very roughly outlined here, we have not yet attempted to develop a conclusive theory of sustainability. We have our doubts as to whether it is even useful or possible to formulate a theory (or theories) of sustainability as something conclusive, regardless of the specific processes or structures to which sustainability refers. We assume that the scientific interest in a better understanding of sustainability cannot be separated from the context of the societal discourses around sustainable development – nor should it be. It appears to us not particularly useful to rigidly fix that which should be in a theory of sustainability; moreover, it would yet have to be determined in reference to which understanding of theory this were being done. For any research which referred to such theories would only be able to operate within the corset of "permitted" solutions to problems, which, however, might not be appropriate to the specifics of a particular concrete sustainability problem. If there is to be a theory, it should, in my view, be a critical theory in accordance with the approach described herein which could describe and explain how, where and when transformations to sustainable development might be possible, and could help identify points of bifurcation and windows of opportunity.

Notes

I would like to thank Florian Keil, Egon Becker and Diana Hummel for their support and critical comments on the manuscript.

1 Although it is not always clear which perspective is being adopted in a certain instance. However, as I would like to demonstrate in the following, a clear understanding will be necessary for a productive debate around new ways for handling the problems of sustainable development in a knowledgeable manner.
2 Ziegler and Ott (2011; see, too, the chapter in this volume) take a different path here. They correctly point out that a transdisciplinary science which addresses issues of sustainable development will increasingly face a debate over quality as thorny as the issue it addresses. The suitable and tested framework for that is that of the scientific discipline. However, in view of the fundamental problems addressed herein, the issue of quality cannot, in my view, suffice as an argument for the establishment of a separate discipline. Rather, the important debate about quality and also about evaluation has been conducted for years in the context of the discourse around transdisciplinarity (cf. Bergmann et al. 2005; Defila & DiGiulio 1999; Jahn 2008; Klein 2008; Späth 2008).
3 On this, see the current debate around large-scale technological measures for countering climate change (Rickels et al. 2011).
4 This model is similar to those developed by Schellnhuber et al. on earth-system analysis (cf. Schellnhuber et al. 2004 and Kates et al. 2001).
5 In the following classification, it is assumed that in all cases, at least action or transformation knowledge will be needed. Otherwise, it would not be possible to identify any problem which might be addressed with the aid of research.

Bibliography

Baumgärtner, S., Becker, C., Frank, K., Müller, B., Quaas, M. (2008). Relating the philosophy and practice of ecological economics: The role of concepts, models, and case studies in inter- and transdisciplinary sustainability research. *Ecological Economics*, 67(3), 384–393.

Becker, E. (2002). *Transformations of Social and Ecological Issues into Transdisciplinary Research*. Paris/Oxford: UNESCO Publishing/EOLSS Publishers, 949–963.

Becker, E. (2012). Social-Ecological Systems as Epistemic Objects. In: Glaser, M., Krause, G., Ratter, B., Welp, M., (eds.). *Human-Nature Interactions in the Anthropocene: Potentials of Social-Ecological Systems Analysis*. London: Routledge, 37–59.

Becker, E., Jahn, T. (eds.) (1999). *Sustainability and the Social Sciences. A Cross-Disciplinary Approach to Integrating Environmental Considerations into Theoretical Reorientation*. London: Zed Books Ltd.

Becker, E., Hummel, D., Jahn, T. (2011). Gesellschaftliche Naturverhältnisse als Rahmenkonzept. In: Groß, M. (ed.). *Handbuch Umweltsoziologie*. Wiesbaden: VS Verlag für Sozialwissenschaften, 75–96. (English translation, see http://de.scribd.com/doc/226742771/Societal-Relations-to-Nature-as-a-Common-Frame-of-Reference-for-Integrated-Environmental-Research)

Becker, E., Jahn, T., Hummel, D. (2006). Gesellschaftliche Naturverhältnisse. In: Becker, E., Jahn, T. (eds.). *Soziale Ökologie. Grundzüge einer Wissenschaft von den gesellschaftlichen Naturverhältnissen*. Frankfurt: Campus Verlag, 174–197.

Bergmann, M., Brohmann, B., Hofmann, E., et al. (2005). *Quality Criteria of Transdisciplinary Research. A Guide for the Formative Evaluation of Research Projects*. ISOE-Studientexte, No. 13. Frankfurt: Institute for Social-Ecological Research (ISOE).

Bergmann, M., Jahn, T., Knobloch, T., et al. (2012). *Methods for Transdisciplinary Research. A Primer for Practice*. Frankfurt/New York: Campus Verlag.

Berkes, F., Colding, J., Folke, C. (eds.) (2003). *Navigating Social-Ecological Systems. Building Resilience for Complexity and Change*. Cambridge: University Press.

Boserup, E. (2010). An interdisciplinary visionary relevant for sustainability. Proceedings of the National Academy of Sciences of the United States of America (PNAS), 107(51), 21963–21965.

Bunders, J.F.G., Broerse, J.E.W., Keil, F., et al. (2010). How Can Transdisciplinary Research Contribute to Knowledge Democracy? In: Veld, R. J. (ed.). *Knowledge Democracy. Consequences for Science, Politics, and Media*. Berlin/Heidelberg: Springer, 125–152.

Crutzen, P. J. (2002). Geology of mankind. *Nature*, 415, 23.

Defila, R., DiGiulio, A. (1999). Evaluating transdisciplinary research. *Panorama: Swiss National Science Foundation Newsletter*, 1, 4–27.

Farley, J., Batker, D., de la Torre, I., Hudspeth, T. (2010). Conserving mangrove ecosystems in the Philippines: Transcending disciplinary and institutional borders. *Environmental Management*, 45, 39–51.

Farrell, K. N. (2011). Tackling wicked problems through the transdisciplinary imagination. Book review. *Journal of Environmental Policy and Planning*, 1522–7200, 13(1), 75–77.

Frame, B., Brown, J. (2008). Developing post-normal technologies for sustainability. *Ecological Economics*, 65(2), 225–241.

Funtowicz, S. O., Ravetz, J. R. (1993). Science for the post-normal age. *Futures*, 25(7), 735–755.

Gibbons, M., Limoges, C., Nowotny, H., et al. (1994). *The New Production of Knowledge*. London: Sage.

Hummel, D., Keil, F. (2006). Nachhaltigkeit und kritische Übergänge. In: Becker, E., Jahn, T., (eds.). *Soziale Ökologie. Grundzüge einer Wissenschaft von den gesellschaftlichen Naturverhältnissen*. Frankfurt: Campus Verlag, 240–247.

Hummel, D., Jahn, T., Schramm, E. (2011). Social-Ecological Analysis of Climate Induced Changes in Biodiversity – Outline of a Research Concept. BiK-F Knowledge Flow Paper No. 11. Frankfurt am Main, www.bik-f.de/files/publications/kfp_nr-11_neu__71c3b9.pdf.

Jahn, T. (2005). Soziale Ökologie, kognitive Integration und Transdisziplinarität. *Technikfolgenabschätzung Theorie und Praxis*, 14(2), 32–38.

Jahn, T. (2008). Transdisziplinarität in der Forschungspraxis. In: Bergmann, M., Schramm, E., (eds.). *Transdisziplinäre Forschung. Integrative Forschungsprozesse verstehen und bewerten*. Frankfurt/New York: Campus Verlag, 21–37. (English translation, see http://de.scribd.com/doc/226742768/Transdisciplinarity-in-the-Practice-of-Research)

Jahn, T. (2013). Wissenschaft für eine nachhaltige Entwicklung braucht eine kritische Orientierung. *GAIA*, 22(1), 29–33. (English translation, see http://de.scribd.com/doc/226742770/Science-for-Sustainable-Development-Requires-a-Critical-Orientation)

Jahn, T., Keil, F. (2006). Transdisziplinärer Forschungsprozess. In: Becker, E., Jahn, T., (eds.). *Soziale Ökologie. Grundzüge einer Wissenschaft von den gesellschaftlichen Naturverhältnissen*. Frankfurt/Main: Campus Verlag, 319–329.

Jahn, T., Bergmann, M., Keil., F. (2012). Transdisciplinarity: Between mainstreaming and marginalization. *Ecological Economics*, 79, 1–10.

Jantsch, E. (1972). Towards Interdisciplinarity and Transdisciplinarity in Education and Innovation. In: CERI (eds.). *Interdisciplinarity. Problems of Teaching and Research in Universities*. Paris: Organization for Economic Cooperation and Development, 97–121.

Kajikawa, Y. (2008). Research core and framework of sustainability science. *Sustainability Science*, 3, 215–239.

Kates, R. W., Clark, W. C., Corell, R., et al. (2001). Sustainability science. *Nature*, 292, 641–642.

Kauffman, J. (2009). Advancing sustainability science: Report on the International Conference on Sustainability Science (ICSS) 2009. *Sustainability Science*, 4, 233–242.

Klein, J. T. (2008). Evaluation of interdisciplinary and transdisciplinary research: A literature review. *American Journal of Preventive Medicine*, 116–123.

Komiyama, H., Takeuchi, K. (2006). Sustainability science: Building a new discipline. *Sustainability Science*, 1, 1–6.

Mittelstraß, J. (2005). Methodische Transdisziplinarität. *Technikfolgenabschätzung – Theorie und Praxis*, 2(14), 18–23.

Rickels, W., Klepper, G., Dovern, J., et al. (2011). *Gezielte Eingriffe in das Klima? Eine Bestandsaufnahme der Debatte zu Climate Engineering*. Study commissioned by the German Federal Ministry of Education and Research. Kiel: Kiel Earth Institute, www.bmbf.de/pubRD/CE_Studie2011-Gesamt-final-Druck.pdf.

Rittel, H.W.J., Webber, M. M. (1973). Dilemmas in a general theory of planning. *Policy Sciences*, 4, 155–169.

Schellnhuber, H. J., Crutzen, P. J., Clark, W. C., et al. (2004). *Earth System Analysis for Sustainability*. Cambridge: MIT Press.

Schneidewind, U. (2010). An institutional reform agenda for the establishment of transdisciplinary sustainability research. *GAIA*, 19(2), 122–128.

Späth, P. (2008). Learning ex-post: Towards a simple method and set of questions for the self-evaluation of transdisciplinary research. *GAIA*, 17(2), 224–232.

Steinfeld, J. I., Mino, T. (2009). Education for sustainable development: The challenge of trans-disciplinarity. *Sustainability Science*, 4, 1–2.

Thompson Klein, J., Grossenbacher-Mansuy, W., Häberli, R., et al. (eds.) (2001). *Transdisciplinarity: Joint Problem Solving among Science, Technology and Society. An Effective Way for Managing Complexity*. Basel/Boston/Berlin: Birkhäuser Verlag.

US Committee of Scientists (1999). *Sustaining the People's Lands: Recommendations for Stewardship of the National Forests and Grasslands into the Next Century*. Washington, DC: U.S. Department of Agriculture.

Vandermeulen, V., Van Huylenbroeck, G. (2008). Designing trans-disciplinary research to support policy formulation for sustainable agricultural development. *Ecological Economics*, 67(3), 52–361.

Verweij, M., Douglas, M., Ellis, R., et al. (2006). Clumsy solutions for a complex world. *Public Administration*, 84, 817–843.

Weinstein, M. (2010). Sustainability science: The emerging paradigm and the ecology of cities. *Sustainability: Science, Practice, & Policy*, 6(1), 1–5.

Ziegler, R., Ott, K. (2011). The quality of sustainability science – A philosophical perspective. *Sustainability: Science, Practice, & Policy*, 7(1), 31–44.

5 The quality of sustainability science

A philosophical perspective

Rafael Ziegler and Konrad Ott

Introduction

Sustainability science has become a recognizable domain of scientific funding. Two notable examples are the program *Forschung für Nachhaltigkeit* (Research for Sustainability), funded by the German Ministry of Education and Research, and the *Science and Technology for Sustainability Program* of the National Academies in the United States. Funding by itself does not legitimize sustainability science. Rather, it calls for reflection on such scientific activities, their key features, and the reasons for them. There is also sustainability science in the sense that there are scientists who regard themselves as sustainability scientists and who claim to do such science. However, neither funding nor a mere presumption to do science is sufficient to establish a scientific field. Sustainability science must continuously reflect on its practice and its key features, to avoid becoming unduly doctrinaire. To this end, we raise from a philosophical perspective four questions regarding key features of sustainability science. How these questions are dealt with strongly influences the quality of sustainability science. The respective choices and positions should be made explicit so as to avoid confusion and to improve understanding of the concept "sustainability science."

This article examines key features of the projects and research activities of sustainability science – these features define our working concept of "sustainability science" or "science for sustainable development."[1] These features are: normativity, the temporal character (urgency) of the research, the inclusion of nonscientists into sustainability science, and the task of understanding social and environmental interrelations. Put briefly, these four features concern the explication and articulation of values and principles (normativity), addressing the temporal relation of the research to what is at stake (urgency), the justified inclusion of nonscientists (participation), and the joint research of natural and social scientists (interdisciplinarity).

These features make sustainability science difficult to evaluate according to the standards of disciplinary science, especially of the natural sciences. The overall field of sustainability science, with its explicit inclusion of normative considerations, seems to rest on shaky ground by the standards of many other disciplinary approaches. However, since the challenges of sustainability are real and unresolved, and a high quality of scientific inquiry desirable, a deeper understanding of these features matters. Philosophical considerations, in particular from the philosophy of science, can *contribute* to this task.[2] For the investigation of the quality of sustainability science, it is of primary importance to ask methodological questions and to examine ways of defining a problem. As important as the development of indicators and tool sets for evaluation is the philosophical task of examining major presuppositions of sustainability science and their justifications. Our approach aims at deep and comprehensive questioning in sustainability science: depth with respect to each feature, comprehensiveness as covering all major features.

We first introduce a famous example to demonstrate that the philosophy of science plays a role by co-structuring the debate in sustainability science. Our illustration is the ongoing dispute between weak and strong sustainability. We show how Popperian and Kuhnian philosophy of science co-structure Neumayer's ([2003] 2010) classic contribution to the debate. In addition, we demonstrate this to be an uptake of philosophy of science that leads to a conceptually problematic way of framing the debate.[3] The article then discusses how a critical reexamination of the Kuhnian and Popperian views can inform an analysis of the four key features mentioned above – and with it shed a different light on the debate between strong and weak sustainability. Philosophy of science so conceived is enabling and its attempt to pose the relevant questions is one contribution to a critical self-understanding for sustainability scientists. Rather than uncritically stating certain features, we reexamine why and under what conditions features are justified, thereby improving the quality of the research. Finally, we draw some tentative conclusions for the emerging culture of sustainability science.

Framing issues – The difficult heritage of philosophy of science

The relevance of philosophy of science for the way questions are asked in sustainability science can be demonstrated via the discussion of weak and strong sustainability. This key debate revolves around the question of whether natural capital, in particular natural resources and natural sinks, should be regarded in principle as substitutable ("if we run out of coal or oil it does not matter, for we will be able to substitute them with another energy source") – weak sustainability – or as complementary ("if we destroy or deplete natural capital such as the world freshwater supplies, there is no alternative for this essential service") – strong sustainability. Here we focus on Eric Neumayer's ([2003] 2010) seminal contribution to this debate.

Weak sustainability (WS) in Neumayer's definition requires "keeping total net investment [or total savings], suitably defined to encompass all relevant forms of capital, above zero." In contrast, *strong sustainability* (SS) "calls for the preservation of the physical stock of those forms of natural capital that are regarded as nonsubstitutable (so-called critical natural capital)." Neumayer states the goal of his argument as follows: "It will be argued here that both paradigms are non-falsifiable under scientific standards. Therefore, there can be no unambiguous support for either weak sustainability or strong sustainability." At the end of this extended debate, he states: "The contest between WS and SS cannot be settled by theoretical inquiry. Nor can it be settled by empirical inquiry." For the present purpose, we need to pay attention to the way in which Neumayer frames the question. *Can the paradigms of WS or SS be falsified?* This question (as Neumayer also indicates via his references) points directly to two seminal contributors to the philosophy of science: Karl Popper and Thomas Kuhn. We will therefore very briefly introduce a few essential points of these respective philosophers so as to highlight the philosophical structure of Neumayer's question.[4]

Karl Popper and scientific method

Karl Popper (1963) influentially argued for the idea that science is distinguished by a scientific method consisting of an evolutionary process of conjectures and refutations. Popper's work has been doubly influential: with respect to reinforcing the meta-idea that science is distinguished by a *method* and his specific idea of *falsification*, which has been endorsed by numerous scientists, as well as – suitably for a discussion of sustainability science – a wider public.

The specification of this scientific method, Popper argues, allows science to be distinguished from pseudoscience (the so-called demarcation problem). Popper believed fields such as psychoanalysis or scientific socialism belong in the domain of pseudoscience because they do not follow the scientific method. Popper did not describe how the fabric of science works in its day-to-day routines. His philosophy of science is prescriptive, since it tells courageous scientists how they should proceed, a method, Popper believed, that would bring about scientific progress in the long run. On the one hand, scientists (should) advance bold and risky hypotheses and, on the other hand, they (should) attempt to derive empirical predictions from these conjectures and seek to refute them. This process of conjectures and refutations is (or should be) in Popper's view at the core of the scientific method. A proposition is only scientific if it is possible to falsify it. Thus, if neither WS nor SS can be properly falsified, both concepts would not belong to the realm of scientific knowledge. If key approaches in sustainability science turned out to be nonfalsifiable pseudoscience, then this way of framing the problem could have serious consequences in general for sustainability science well beyond the focus of Neumayer's claim.

The situation looks less painful for sustainability science if empirical falsification is perceived as a special case of refutation. There are many controversies that cannot be settled by empirical falsification of risky predications derived from a theory. For example, ethicists may refute specific claims by means of analysis of the concepts and the internal coherence of a theory (Neumayer himself engages in this kind of logical argumentation). Here, nonempirical shortcomings such as circularity, non sequitur, self-contradiction, absurd implications, and so forth count as counterarguments. There are thus plausible refutations beyond empirical falsification.

Thomas Kuhn and scientific community

Only Kuhn's (1996) paradigm account of science has been similar in scientific and popular influence in the twentieth century. Paradigms, in one key meaning of the definitive term in Kuhn's work,[5] offer a vision of what scientific work ("puzzle-solving") is worth performing in terms of theory articulation, empirical experimentation, and measurement, and a vision that determines which scientific work is secondary or even illegitimate. A paradigm in this sense includes generalizations along with preferred instruments and methods. It is furthermore structured by ontological commitments about elements and concepts and powered by the faith that nature can be fit into the box of the paradigm via puzzle solving (such as the often brilliant work of more elegant theory formulation and extension or more precise measurements).

Kuhn describes the social structure of science as one of particular scientific communities that are constituted by a shared faith in a paradigm. In his view, the scientific community is the supreme authority for validating and assessing scientific claims. Scientific claims are adopted and rejected according to criteria that stem from the paradigm itself. Students are initiated into the scientific community via textbooks, academic study programs, and laboratory training, and they adopt basic axioms, concepts, and mindsets. Specialized conferences and peer-reviewed journals make it possible to assure the quality of research done within the community. In such ways, normal science becomes established.

In light of Popper's and Kuhn's views on science, the philosophical structure of Neumayer's question emerges – and is puzzling! From a Popperian perspective, the structural process of science is one of conjecture and refutation with falsification as the selection, or rather elimination, criterion. From a Kuhnian perspective, scientific work mostly takes place in paradigm-based normal science. There will be scientific revolutions and new paradigms will emerge and take hold according to Kuhn, but the selection criterion for the new paradigm is not one of falsification. Moreover, falsification plays little role for (faith-based) normal science. We thus face the following dilemma: either WS or SS really are genuine paradigms – but then we should not expect any attempts at falsification, rather "puzzle solving" (much of such puzzle solving is in evidence in the materials Neumayer cites) – or WS and SS are falsifiable. Paradigms are not falsifiable according to Kuhn's rich account of the history of science and arguably also for conceptual reasons (for example, the holism of paradigms makes it unclear what would have to be rejected if an experiment is to be falsified). In short, viewed in terms of these philosophies of science, Neumayer's guiding question is indeed a difficult one, not only because of empirical problems (missing or incomplete data on resource availability, substitution elasticities, and so forth), but because conceptually the question – can paradigms be falsified? – is problematically stated. That paradigms cannot be falsified is a conceptual truth and Neumayer's thesis is in this sense correct – but this of course is hardly what he meant to show.[6] No case studies or secondary literature are required for this result.

Moreover, this uptake of the philosophy of science has further problematic implications. "Normative positions are nonrefutable," according to Neumayer. There are two readings of this claim. First, it can be justified in the sense that a person's violation of a normative proposition does not refute the proposition's validity. A corrupt politician does not falsify the validity of anticorruption legislation. Instead, he demonstrates the difficulty of its effective implementation. The Popperian language of risky predictions and falsifications, and its classic example (relativity theory), tempts us to exclude or ignore genuine ethical methods of refutation. An example is John Rawls's (1999) classic method of reaching a reflective equilibrium, which draws on ethical convictions as well as a procedural method ("the veil of ignorance") to reach an outcome motivated by a coherentist epistemology (see also Scanlon 2003).[7] In a second reading, Neumayer seems to endorse some variant of metaethical noncognitivism. His claim that there might be a "persuasive case" in favor of a specific concept of sustainability could be informed by emotivism that regards normative statements as mere expressions of emotive attitudes. Emotivism is by no means an uncontested metaethical theory, as it cannot distinguish between the convincing force of reason and the persuasive force of rhetoric (Ott 1997). Under emotivist premises, the question of how the quality of ethical reflection within sustainability science might be assessed becomes somewhat pointless or must be replaced by interviews about how well and badly people feel within a given project. If the project were performed in a good mood, the ethical quality would be high. Given this consequence, we would not like to adopt an emotive approach to assess quality in the ethical dimension of sustainability science.[8]

If normative statements are not refutable in laboratories or on scientific expeditions, it does not follow that they are necessarily unscientific. But it would be unscientific not to use the methods proper to ethics. Because the debate between WS and SS depends strongly on ethical arguments about our responsibility to future generations, about precautionary motives, and about our relationship to the natural environment, excluding normative propositions from method-based investigation amounts to a problematic way of posing the question – more precisely, to an incomprehensive way.

This analysis of the structure of Neumayer's argument demonstrates that philosophical questions play a role in the analysis of sustainability science and the self-understanding of sustainability scientists. One might abstract them away in the routines of individual projects, but one should not overlook them in basic debates. If sustainability science is to stand for a distinctive way of doing science, the philosophical dimensions of this mode need to be considered. We submit that both Kuhn's focus on the scientific community and Popper's call for a scientific method continue to raise important questions. The point, however, is not to uncritically accept their philosophies, but to reconsider them in the respective context. In the next sections, we therefore deal with their heritage for thinking about key features of sustainability science. By doing so, we follow the pathway Neumayer has opened, but add that there are different viable pathways for the framing of questions in sustainability science.

Sustainability science

In this section, we wish to deepen the understanding of our four key features of sustainability science that its practitioners have identified as distinguishing sustainability science in a particular, and even peculiar, way.[9]

Normativity: Sustainability science explicitly acknowledges a normative context, that of sustainability or sustainable development (Clark & Dickinson 2003). As "sustainability" and "sustainable development" are contested concepts, many definitions and approaches have been argued for. However, it seems fair to say that the so-called Brundtland definition – "sustainable development is development that meets the needs of the present without compromising the ability of future generations to meet their own needs" – defines a vague space of global intergenerational and intragenerational justice and development that, nevertheless, no specific or more rigorous definition can ignore (Jacobs 1999). If so, any concept of sustainability must clarify notions and theories of justice with respect to development. This clarification is by no means an easy task and we will return to it below.

Urgency: A commitment to the fulfillment of human needs in a world where even the basic requirements of a large part of the human population are often not met implies a dimension of urgency. How can science and technology help move society toward a more sustainable future (Clark & Dickinson 2003)? There is an ethical supposition in claims of urgency: as moral persons, we are not neutral to whether a specific problem might be addressed now, in some decades, or even in centuries. Fermat stated a theorem in the seventeenth century, but did not disclose the proof. It took three centuries until Andrew Wiles and Richard Taylor did so; in the intermediary time those interested simply had to wait and/or puzzle. The patience of the puzzle solver is a virtue. In puzzle-solving science, one might trust that all major problems will be solved in the longer run and that science will, in the end, discover some ultimate truth (Peirce's "final opinion") about how the universe is. Meanwhile, down on earth, there is suffering, injustice, and devastation of the biosphere. The puzzle-solving scientific attitude can abstract away from such pressing concerns, transforming them into private opinions a scientist may (or may not) hold. However, in the case of sustainability science these moral concerns are intrinsic. Those whose needs are to be met may simply no longer be alive in the long run. There is still another aspect of urgency: in the case of climate change the risks associated with waiting for better science might simply be judged too high. A purely scientific attitude can become a source of risk in sustainability science. As Hiroshi Komiyama and Kazuhiko Takeuchi (2006) put it: "The search for solutions cannot wait."

Inclusion of nonscientists: Sustainability science typically endorses a commitment to the inclusion of nonscientists in the process of research itself. Funding bodies might even require the satisfaction of this condition. As Kates et al. (2001) observe, "Combining different ways of knowing and learning will permit different social actors to work in concert, even with much uncertainty and limited information." Sustainability science thus supposes that nonscientists can contribute to projects in the field in ways that the scientists involved cannot substitute for. The inclusion of nonscientists and its justification is further discussed below.

Interrelation of environment and society: Sustainability science seeks to "understand the fundamental character of interactions between nature and society" (Kates et al. 2001; see also Renn 2008), to find joint ways in which natural and social scientists can improve the understanding of environment–society relations. Typical tools for such attempts are scenario techniques that depend on information and causal mechanisms from natural and social sciences. Another example might be coupled models that shed some light on the interactions between human and natural systems.

In the subsequent sections, we discuss the questions raised by these features and their contribution to the quality of sustainability science. In doing so, we further engage with the weak and strong sustainability debate and its framing in our attempt to contribute to a critical and enabling philosophy of science.

Why include nonscientists?

An important contribution, explicitly informed by the philosophy of science, is the postnormal science proposed by Silvio Funtowicz, Jerome Ravetz, and others (Funtowicz & Ravetz 1991; 1993; van der Sluijs & Funtowicz 2008). This approach specifically focuses on the inclusion of nonscientists (as a matter of extended peer review). Postnormal science is explicitly situated in a sustainability context:

> The new global environmental issues . . . are global in scale and long term in their impact. Data are . . . radically inadequate. Science . . . can frequently only achieve at best mathematical models and computer simulations, which are essentially untestable. On the basis of such uncertain inputs, decisions must be made . . .
>
> (Funtowicz & Ravetz 1991)

This context of sustainability science calls for a revision of the organization of science:[10] the scientific community, in the context of sustainability issues, must open itself to an extended peer review and the extended facts it might offer. Put differently, the Kuhnian community structure, which gives the scientific community supreme authority, no longer applies. As Funtowicz and Ravetz (1991) note, this can be observed as a simple matter of external pressure. To the extent that scientists are "manifestly incapable of providing effective conclusive answers to the many problems they confront," administrators, politicians, and others are able to "force" their way into the dialogue. However, there is also a separate series of arguments for the inclusion of nonscientists in sustainability science.[11] We discuss first five epistemological, then three political, and finally one ethical argument for the inclusion of nonscientists in project-based sustainability science.

1   *Local knowledge:* The inclusion of nonscientists opens sustainability science to local knowledge and tacit knowledge considerations. Funtowicz and Ravetz (1991) assert that "knowledge of local conditions may not merely shape the policy problem, it can also determine which data is strong and relevant" (see also Renn 2008). Thus, the inclusion of nonscientists might be relevant for both problem formulation and for contextual knowledge application.

Local knowledge is found in laypersons and it may also be stored in literature that does not count as scientific. According to contemporary standards of peer-reviewed journals, such literature is very often "dark grey." Local knowledge often comes in "thick" narratives that are not "stored" in the same way as disciplinary knowledge.

2 *Bias:* Funtowicz and Ravetz (1991) contend that "experts lack practical knowledge and have their own forms of bias." Normal science involves a process of initiation: assumptions have to be internalized, methods learned – in short, a paradigmatic view acquired. The result is a certain way of seeing the world: we see evidence of this when, for example, laypersons strongly react to the economists' point of view. Because biases must remain unnoticed to be biases, the antidote against biases must come from outside. The inclusion of nonscientists can serve as an antidote against specialization and can help expose the limits of science. For instances, scientists are often ignorant about history while history plays an important role for local people.

3 *Self-criticism and normal science:* Precisely because academic science has a strong institutional character that involves hierarchies, careers, and hence the life prospects of people, internal criticism may be difficult or even rare (Betz 2006). Again, outside perspectives not so constrained can be helpful in engaging in such criticism. Laypersons do not have blind faith in science and often challenge scientific claims. In this way, the scientific virtue of a critical attitude is turned against science from the outside.

4 *Alertness:* Normal science can be compared to a large tanker. It is the tanker of science at sea and it is difficult to change its course once it has picked up speed. Research programs involve significant human and monetary investments and paradigm work on measuring and theory articulation is likely to have a long-term perspective. As a result, scientists as a community may have difficulty being alert to novel challenges that do not easily fit into their theoretical outlook. Nonscientists are not so constrained; hence, they can serve the function of communicating novel issues, thereby possibly making the ship of science more responsive.

5 *Conjectures:* Conjectures require imagination. Imagination is, like prudence or even wisdom, not only found among scientists. The inclusion of nonscientists may open the scientific communities to new conjectures: wild ideas, naïve questions, and unexpected observations, that the scientific community has the resources to state rigorously, refine, or refute.

6 *Care and concern:* Funtowicz and Ravetz (1991) write that "those whose lives and livelihood depend on solutions of the problems will have a keen awareness of how general principles are realized in their 'back yards.'" Science that aims to have a practical influence must be especially cautious with respect to the real-world impacts it may have. To the extent that people most affected by environmental issues are not generally scientists, the care argument is sociologically plausible: those most affected are likely to care the most, and hence care that the policy instrument (or similar) is appropriate. In medicine, it is the patient who must live with the consequences of a physician's

recommendation for surgery. Because of this, the ultimate decision is up to her (informed consent). In similar ways, local stakeholders have to cope with the consequences of projects designed by scientific experts.

7 *Timing:* If sustainability science seeks to contribute to practical problem solving, then generally timing will be one component of successful science. For example, if a scientific report, however brilliant, misses the window of opportunity provided by an election cycle, it might be practically useless. Here, too, the inclusion of nonscientists may offer insight. Such inclusion also gives scientists a better understanding of the affected people's perception of the pressure and urgency of a given problem (for example a problem could be less urgent for local people than the scientists believe!).

8 *Power:* Nonscientists may not only offer insight, but they can also generate the power to help advance a proposal resulting from sustainability science. Nonscientists who are informed and have the necessary influence can help effectively communicate or even implement a policy proposal (Bergmann 2008).

9 *Normativity:* A normative science needs to take care with respect to the social values it seeks to achieve or promote. However, as Funtowicz and Ravetz (1991) note, values are in dispute. Precisely for this reason, it seems important to make this dispute public and not to leave science with the decision of which values to prioritize (Renn 2008). The inclusion of non-scientists can contribute to this end. Scientists as such are not experts in value judgments. Ethicists may offer skills for the investigation of normative intuitions and their implications, historians may offer insight into the contexts of such intuitions, and so forth. However, here too bias and limited self-criticism can pertain. Scientists should not have ultimate authority in moral matters.

These various arguments partly complement one other, and may also be in many contexts quasi-independent. It is conceivable that in a context concerning basic needs, the value dimension is trivial and uncontroversial. This does not mean that there is no value dimension in this context, but only that it may justifiably fade into the background as far as the possible inclusion of nonscientists is concerned. More generally, it seems that some set of these arguments ought to be made explicit for the specific context of the sustainability project at hand. Put differently, for each sustainability science research project with nonscientists included, the various epistemological, political, and normative relations between scientists and nonscientists ought in principle be made explicit. They are not always the same: they may not always have the same weight and the design consequences (the question of *how* nonscientists are included or participate) are accordingly also likely to vary.

These reasons indicate that one criterion for the quality of sustainability science is an explicit rationale for the inclusion of nonscientists in a given project. In terms of the evaluation of sustainability science projects, this point concerns especially *ex ante* and intermediary evaluations. That there are reasons for the inclusion of nonscientists is here not in doubt, but what is required is that these reasons are made explicit and are specified according to the design of a given project. In his discussion, Neumayer does not explicitly take this feature into account for his problem formulation, but where he implicitly notes it, it sug-gests a tendency in favor of strong sustainability. For example, discussing climate change, he notes that

> voters and politicians who favour decisive and urgent action . . . are con-cerned that climate change is like no other and that its sheer scale and extent of damage threatens to create a new bio-physical world that either leaves the future worse off or violates the inalienable right to enjoy natural capital.
>
> (Neumayer [2003] 2010)

The dogma of participation

The establishment of sustainability science noted at the beginning of this article also means that some funders mandate the participation of nonscientists. In such cases, inclusion does not need to be justified, but becomes an expectation or sim-ply a dogma of sustainability science. However, one can endorse the nine reasons just mentioned and remain critical of dogmatic ways to perform participation for the sake of funding requirements. We may face such dogma if participation and inclusion seem to be mere add-ons to a given project, are disconnected to the scientific objectives, or do not rely on a sound concept.

For this reason, Wolfgang Zierhofer and Paul Burger (2007) have a valid point when they question whether the inclusion of nonscientists in transdisciplinary research always serves epistemic ends. They define transdisciplinary research "*formally* by interdisciplinarity and participation (of nonscientists), and problem-oriented research is its main *epistemic end*."

Problem-oriented research in their understanding aims to reduce knowledge gaps that "hinder some stakeholders or institution to pursue certain actions." Based on a survey of sixteen transdisciplinary research projects, they found that few projects really investigate goals or knowledge objectives. They conclude that transdisciplinary research should not be considered a distinct mode of knowledge production. Instead, it "should be considered rather a class of epistemically and methodologically heterogeneous research activities which are only formally uni-fied by the two general properties 'interdisciplinary' and 'participatory.'"

Skepticism as to the inclusion of nonscientists is reasonable in view of par-ticipation as dogma. However, Zierhofer and Burger's conclusion that transdis-ciplinary research is "not a distinct mode of knowledge production" does not logically follow from the observation of a sample of empirical examples. More-over, their conclusion seems to be the consequence of a formal description of transdisciplinary research that does not specify a domain of investigation, which could be numbers as in mathematics, life as in biology, the commitment to sus-tainability as in sustainability science, and so forth. These domains of investi-gation stand for distinct epistemic ends (What is number? What is life? What is sustainability?). Once we have stated these domains, we can ask whether transdisciplinary research contributes to the respective ends. For example, sustainability science focuses on the promotion of normative sustainability goals and to this end on an improved understanding of nature–society relations. The inclusion of nonscientists can serve this end (see the previous list of arguments). Therefore, transdisciplinary research in conjunction with a domain of investigation does seem to yield distinct modes of knowledge production.

As Zierhofer and Burger's (2007) survey of research projects shows, many of them relied in practice on nonscientists only for strategic reasons. They benefit from a dogma of participation and here the inclusion of nonscientists may not serve epistemic ends. But sustainability scientists should examine what relationships between scientists and nonscientists may promote the issue at hand. Therefore, in our view a criterion for the quality of sustainability science is an explicit statement why nonscientists are included and a clear concept of how participation should be performed and how the results should contribute to the overall results.

Why the pathos of urgency? The temporal horizon

We tend to think that whether a geometric proof is valid is independent from its discovery by Greek, Indian, or other mathematicians. The context of discovery is distinct from the context of justification. According to this view, it is the reasoning for a scientific claim that counts, not its timing. We say that a scientific claim is valid if it can be shown to be a condition of the world, according to a specific observation or laboratory method that verifies or confirms the claim (this method usually involves a specific community structure for confirmation and testimony of experiments and observations). Such conditions of the world can have a temporal reference. For example, the passenger pigeon – once an abundant species in North America – is supposed to have become extinct in the early twentieth century. A scientific claim (or entire set of claims) can involve a reference to a specific time or to a temporal dynamic (such as the once abundant passenger pigeon becoming extinct). However, such temporal references are irrelevant with respect to the validity of the scientific claims.[12]

Many events and temporal dynamics are relevant within sustainability science. "Urgency" is determined by temporal considerations (how much time do we have?) as well as ethical stakes (how important is the event/dynamic?). For example, predictions and forecasts regarding single events and dynamics of stocks are frequently related to human options. If global temperature is likely to increase by two degrees within the next generation, this can affect environmental security (for example, shelter due to increased risks of floods). Accordingly, there can be questions of mitigation (fight temperature increase) and adaptation (improve shelter). As the adaptation example shows, the relevance of scientific claims is not dependent on the human capacity to influence the occurrence of an event or the pattern of a dynamic. In any case, sustainability science is interested in the dynamics of specific stocks and flows over time. These dynamics (Aristotle's *kinesis*) are perceived from the normative perspective: in sustainability science one must, *ceteris paribus*, engage oneself against stocks of pollutants, declining stocks of resources, increasing stocks of greenhouse gases, etc. As in the case of atmospheric greenhouse gases, the dynamics of increase give reason to claim that mitigation is urgent. If a lake is close to collapse or a species is near extinction, action is urgent. Many stocks are goods that are components of the overall fair bequest package we owe to future generations. If so, sustainability science must schedule the relationship between stocks and time. A normative approach to the kinetics of stocks is required. Quite often, there will be a window of opportunity. We can call this the *kairos*, the opportunity to act.

The quality of sustainability science is codependent on an explicit way of dealing with urgency: How do stocks change over time? What are the temporal windows? How can long-term objectives be combined prudently with first steps and a transition period? In our view, these questions do not necessitate a departure from sound scientific standards, but augment them. The pathos of urgency as such clearly does not make any claim a scientific one. Scenarios being presented in a context of urgency must *in principle* be open to disciplinary scrutiny and critique. Even the claims of urgency themselves must be open for refutation. What is required is the explicit contextualization of scientific claims (and practices) in a temporal framing of dynamics and events. Whether a scientific claim is considered as evidence and a reason for action is ultimately an ethical question. (This establishes a double link to the inclusion of nonscientists: Who decides on ethical stakes? Who has knowledge of and influence on windows of opportunity for action?)

These questions, we submit, also need to be asked for the weak versus strong sustainability debate. Consider the example of energy substitution, such as the substitution of nonrenewable oil with renewable solar energy that Neumayer discusses. There are optimistic scenarios that suggest substitution is possible and there are pessimistic scenarios that put the possibility of substitution into doubt. As Neumayer ([2003] 2010) notes, "Which of the two projections will be closer to reality we do not know." Again, we need to pay attention to the formulation of the question. No doubt, there are energy optimists and energy pessimists, but what, in this context, is the meaning of "closer to reality?" The discussion above suggests that for a sustainability evaluation of these scenarios we would have to ask whose needs are likely to be affected and how and when they will be affected (with respect to the question of substituting oil with solar power). With regard to urgency, WS would likely rely on economic wisdom about how depreciation of a resource motivates the search for substitutes, while SS would recommend political measures to speed up such substitution. In such matters, there is no such thing as empirical "closeness to reality." "Closeness to reality," we submit, requires an account of these questions of needs and urgency without which a dimension of sustainability science is missing. Only with these questions addressed can we discuss and compare which energy scenarios we would like to base our decision on. Ethico-temporal urgency is a condition of asking the question.

Why must various disciplines work together?

Sustainability science, it will be recalled, seeks to understand the "interactions between nature and society," and it is in principle plausible that it needs to draw on the knowledge of both natural and social scientists, as well as the humanities and vocational disciplines (such as engineering, law, and medicine) to advance this understanding. As a minimum question of quality, the various scientists working on the respective issue should be included (Jahn 2008). For example, research on a problem with floods requires hydrological (and possibly climatological) knowledge, but also political knowledge regarding the societal actors and their coalitions.

A closely related second question of quality is the hierarchy of the disciplines involved. Does one discipline define the problem and simply add the other disciplines so that the basic perspective on the problem is essentially disciplinary (compare the example below)? If there is a hierarchy, what is the reason? One nonhierarchical approach is to start from the societal problem (rather than the scientific puzzle of a discipline).[13] Working together is then a process of joint problem analysis (Wätzold 2009). Scenario techniques and models can serve as tools for joint work in this sense. Scenario techniques are one example of a family of models, which suggests a joint method for various sciences. Moreover, scenarios and other tools can themselves be included in integrated sustainability approaches, such as the embedded cases study approach for sustainability learning (Scholz et al. 2006).

In light of the discussion of urgency and scientific validity, we need to recall that problem-oriented science is not something different from scientific practice (and its methods, data, observations, and so forth). In establishing a knowledge base, sustainability science consumes the results of scientific research. It frequently relies on normal science. Therefore, sustainability science is hard to reconcile with philosophies of science that are highly critical of modern science. A third question of quality in this category is whether sustainability science produces results that are communicable or translatable into specific disciplines and open to the critique and scrutiny of disciplinary science and its systems of peer review.[14]

Again, the debate of weak versus strong sustainability can serve as an instructive illustration of this feature of sustainability science. Both paradigms presuppose some ideas of how humans and natural systems are related. We here make three observations with respect to the nature–society relation:

1　The definitions of weak sustainability, strong sustainability (see above), and of natural capital[15] and their terminology originate in economic thought about investments, substitutes, complements, capital, and so forth. Thus, it is already a challenge to translate the weak versus strong debate into a genuine debate of social *and* natural science.

2　The debate issues from another debate between much wider paradigms: those of neoclassical economics and ecological economics.[16] Roughly put, the first paradigm conceives of the economy as an autonomous entity in which economic growth can be examined and explained without reference to exogenous variables. Endogenous growth is in principle unlimited. The second paradigm conceives of the economy as a subset of the biosphere and claims that economic growth cannot be explained without reference to the enveloping biophysical system that also limits economic growth. The anomaly in the Kuhnian sense is the problem of substitution (the old neoclassical paradigm is pushed to defend the increasingly contested claim that natural resources and services are substitutable). *Prima facie*, the paradigm of ecological economists necessitates nature–society integration due to its image of the economy as a subset of the biosphere. Its paradigmatic image is one that fits well with respect to sustainability science, whereas the same cannot be said, at least at first sight, with respect to neoclassical economics.

3   Precisely because the debate is in the first place one between economic paradigms, we need to pay attention to the structure of the argument and to the burden of proof. Here we find the following structure in Neumayer's ([2003] 2010) discussion of the debate. He subjects the four premises of weak sustainability to the logical and empirical objections of opponents,[17] concluding that SS proponents cannot decisively refute WS because their objections are inconclusive or logically flawed. But there is no complementary examination of the premises of strong sustainability.[18] In short, Neumayer does not ask whether proponents of WS have good arguments to put the SS premises into doubt. Therefore, the burden of proof is not applied in an evenhanded manner.

We submit that the normative considerations, along with the observation that this very debate has a disciplinary bias (it is in the first place posited as an economic debate, in which ecologists do not really have a say), suggest a reasonable argument in favor of strong sustainability. The evidence is that ecologists clearly tend toward the nonsubstitution view (see e.g. MEA 2005). Indeed, some of them might not accept the terms of the debate as meaningful to begin with. How could life-supporting ecosystems possibly be substitutable? Even minute artificial biosphere projects have failed.

Why do ethical considerations matter?

Even for Popperians, as we noted above, scientific method is not reduced to empirical falsification. It is all the more important not to simply ignore normative questions because they are not falsifiable via risky predictions. Normativity is a key feature of sustainability science. Under a broad conception of science (as in the continental tradition of *Wissenschaft*) this is not as problematic as under a narrow conception of science. Many disciplines are intrinsically related to and connected with ethical questions (e.g. medicine, technology, ecology, architecture, economics, psychology, history). Scientists might abstract away such ethical questions, but they should not be ignorant about the closeness of their discipline to ethics. It might be beneficial for specific research (experiments) to abstract away all social concerns; however, from this premise it cannot be inferred that such a move would be beneficial for whole disciplines. This rejection of value-free dogmatism often has been stated in critical theory of science and it can be supported even by Max Weber's critical analysis of the fact–value distinction (Ott 1997).

Because sustainability science incorporates members of different disciplines, its general ethical framework – with all its pitfalls – must become transparent. How can there be sound ethics within the realm of science and, especially, within the field of sustainability science? We define ethics as being a critical reflection and analysis of prescriptive claims of different kinds (e.g. metaethical, moral, axiological, prudential, legal-political). Ethical inquiry investigates how prescriptive claims (How should we act?) can be substantiated by means of argument. Given this definition, we would like to propose the following considerations regarding the quality of sustainability science with respect to normativity.

1   If science, in general, often comes close to ethics and implicitly has a normative dimension, then it is a minimum requirement to make norms and values explicit to both scientists and nonscientists. Clearly, this is not easy, since humans are always engaged in moral affairs and often the borderline between facts and values is passed unnoticed. This is simply human, but in science it is "all-too-human." High quality in the ethical dimension of sustainability science implies a sharp awareness of the *haarfeine Linie* (Max Weber's "capillary line") between facts and values. Scrutiny and honesty in dealing with the fact–value distinction are required in sustainability science. Very often, sustainability science projects make use of specific concepts and measures (e.g. ecological footprint, ecosystem approach, safe biological limits, critical loads, environmental impact analysis, integrated water management) that entail values and objectives. The obligation of transparency applies to them as well. It also applies to hybrid concepts such as biodiversity (Potthast 2006). This obligation is not specific to sustainability science, but is certainly very important for it.

2   An account of the various values at stake is also a matter of a more comprehensive theoretical articulation. On the general and vague level of sustainable development as a contested concept there are certain essential ethical questions regarding what to sustain and why to sustain (Dobson 1998). These questions need to be substantiated and this quickly leads to difficult nontrivial questions. Does moral obligation diminish with temporal (and physical) distance and does it come close to zero after three generations? Do future persons hold rights in the present? Would strong care for posterity imply an individual duty for procreation? Moreover, values are in dispute – there are conflicting intuitions within the domain of sustainable development. In addition, sustainable development stands for value considerations among other value considerations. These difficult questions and challenges suggest that at least large-scale sustainability projects will need to draw on the tools of ethics for the work of theoretical articulation and clarity (so

important where there are activist urges) – with the above-noted qualification that professional ethicists and other scientists do not have ultimate moral authority. No doubt this made sustainability projects, in practice, a tightrope walk.

3   Given a commonly shared vague commitment to sustainable development, how can we specify it according to concepts, temporal and spatial scales, guiding visions, objectives, measures, and implementation schemes? The underlying problem is that there are norms and values to be addressed *all the way down* from sophisticated ethical puzzles to very specific problems of, for instance, how to design catchment schemes for water in landscapes under some legal circumstances. For this reason, it seems useful to distinguish various theoretical layers (Schultz et al. 2008). At one end of the spectrum is a layer of principles of justice and development, at the other end are indicators and monitoring devices for very specific domains (e.g. local water management). These distinctions are *inter alia* useful for distinguishing different domains of refutation. For example, empirical falsification based on prediction is irrelevant on the level of principles of justice and development. On this level, various (meta)ethical considerations and methods allow for a highly sophisticated discussion of normative ideas (including refutations, such as the refutation of utilitarianism in the reflective equilibrium).

Transparency as intrinsic ethos in science, (meta)ethical explication of basic assumptions in any concept of sustainability, sustainability embedded in the system of ethical beliefs, and last but not least, specific conflict analysis within single projects are some parameters that define sustainability science's overall ethical quality. This implies that more ambitious sustainability science projects should incorporate ethical expertise. Such expertise cannot be substituted by good will and political correctness.

Normativity as a key feature of sustainability science also has implications for the weak versus strong sustainability debate. As noted, the burden of proof in this debate should be evenhanded and thus the premises of weak *and* strong sustainability should both be critically examined.[19] For example, the premise that we are largely uncertain or ignorant about the detrimental consequences of depleting natural capital is not just a faith-based assumption, but a premise that has been justified. A key argument concerns the multifunctionality of many ecosystems. As soon as we move away from the economic focus on resources such as oil and the (seemingly) simple substitution questions they pose, and as soon as we move to ecosystems and their services, then the premise that we are largely uncertain about the detrimental consequences of depleting natural capital is empirically the state of the art (MEA 2005). As far as we know, WS proponents have no decisive objection to this premise and attempts to substitute ecosystems in artificial biosphere experiments have failed.

This argument is closely linked to the fact that ecosystems provide a variety of benefits to humans and other living beings and thus provide a nexus of human values. Not just economic, but also aesthetic, recreational, and spiritual benefits are associated with cultural ecosystem services. Even if diverse groups do not value these services for the same normative reasons – not just preferences – there is still an overwhelming, if ill-defined, general support to sustain natural capital. These and other normative considerations suggest in our view a *prima facie* plausibility of strong sustainability for normative reasons.[20] They are all open to critical refutation. Note, however, that they do not yield any a priori decisions of what to sustain or how to sustain. Here thinking in levels of theory is useful. Ecosystem approaches and the ethical considerations they involve support a convincing case for strong sustainability *in general*. Thus, we reach exactly the opposite conclusion as Neumayer, who makes a persuasive case for *specific types* of natural capital. In our view, there is a convincing case that natural capital in general ought to be preserved, whereas turning to specific practical domains of application ensures much controversy with respect to specific issues of conservation or preservation, not least due to the many value considerations quite independent from sustainability.

Conclusion

This article first explores the way in which philosophy of science constructs a key debate in sustainability science, showing how philosophy of science can thereby become a problematic heritage. We have also argued that a critical examination of this heritage points the way to an enabling, critical reexamination of the way sustainability science understands itself. Table 5.1 summarizes the central considerations of the respective views. The quality of sustainability science is in our view a matter of constantly stating and reexamining the reasons for the inclusion of nonscientists, the normative issues at stake (and in conflict), the temporal relation of the research to the stakes at hand, and finally, the cooperation of the relevant natural and social sciences based on joint problem formulation. Keeping

Table 5.1 Comparison of approaches

	Popper	*Kuhn*	*Neumayer's Framing*	*Sustainability Science*
Structure of science	Conjecture and refutation in open society	**Paradigms** of scientific communities	**Paradigms**	Conjecture and refutation (in a wide sense) in hybrid communities
Selection criteria for the quality of scientific claims	**Falsification**	Sociological (scientific community as ultimate source of authority)	**Falsification**	Explicit normativity Justified inclusion of nonscientists Explicit temporal reference of research to what is a stake Cooperation of relevant natural and social scientists based on joint problems

Source: Authors.

in view the debate of weak versus strong sustainability throughout our discussion of these key features, we conclude that comprehensive questioning supports strong sustainability.

The key features of sustainability science do not yield indicators or evaluation tools that every sustainability science project has to meet. Rather, they concern background considerations that in different contexts are important and that scientists will have to judge as particularly relevant.[21] Arguably, only large research programs that have the resources can be expected to consider all features in depth.

The last point suggests that it could be useful to conclude in terms of a culture of sustainability science – in terms of a more general understanding shared by members who in any specific situation will have to make choices and focus on specific issues. If culture is understood as shared norms and values, the culture of sustainability science is a "thin culture": the normative commitment is vague and more precise conceptions of sustainability and sustainable development are contested. Still, there is a general normative commitment as well as a commitment to the inclusion of nonscientists, to the consideration of urgency, and to the cooperation of natural and social scientists.

In view of these criteria, the culture in question is not homogeneous but hybrid, bringing together natural and social scientists and nonscientists. If the Kuhnian view tends toward a homogeneous community of the "initiated," and if the Popperian view tends toward a society of "atomistic" individuals (Popper, 1945), then the present perspective tends toward a third view of a methodologically heterogeneous culture with shared, thin values and in dialogue with nonscientists. The image of a seaport comes to mind where the adventures of "science at sea" (Neurath 1932) meet with the people from the land and their needs.[22] A specific feature of this idea of culture is a commitment to bring together different perspectives. This diversity is the key "division of labor" for this culture and the key to the wealth it seeks to sustain and foster.

Culture also stands for cultivation and improvement. Taking seriously, not dogmatically, the key features of sustainability, science can foster its cultivation, or so we would suggest. Questioning can be deep and comprehensive. For a specific project, the deep questioning of one or two features might be irrelevant (for example, because the relevant temporal and ethical questions are obvious). For sustainability science as a whole, however, questioning must be deep and comprehensive. The fulfillment of this requirement no doubt makes sustainability science as much an idea as a reality.

Notes

1 In addition to this journal, contributions to sustainability science are regularly published in a special section of the *Proceedings of the National Academy of Sciences of the United States of America* as well as numerous other journals (for a current list as well as further resources see http://sustainabilityscience.org/document.html?type=journal). Important, frequently overlapping research communities contributing to sustainability science include resilience research, common-pool research, socio-ecological research, transitions research, and vulnerability research. For the discussion in this paper, the

ecological economics community is particularly important, as one of the cofounders of the field, Herman Daly, made major contributions to the weak versus strong sustainability debate (see e.g. Daly 1996).

2 It is in this respect that we hope to contribute to the discussion of the quality of sustainability science and thus pragmatically its evaluation. We deliberately say "contribute" as we do not claim that philosophy of science somehow delivers "the" method of sustainability science. In our view, sustainability benefits from a diversity of methods. One contribution of the philosophy of science is to make explicit and discuss the presuppositions about science that co-structure fundamental disputes such as the one between strong versus weak sustainability.

3 There is probably a link here to the French tradition of epistemology and its examination of the role of the philosophy of science as in Lecourt's account of a historical epistemology (Lecourt 1969).

4 The secondary literature on Popper and Kuhn is enormous. Here we cannot discuss the many critical points that have been raised with respect to these philosophies, amendments, and refinements. Our only goal is to delineate as clearly as possible how they influence the way the question is posed in our case study.

5 Kuhn notably also uses the term in the sense of a scientific achievement: "Research firmly based upon one or more past scientific achievements, achievements that some particular scientific community acknowledges for a time as supplying the foundation for its further practice" (Kuhn 1996). It is not clear that WS and SS are "paradigms" in this sense. Rather, they seem to depend on a wider dispute between the neoclassical growth model and ecological economics. Underpinning these we have, respectively, Solow's (1956) growth model and Georgescu-Roegen's (1971) work on the entropy law and the economic process as scientific achievements on which other scientists built. We would like to thank an anonymous reviewer regarding the need to clarify these different meanings of "paradigm."

6 Note that Neumayer is well aware of the problem that any simple view of falsification is implausible and we therefore by no means want to charge him with this mistake. Rather, our goal is to draw the conclusion from this insight. If "simple falsification" is implausible, what is the implication for theory choice in sustainability science (or for decision on "correctness" as Neumayer puts it)? Our response to these questions is the discussion of the four features of sustainability science and their justification.

7 Rawls's method of reflective equilibrium is based on a) a hypothetical situation of choice ("the original position") that allows the comparison of various approaches to justice (Kantian, utilitarian, intuitionist, and so forth), and b) a consideration of our considered ethical judgments (for example: "racist discrimination is wrong"). Reflective equilibrium is a state of coherence between the conclusions arrived at in the original position and one's considered judgments. Achieving reflective equilibrium requires adjustments both in the formal reasoning of the original position and of (some) considered judgments or basic intuitions about justice.

8 Also note that Neumayer relies on a Kantian approach to make the case why we should care about future generations. A Kantian approach is not only inconsistent with emotivism, it also shows that performatively it is not possible to conceptually introduce the debate without drawing on ethical arguments (Neumayer's own skepticism elsewhere notwithstanding).

9 There are very close family ties between sustainability science and other research programs including integrative and transdisciplinary environmental research (Renn 2008) or social-ecological research (Jahn 2008). This article does not compare these approaches. However, we believe that our conclusions regarding the quality of sustainability science by and large also pertain to these other "family members."

10 Funtowicz and Ravetz (1991) put much weight on the distinction of quality and certainty (as logically independent attributes of knowledge). However, we are not sure that this argument succeeds and, moreover, whether it does not unnecessarily

overstate the role of certainty for science. For example, neither Popper's risky predictions nor Kuhn's normal science put fundamental weight on certainty.

11 These arguments are not directly stated as such by Funtowicz and Ravetz (1991) but are, where indicated, inspired by them and others. In the following paragraphs, we use the language of inclusion of nonscientists rather than the extended peer review because it is *prima facie* unclear in what sense a nonscientist is a "peer." As the discussion will show, there is more than one reason for the inclusion of nonscientists and even for their equal standing in a scientific project. However, whether this makes them peers is debatable and possibly obscures the point that the relation between scientists and nonscientists is by no means trivial, but is rather multifold and contextual. In their discussion of research evaluation, Bergmann and Schramm (2008) speak of "expert review." The need for the inclusion of nonscientists has been widely recognized in sustainability science. For a review of major problems associated with the idea of sustainability scientists as "separate" researchers offering society the facts, see van Kerkhoff and Lebel (2006).

12 This time-independence of validity seems consistent with the "biography of Athena" (Daston 2001), that is the discovery of different ways of establishing valid claims in history and the associated rationalities.

13 "Problem-solving" will only acquire a societal meaning if nonscientists are included in problem formulation. This is another instance of the codependence of the four features of sustainability science discussed here.

14 For the reasons discussed in this paragraph, we are no advocates of sustainability science as a new "super-discipline" or "supra-discipline" (Jahn et al. 2012, p. 4). To the contrary, interdisciplinarity is a constitutive feature of sustainability science as discussed here.

15 Neumayer (2010) defines natural capital as "the totality of nature – resources, plants, species and ecosystems – that is capable of providing human beings with material and nonmaterial utility."

16 See also note 5.

17 As noted by Neumayer (2010), natural resources can be substituted with other natural resources; price signals overcome resource constraints; man-made capital will substitute for natural resources; and technical progress eases resource constraints.

18 Neumayer (2010) himself notes the following key reasons (based on Spash 2002): we are largely uncertain/ignorant about the detrimental consequences of depleting natural capital, natural capital loss is often irreversible, some forms of natural capital provide basic life-support functions, and individuals are highly adverse to losses in natural capital.

19 See note 17.

20 We introduce here only one argument, but see Ott & Döring (2008) for an extended discussion.

21 See Peterson (2006) on the importance of judgment for interdisciplinary environmental science.

22 A point that is important for science as research just as much as for science as education (Ziegler 2008).

References

Bergmann, M. (2008). Grenzüberschreitung und Integration: Die formative Evaluation transdisziplinärer Forschung und ihre Kriterien (Boundary transgression and integration: The formative evaluation of transdisciplinary research and its criteria). In: M. Bergmann & E. Schramm (Eds.). *Transdisziplinäre Forschung. Integrative Forschungsprozesse verstehen und bewerten* (Transdisciplinary Research: Understanding and Evaluating Integrative Research Processes), 149–176. Frankfurt: Campus Verlag (in German).

Bergmann, M., & Schramm, E. 2008. Grenzüberschreitung und Integration: Die formative Evaluation transdisziplinärer Forschung und ihre Kriterien (Boundary transgression and integration: The formative evaluation of transdisciplinary research and its criteria). In: M. Bergmann & E. Schramm (Eds.). *Transdisziplinäre Forschung. Integrative Forschungsprozesse verstehen und bewerten* (Transdisciplinary Research: Understanding and Evaluating Integrative Research Processes), 149–176. Frankfurt: Campus Verlag (in German).

Betz, G. (2006). *Prediction or Prophecy? The Boundaries of Economic Foreknowledge and Their Socio-Political Consequences.* Wiesbaden: Deutscher Universitäts-Verlag.

Clark, W., & Dickson, N. (2003). Sustainability science: the emerging research program. *Proceedings of the National Academy of Sciences of the United States of America* 100 (14), 8059–8061.

Daly, H. (1996). *Beyond Growth: The Economics of Sustainable Development.* Boston: Beacon Press.

Daston, L. (2001). *Wunder, Beweise und Tatsachen. Zur Geschichte der Rationalität* (Miracle, Proofs and Facts: On the History of Rationality). Frankfurt: Fischer (in German).

Dobson, A. (1998). *Justice and the Environment.* Oxford: Oxford University Press.

Funtowicz, S., & Ravetz, J. (1991). A new scientific methodology for global environmental issues. In: R. Costanza (Ed.). *Ecological Economics: The Science and Management of Sustainability,* 137–152. New York: Columbia University Press.

Funtowicz, S., & Ravetz, J. (1993). Science for the post-normal age. *Futures* 25 (7), 735–755.

Georgescu-Roegen, N. (1971). *The Entropy Law and the Economic Process.* Cambridge: Harvard University Press.

Jacobs, M. (1999). Sustainable development as a contested concept. In: A. Dobson (Ed.). *Fairness and Futurity,* 21–45. New York: Oxford University Press.

Jahn, T. (2008). Transdisziplinarität in der Forschungspraxis (Transdisciplinarity in the research-practice). In: M. Bergmann, E. Schramm (Eds.). *Transdisziplinäre Forschung. Integrative Forschungsprozesse verstehen und bewerten* (Transdisciplinary Research: Understanding and Evaluating Integrative Research Processes), 149–176. Frankfurt/ Main: Campus Verlag (in German).

Jahn, T., Bergmann, M., & Keil, F. (2012). Transdisciplinarity: Between mainstreaming and marginalization. *Ecological Economics* 79, 1–10.

Kates, R., Clark, W., Corell, R., Hall, J., Jaeger, C., Lowe, I. . . . Svedlin, U. (2001). Sustainability science. *Science* 292 (5517), 641–642.

Komiyama, K., & Takeuchi, K. (2006). Sustainability science: building a new discipline. *Sustainability Science* 1 (1), 1–6.

Kuhn, T. (1996). *The Structure of Scientific Revolutions,* 3rd Edition. Chicago: University of Chicago Press.

Lecourt, D. (1969). *L'Epistémologie historique de Gaston Bachelard* (The Historical Epistemology of Gaston Bachelard). Paris: Vrin (in French).

Millennium Ecosystem Assessment (MEA) (2005). *Ecosystems and Human Well-Being: Synthesis.* Washington, DC: Island Press.

Neumayer, E. ([2003] 2010). *Weak Versus Strong Sustainability: Exploring the Limits of Two Opposing Paradigms,* 3rd Edition. Northampton, MA: Edward Elgar.

Neurath, O. (1932). Protokollsätze (Protocol statements). *Erkenntnis* 3, 204–214 (in German).

Ott, K. (1997). *Ipso Facto – Zur ethischen Begründung normativer Implikate wissenschaftlicher Praxis* (Ipso Facto – On the Ethical Substantiation of the Normative Implications of Scientific Practice). Frankfurt: Suhrkamp (in German).

Ott, K., & Döring, R. (2008). *Theorie und Praxis starker Nachhaltigkeit* (Theory and Practice of Strong Sustainability), 2nd Edition. Marburg: Metropolis-Verlag (in German).

Petersen, T. (2006). Phronesis, Urteilskraft und Interdisziplinarität (Phronesis, judgment and interdisciplinarity). In: S. Baumgärtner, C. Becker (Eds.). *Wissenschaftsphilosophie Interdisziplinärer Umweltforschung* (Philosophy of science of interdisciplinary environmental research), 25–40. Marburg: Metropolis (in German).

Popper, K. (1945). *The Open Society and Its Enemies*. New York: Routledge.

Popper, K. (1963). *Conjectures and Refutations. The Growth of Scientific Knowledge*. New York: Routledge.

Potthast, T. (2006). Umweltforschung und das Problem epistemisch-moralischer Hybride (Environmental science and the problem of epistemic-moral hybrids). In: S. Baumgärtner, C. Becker (Eds.). *Wissenschaftsphilosophie interdisziplinärer Umweltforschung* (Environmental research and the problem of epistemic-moral hybrids), 87–100. Marburg: Metropolis (in German).

Rawls, J. (1999). *A Theory of Justice*, Revised Edition. New York: Oxford University Press.

Renn, O. (2008). Anforderungen an eine integrative und transdisziplinäre Umweltforschung (Requirements for integrative and transdisciplinary environmental science). In: M. Bergmann, E. Schramm (Eds.). *Transdisziplinäre Forschung. Integrative Forschungsprozesse verstehen und bewerten* (Transdisciplinary Research: Understanding and Evaluating Integrative Research Processes), 119–148. Frankfurt: Campus Verlag (in German).

Scanlon, T. (2003). Rawls on justification. In: S. Freeman (Ed.). *The Cambridge Companion to Rawls*, 149–167. New York: Cambridge University Press.

Scholz, R., Lang, D., Wiek, A., Walter, A., & Stauffacher, M. (2006). Transdisciplinary case studies as a means of sustainability learning. *International Journal of Sustainability in Higher Education* 7 (3), 226–251.

Schultz, J., Brand, F., Kopfmüller, J., & Ott, K. (2008). Building a theory of sustainable development: Two salient conceptions with the German discourse. *International Journal of Environment and Sustainable Development* 7 (4), 465–482.

Solow, R. (1956). Contribution to the theory of economic growth. *The Quarterly Journal of Economics* 70 (1), 65–94.

Spash, C. (2002). *Greenhouse Economics – Value and Ethics*. London/New York: Routledge.

Van der Sluijs, J., & Funtowicz, S. (2008). Sozialökologische Transformation bedingt neues Verhältnis von Wissenschaft und Politik (Social-ecological transformation requires a new relation between science and politics). In: J. Dellheim, G. Krause (Eds.). *Für eine neue Alternative. Herausforderungen für eine sozialökologische Transformation* (For a New Alternative: Challenges for a Socio-Ecological Transformation), 63–81. Berlin: Karl Dietz Verlag (in German).

Van Kerkhoff, L., & Lebel, L. (2006). Linking knowledge and action for sustainable development. *Annual Review of Environment and Resources* 31, 445–77.

Wätzold, F. (2009). *Interdisziplinarität am Beispiel der Zusammenarbeit von Ökologie und Ökonomie* (Interdisciplinarity: An exemplary discussion of the co-operation of ecology and economy). Public Lecture, Historisches Institut (Institute of History), University of Greifswald, 18 November (in German).

Ziegler, R. (2008). Science on the marsh: On the ground of education (for sustainable development). In: S. Allen-Gil, L. Stelljes, O. Borysova (Eds.). *Addressing Global Environmental Security Through Innovative Educational Curricula*, 11–26. Berlin: Springer.

Zierhofer, W., & Burger, P. (2007). Disentangling transdisciplinarity: An analysis of knowledge integration in problem-oriented research. *Science Studies* 20 (1), 51–74.

6 Transdisciplinary humanistic sustainability theory

Justice, governance, blocks

Felix Ekardt

Epistemological and definitional foundations

In accordance with the goals of this volume, this paper presents an approach for a transdisciplinary humanistic sustainability theory which has been developed in greater detail elsewhere. Editorial requirements have demanded that this presentation be compressed to one fiftieth, which leaves space for only the modules, theses and results; I will therefore have to refer the reader to the original, more detailed work titled *Theorie der Nachhaltigkeit* (*Theory of Sustainability;* Ekardt 2011) for the specific argumentation, both normative and empirical, regarding the various points, and the discussion of the sometimes concurrent, sometimes countercurrent, literature. Where appropriate, I will provide references to the relevant sections of that work.

Methodologically, this approach is a contribution to transdisciplinary sustainability research – meaning it is oriented toward current problems, and not toward the established academic boundaries. The key aspect – and the focus of the paper – is therefore not the natural-scientific, but rather the humanistic aspect. I view sustainable development not only as the establishment of a permanent, globally practicable and future-capable mode of life and economics, but rather as a complex array of problems, involving a wide range of social-scientific and humanistic disciplines – law, political science, sociology, economics, theology, psychology, philosophy, etc. A comprehensive understanding of sustainability, in my view, must include:

(a) definitional clarity of the term sustainability (*definitional level;* ibid., 1C);
(b) a descriptive analysis of the existing situation, how sustainable societies are measured by that standard, and which developments and tendencies to date can be described in that respect (*existing-situation level;* ibid., 1B); since this can be only partially resolved by social science, this is primarily the place for natural-scientific sustainability research;
(c) the likewise descriptive question as to what external blockages and motivation situations are essential or causal for the achievement of, or failure to achieve, the transformation to sustainability, and which statements can be made regarding human ability to learn; the latter may include natural-scientific

research results, inasmuch as biological factors are involved (conditions of transformation or the *causal level*; ibid., 2);

(d) the normative question as to why sustainability is desirable, and by derivation, what its exact substance is (*requirement level*; ibid., 3, 4);

(e) how much sustainability is required from a normative point of view, considering other contesting interests, such as "short-term growth," including the aspect of which institutions are responsible for answering this question, and what leeway for decision-making exists (*consideration-of-interests level*; ibid., 5); and

(f) the funding, governance and/or steering instruments capable of effectively implementing goal determination at levels (d) and (e), including "bottom-up" measures, such as learning processes, or sustainability education, more corporate self-regulation, and the question as to the blockages, possible actors, strategies, etc. (implementation, steering or *governance level*; ibid., 6, 7); for the natural-science side, the question as to the technological possibilities also arises, the actual use of which is affected by the governance aspect.

These aspects are all very important. However, in the scientific – and, even more so, in the political – debate, they are rarely distinguished clearly. Nonetheless, such a distinction between levels is obviously important, especially in view of the epistemological distinction between what is and what should be: items (b), (c), and (f) are questions of what is, while (d) and (e) are questions of what should be. Whether, for example, there are good reasons for the goal of sustainability (the normative justification) is a different question from that as to the factual motives which drive us toward implementing sustainability, or keep us from doing so (the descriptive explanation) – or the question as to which means will be needed to in fact effect that implementation. Nonetheless, these questions naturally build one upon the other:[1] for example level (c) essentially informs level (f). Moreover, the distinction between "subjective" and "objective" is not the same as the distinction between what should be (normativity) and what is (factuality/empirics). These epistemological distinctions can also be substantiated in greater detail (ibid., 1D III).

By the same token, the definition of content and distinction is a factor in formulating the levels. Definitions, i.e. the simple linguistic identification of matters (level [a]), are ultimately arbitrary, unlike their knowable, and hence non-arbitrary contents (levels [b] through [f]). If I wished, I could call a piece of furniture a "squirrel" instead of a "chair" (definition). What is non-arbitrary, however, is whether an item in front of me is in fact a chair, whether or not chairs in fact exist, whether they are square or round, etc. (content).[2] The same is true of sustainability: of course, I could easily "define" a condition X – for example, a world completely unsuitable for human life – as one to be called "sustainable," for definitions merely serve the purpose of problem-free understanding; they are neither true nor false. The question of whether the realization of such a condition is a justifiable normative demand, and that as to the descriptive cause for either meeting this demand or not doing so, is on the other hand a question of content, which is epistemologically accessible, and hence non-arbitrary/subjective. The question that both facts (ibid., 1D I) and norms (ibid., 3F) can be objectively recognized – with some residual fuzziness – is one that requires clarification, but can ultimately be answered in the affirmative.

Definitionally, justice means the rightness of the order of human cohabitation, just as truth means the factual correctness of a statement. Social distributive justice as a category of material issues of distribution is only a part of that (ibid., 1D III 2). Sustainability defines the political/ethical/legal demand for more intertemporal and global justice, in other words, the demand for permanent and globally maintainable modes of life and economics (ibid., 1C I). A three-pillar concept of sustainability, on the other hand, is misleading and out of place for a number of reasons that cannot be addressed in detail here. In particular, it would potentially distract greatly from the core intent of the principle, which is the creation of permanent and globally maintainable conditions of life (ibid., 1C II).[3]

Epistemologically, it is necessary to distinguish between theoretical, normative and instrumental rationality. The last of these, addressed by economists, sociologists and others, is hence not the only form of rationality (ibid., 1D II). The basis for this distinction, and hence, too, in transdisciplinary sustainability, is the distinction between *what is* and *what should be*, and – not parallel, but rather perpendicular to that – the distinction between the *objective* and the *subjective*. Facts are basically objectively ascertainable. While difficulties of proof and uncertainties are also major factors, with respect, also, to sustainability, they do not affect this fundamental truth (ibid., 1D I). In this context, the law is concretized ethics, embellished with sanctions, and ethics may be capable of providing universal justification for the basic principles of law. The entire present theoretical approach thus results in a parallelization of ethical and human rights-interpretative statements (ibid., 1D III, 3F). Such terms as justice, law, politics, constitution, governance, or anthropology/social theory require and receive clarification, as do the forms of normative and descriptive research used in the present sustainability perspective. Nonetheless, the proposal of policy options contrary to broadly held views is not in and of itself normative; in all these respects, the possibilities and limits of judicial methods of interpretation are relevant (ibid., 1D III, 2–5).

The existing-situation level of sustainability

With respect to the existing situation of sustainability, the current fixation of the political debate upon financial crises, growth, social insurance, the war on terror, and jobs, as constant diversions from the issue of sustainability is a serious problem (ibid., 1A). Rather more important for the permanent and global maintainability of modes of living and of economics would, for example, be an appropriate handling of such issues as energy, climate and resources. Taken together, these three areas will require a fundamental change in our approach to the issues of fossil fuels – meaning essentially a total abandonment of their use by 2050 in the areas of electric power, heat, fuel and material utilization – and of land use, if we are to avoid catastrophic damage, particularly as the result of climate change, with millions of dead, international and civil wars over diminished resources, massive migrations, huge natural disasters and exploding oil and gas prices, with correspondingly extreme economic damage (the classic work in that regard: Stern 2007). Contrary to widespread perception, natural scientists are calling not for a 50% reduction in greenhouse gas emissions, but more like an 80% reduction, if such scenarios are to be avoided.[4] Germany and the EU are in no sense "leading the way" in terms of per capita emissions, or with respect to supposed reductions thereof, the latter having been achieved entirely by mathematical trickery, the shift of production to the emerging markets, the financial crisis and the industrial collapse of East Germany in 1990.[5] Of course, sustainability cannot be reduced to issues of climate and energy; other resources, such as water and phosphorus, are of existential importance, and are also being massively overused (Ekardt 2011, 1B I).[6]

Such issues bring sustainability into conflict with the universally dominant concept of growth. However, endless growth is somewhat difficult to imagine in a world that is not endless, and renewable resources may have only an incremental effect on that, for, as an example, solar automobiles and solar panels, too, use resources which are threatening to become scarce very soon. Moreover, the magnitude of the challenge we face with regard to climate change will force us in the long-term – by contrast with the medium-term, in which the innovation potentials of energy efficiency and renewable energy resources are to take affect – to seek a way out of the growth paradigm, as opposed to merely "increasing efficiency"; the same is true of threatening rebound effects. And "qualitative growth" of a purely ideal nature may not be able to solve these problems. According to all our experience, such ideal growth is itself materially based; moreover, it is difficult to conceive of a steadily – and hence, ultimately, exponentially! – ever-improving quality of such nonmaterial "assets" as social care, health, music ability, or the enjoyment of nature or the arts, in any way that makes sense. This indeed seems not really to be a problem, since the issue of the effects, for instance with regard to social systems, would appear to be manageable, and since growth has in any case had very little to say to date about such issues as human happiness (ibid., 1B II).

The conditions for social transformation toward sustainability

The transformation toward more sustainability, which, as the latest data on the climate and on resources indicate, has to date essentially proven to be a failure, both nationally and globally, has its origins in the dual vicious circle of politics/the electorate, and economics/the consumers (ibid., 2A). That vicious circle is not caused primarily by a lack of knowledge about sustainability with respect to natural scientific, economic, legal or ethical information (ibid., 2B); rather, the key factors, both for politicians and businesspeople and for voters/consumers alike, are conformity, such feelings as convenience, a lack of long-term orientation in space or time, psychological displacement/repression, failure to think in complex causalities, etc., as well as selfishness, traditional values, path-dependencies, structures of collective assets, etc. (ibid., 2C). All these factors are manifested in individuals and as a "structure." Perpendicular to them, we could say that the lack of sustainability is based on a mixture of biological, cultural and external factors. Especially the cultural background of the modern economy, natural science and technology have emerged in a complex interaction with originally religious, today often secularized, but nonetheless persistent, value attitudes (ibid., 2D). It is from this that the essential basic statements on the possibilities and the – all too obvious – limits to the human ability to learn, as well as the necessary, and ultimately global, transformation of society to sustainability, will ultimately result (ibid., 2E).

Universal theories of justice as the basis for sustainability

In order to find an ethical and legal justification for sustainability, a new justification for universal justice, or a demonstration of the objectivity of normative statements, is first of all needed – otherwise, the standard for further steps will be lacking – with, however, considerable leeway for the consideration of interests, and with no discussion of the "good life," as it is not possible to make meaningful statements about that. The normative theory of justice should not be confused with the descriptive study of the anthropology/social theory concept of humankind (ibid., 3A, 3G).

The version of universal justice developed and defended by the present sustainability perspective as the basis for ethics and law, and hence, too, for the concretization of sustainability, is a heterodox discursive ethic as the basis for a revised ethical and legal-interpretive concept of liberal democracy based on the division of powers, and its central positioning of human rights, both nationally and transnationally. In each case, a *lack-of-alternatives argument*, an *elenctical argument* and a *burden-of-proof argument* initially justify the possibility of rationality in questions of how things should be, and hence, too, human dignity and impartiality as the – sole – universal principle of justice. This is then true not only in discourse, but also in action, and even toward potential discourse partners – in other words, towards all people. From this principle flows a comprehensive universal right to freedom not limited only to certain areas of life, to democracy based on the division of powers, and to have freedom established in written legal form. This overall approach develops the classical discourse ethic, e.g. of Karl-Otto Apel, and to some extent, too, of Jürgen Habermas, and revises and extends them in a number of key points (ibid., 3E–F).

By contrast, approaches such as contextualism or skepticism, as well as metaphysical approaches and cost-benefit analyses based on factual preferences, and such other forms of liberalism as that of Rawls, which compete with this discourse-ethical, liberal-democratic universalism, have proven to be nonviable options. Also unconvincing are all kinds of concepts which consider normativity as *per se* subjective, which are unscientific or axiomatically established, which take empirical anthropology as their point of departure and end up at normative theory, or which are based on any "scientifically" or otherwise empirically derived normativity (ibid., 3B–D). Moreover, a number of purported objections to any heterodox universalistic discourse ethic, based on such buzzwords as "rational dictatorship," "threat to democracy," "ignorance of cultural roots," "colliding nationalities," "doubtful implement ability," etc., are all ultimately likewise unconvincing (ibid., 3G).

Principles of sustainability: A new understanding of freedom – Ethical and legal

In order to ascertain concrete, normative criteria for sustainability, a new ethical and legal interpretation of human rights[7] designed to overcome a primarily economically oriented concept of freedom, but also, conversely, to prevent the threatening abolition of freedom, e.g. through an eco-dictatorship (a dual threat to freedom), is central. All statements on justice are statements regarding the social level. Individual ethical duties, beyond that of the establishment of a just – and hence also sustainable – societal order, are difficult to conceive of, not only due to their weak implementability, but also due to the very fact of their insufficient concretizability (ibid., 3A, 4A). One reason that human rights are always mediated via state authority is that they have their origin in the interpersonal relationship between individuals (ibid., 4A). Human rights consistently prove, ethically and legally, to be rights of freedom and of the preconditions for freedom. The distinction between negative and affirmative freedoms is unconvincing; equally unconvincing, both ethically and legally, is the concept – which exists even in Europe and in international law – that human rights protect only certain select, supposedly particularly valuable, freedom-related actions (ibid., 4C I).

The principle of human dignity, understood as the mandatory respect for the autonomy of the individual, in other words the principle of self-determination, and the principle of impartiality, understood as the mandatory independence of specific perspective, are not basic rights, nor are they intrinsically capable of stating anything at all about a particular concrete ethical or legal case. They are rather the justifying and interpretation-guiding foundations for freedom, and hence, too, for a sustainability-oriented new interpretation of freedom, of the rules of the balanced consideration of interests, of democracy based on the separation of powers, etc. For this reason, the popular question as to whether human dignity itself is subject to balanced consideration or not does not even arise. The oft-cited supposed human dignity formula of "the value of the human being *per se*," and the "prohibition against making someone a mere object," are not central to the concept of dignity. For a number of reasons, human dignity and human rights also apply to severely mentally handicapped people who are hence incapable of engaging in discourse. All this – and everything else in the following and elucidated in Sections 4 and 5 of my book – applies in liberal democracies on the bases of national law, and, under European law and international law in nation-states, in the EU, and also for international institutions and organizations, and it is also ethically valid (ibid., 4B). Moreover, under a further interpretation, this and everything following also apply, thanks to the legal construct rooted in international law and to general legal principles, not only ethically, but also legally with regard to countries and international institutions which have signed no human rights treaties or established no such constitutional standards. An example is the elementary right to food and water, which is central to sustainability, and derivable as a right to the preconditions for freedom (ibid., 4E III).

Thus, the right to the elementary preconditions for freedom, including life, health, and minimum subsistence in the form of food, water, security, climate stability, elementary education, the absence of war and civil war, etc., exist ethically, and, even beyond their partially explicit established norms, in national law, European law and international law. This is only slightly vague; however, it is not reduced to "average" needs, but also protects the weakest. The possible alternative to this concept of freedom, an ethic based on abilities or needs, should be rejected due to a number of logical problems, problems of implementation, and effects which have little to do with freedom (ibid., 4C II-III). On the other hand, the protection of additional conditions which promote freedom, while not enjoying the status of a human right either ethically or legally, certainly does deserve recognition (ibid., 4C IV).

For a number of reasons, freedom, including its elementary preconditions, is deserving of legal and ethical protection, which must extend intertemporally and globally, across borders. This leads to a human rights-based theory of sustainability, i.e. the imperative for permanent and globally maintainable conditions of life. Which public authority should, in case of need, be mandated to implement freedom, i.e. in the form of the struggle against poverty, will be derived below (ibid., 5B, 5C II 3), from the institutional rules. Familiar counterarguments against intertemporal global protection of basic rights, such as the future-individual paradox (related to the "non-identity problem," discussed in Chapter 9), or the reference to the unknown preferences of future generations, are ultimately unconvincing. Nor is there such a thing as a collectivistically coined imperative for the "preservation of humankind." Such national goals as environmental protection or the welfare state only constitute the establishment of supplementary goals in statutory form, as an expression of additional conditions which promote freedom (ibid., 4D); the principle of precaution can be categorized as a subset of human rights (ibid., 5C II 2).

For a number of reasons, the expansion of human rights in accordance with sustainability equally guarantees both "immunity" and "protection," both ethically and legally, and on a national and a transnational basis – although these two terms are hard to distinguish. The one means the right to protection *against* the power of the state, the other the right to protection *by* the power of the state; otherwise, they would be useless for sustainability. These realizations are not obviated by certain widespread objections against the recognition of stronger protective fundamental rights, such as democracy, the balance of powers, the lack of individual reference or the priority of the rights of immunity. The classical distinction of action vs. refraining from action, and, moreover, also deontology vs. consequentialism in ethics, thus latently lose their foundations (ibid., 4E I–II, 3A). Only by means of the totality of these human rights-interpretive steps will a fundamental right to protection against climate change, the exhaustion of resources, etc., and hence concretely normative sustainability criteria, become conceivable. However, the details will of course only emerge from the theory of the balanced consideration of interests and institutions (ibid., 5).

Moreover, human rights-based freedom also includes responsibility for the consequences of activity in the sense of the requirement to assume ethical and legal responsibility for the consequences of actions one has freely chosen to perform. These consequences, such as climate change, may also be "artificially" internalized, e.g. through energy fees. "Responsibility" in this case means not only the fact of having been assigned to assume a certain task, the performance of duty, voluntary charity, etc., but rather, too, the "polluter-pays" principle (ibid., 4C V). On the other hand, no complementation of a normative sustainability theory for the purpose of an environmental-ethical patho-centrics or eco-centrics is possible; nonetheless, environmental protection is comprehensively justified, both ethically and legally (ibid., 4F II).

Generally, freedom is limited only by the freedom of others, including the elementary and extended prerequisites for their freedom, but not by any form of the common good etc., a concept which should rather be rejected (ibid., 4F I). Questions of the "good life" cannot be regulated, for which reason sustainability measures cannot be ethically or legally justified by reference to any potential enhancement of the "inner happiness" of those whose freedom is being limited, but rather only by reference to the protection of the freedom and the prerequisites for freedom of others. For the real implementation of sustainability, on the other hand, that hope for greater happiness, including the associated learning processes, is central (ibid., 4F IV, 6A II). All these basic principles also define the correct ethical and legal measure of policies of social redistribution. The role of the concept of equal opportunity will necessarily be much smaller in this context than is generally assumed. In any case, the ideal of true material equality of distribution must be rejected for a number of reasons. The central issues of social distribution are rather those related to global poverty, the threatening effects of climate change, and the fact that economic globalization could undermine the foundations of the welfare state worldwide (ibid., 4F III).

Consideration of interests, institutions, and rules for ascertaining the facts: Ethics and legality beyond cost-benefit analysis

Ethical and judicial decisions can be reconstructed as the balanced consideration of two sides of a problem – not only in exceptional cases, but ultimately in all cases. These considerations involve balancing various freedoms, elementary preconditions for freedoms, additional conditions which promote freedom, and everything derived from the above – and that is as it should be. Here, the scope of options of "higher" decision-making bodies is generally considerably greater than that of "local" decision-makers. Any sustainability decision is thus characterized by normative, and not only by factually referenced, insecurities – as risk theory suggests. Concrete problems, such as "strong vs. weak sustainability," or, too, the relevance of particular arguments, such as the polluter-pays principle or the performance principle, can only be ascertained on the bases of that framework, based on the *theory of balanced consideration of interests* (ibid., 5A).

A sustainability theory which seeks to be normative – both ethically and legally – must at the same time establish itself as a revised version of the democratic theory of the separation of powers, which, in addition to substantive rules of the balanced consideration of interests, also establishes institutional rules and makes vague talk about "leeway for formulation" more precise. Which public authority is to undertake the compromise between the freedoms of the various citizens, and hence realize sustainability, is on the one hand a question of the balance of power between the legislative, the executive and the judiciary, and, on the other, a question of the level of legal authority responsible in a certain instance: international institutions, the EU, the nation-state or, in Germany, the states. That authority which is best suited in a particular case should assume the duty in question, formally limited by the framework of the established system of competences. The respective duty of the citizens to bear burdens is determined ethically and legally, nationally and transnationally, by the theory of balanced consideration. It refers first of all to the legislative authority, although usually – in the interpretation of standards, or in cases in which leeway for assessment and the consideration of interests has been explicitly opened up – some elements of the process of the consideration of interests are passed on to the administrative authority or to the courts. Beyond that, the respective oversight institutions are instructed, by means of a complex network of parliaments, executive organs and courts, to only ensure, through their oversight mechanisms, that the rules of a balanced consideration of interests are followed (ibid., 5C II 3).

Those primarily affected by the lack of sustainability today are not those who participate in elections for today's parliaments and governments, but rather future generations, and also people in other countries. Non-sustainable measures can therefore not simply be justified as "what has, after all, been democratically decided"; hence, sustainability is in a relationship of friction with democracy, while at the same time having an affinity to it, since it requires democratic discourse and learning processes. For a number of ethical and legal reasons, no form of eco-dictatorship can be considered viable. Sustainability-oriented institutional innovations of the existing form of democracy based on the separation of powers can, however, only be considered appropriate to a very limited extent. The key goal is that those institutions which have proven themselves be internationally strengthened. Moreover, a trusteeship authority for the interests of the future should be created (ibid., 5B).

The correct rules of balanced consideration of interests, which alone can lead to concrete normative sustainability statements, can be attained by means of a mature consideration-of-interest theory reoriented toward a multi-polarity parallel in its legal and ethical aspects, as a further development of the principle of proportionality. This theory would thus be derived both from liberal principles and from the distinction between what is and what should be (ibid., 5C I, 5B). General talk about "leeway for decision-making," "radical democracy," or skeptical general doubt regarding the definability of normative, and even substantive issues, provide no convincing alternatives, for a number of reasons (ibid., 5B). Also derivable are rules for factual ascertainment, a new human rights-based understanding of precaution – i.e. protection against dangers which are remote in time or uncertain in their cause – and a sharing of the burdens of substantiation and proof in cases of uncertain factual situations, for example regarding climate change, in the process of a balanced consideration of interests under German, European and international law. The idea that precautionary measures can protect us against dangers "for sure," even in the incomplete form that they exist today, has been refuted, thereby rendering more precise, and to some extent modifying, both common judicial analyses and sociological risk theory. In view of continual considerable growth in sustainability information, rules are emerging for new knowledge derived from evaluation and new knowledge derived from facts, and, built upon that, a change in the decisions taken by public authorities (ibid., 5C II 2). The same is true for procedural rules in national and transnational – e.g. sustainability – legislation and administration, for statements on participatory democracy, and on extended sustainability-related litigation rights, as well as for the dismantlement of formal barriers against effective participation and for effective legal protection (ibid., 5C II 3).

In the ping-pong game of national and transnational powers, the violation of the rules of balanced consideration, fact gathering and procedure have created the duty for a revision of decisions, taking into account the rules previously violated. In the case of existing climate policy, such violations have involved, for example, the factual basis of existing climate policy, the polluter-pays principle, and the lack of orientation toward any well-founded, adequate, at least somewhat (including global and intertemporal) equal protection of the prerequisites for freedom. Moreover, a non-transparent and often largely ineffective mixture of instruments, such as that which exists today, is problematic not only in terms of democracy, but also in terms of fundamental rights. Such realization is in essence also applicable for sustainability beyond the climate issue. In brief, there is in fact such a thing as a duty to achieve greater sustainability – both ethically and legally (ibid., 5C IV).

All this can also be seen as an alternative to the kind of economically oriented cost-benefit analysis which ultimately represents a disguised form of utilitarian Hobbesian ethics. This is deserving of criticism even aside from its grounding in preference theory: often, it operates with no realistic natural-scientific factual basis, and it is moreover still overly entangled in the growth orientation of neoclassical economics. Moreover, its methods of quantification and discounting are inoperable, for very fundamental reasons. A clearly deflationary and changed cost-benefit analysis should of course retain its key function as an – important – subordinate aspect of a legally/ethically based consideration-of-interests theory: that of a tool for processing facts (ibid., 5C III.)

Sustainability governance: Beyond the "mix of instruments," "self-regulation" and "purely technological" options

Sustainability cannot be successfully implemented on a purely technological basis. The reasons for the limits to growth are at the same time the limits to *exclusive* dependence on more resource efficiency and more renewable resources. Sufficiency, in the sense of absolute reductions of resource use and greenhouse gas emissions, must always also be a factor due to the wide and threatening array of ambivalences and, often, the overestimation of the potential of renewable resources. Some technical options, such as CCS, nuclear energy, geo-engineering, etc., are absolute nonstarters for a number of reasons; one exception might be the sequestration of carbon to be immediately recycled in bioenergy power plants ("negative emissions"; ibid., 6A I).

Self-serving economic/pacifistic, ethical and eudemonistic (happiness-oriented) considerations could make a true global turn toward sustainability possible, which would even include sufficiency, if one were only to reflect on it correctly. That would, however, require a ping-pong game with political/legal stipulations. From the point of view of citizens, these factors would require a process of learning and of the capacity to learn; of course, such educational approaches face multiple barriers. Certainly, no normative statements or mandatory measures are possible regarding happiness, but nonetheless, there are clear indicators of the capacity of sustainable lifestyles to promote happiness (ibid., 6A II). While voluntary corporate social responsibility (CSR) and consumer engagement can be useful in supporting needed political/legal stipulations, they cannot replace them. They will fail due both to problems of knowledge and to the lack of adequate concreteness of what is being "demanded" of corporations and consumers, and especially due to the many problems described above (ibid., 2), in which all commitment to sustainability to date has been entangled. Moreover, there are a number of additional general problems, outlined below, involving the approach of addressing the single company or the individual citizen (ibid., 6B).

At the policy level, we have seen an impressive array of sustainability programs, packages and targets, internationally, at the European level and nationally, although the list of successes, even in such countries as Germany, is less than impressive. This applies, too, to such much discussed stipulations as the Climate Framework Convention and the Kyoto Protocol (ibid., 6C).

The existing state of sustainability governance shows a spotty picture in terms of administrative law, information policy, state subsidies and the issuance of government contracts (ibid., 6D I, III). In Germany, the Renewable Energies Law, with its model of "non-state subsidies," is usually seen as the greatest success (ibid., 6D II, 6E V 1). Overall of course, existing sustainability regulation involves a variety of points of friction, which are in part caused by the limits to growth and the transition to the idea of sufficiency, and which in any case cannot be resolved by addressing single companies or single products. The key terms here include: rebound effects, resource-based/sectoral/spatial displacement effects, weaknesses of targeting and implementation, problems of representation, and problems of cumulation (ibid., 6D IV).

The best structural answer for such problems with respect to the greenhouse issue, as well as for resource issues in general, is a *quantity-control* model, under an expanded understanding of the term, involving price boosts via the certificate markets or a fee-based system, for only in this way can the above-stated problems be addressed, while adequately taking into account the motivation of citizens, companies and politicians as diagnosed in the above anthropology, and at the same time guaranteeing an optimum solution with respect to the aspect of freedom (ibid., 6E I). Of course, the existing EU emissions-trading process in the climate area solves virtually none of the above-listed problems (ibid., 6E II 1); the same is true of such existing tax laws as the German eco-tax (ibid., 6E II 3). The lack of perspective, too, in the current and upcoming global climate protection system can be seen in a particularly exemplary manner in the "Clean Development Mechanism" (ibid., 6E II 2).

In the energy and climate areas, quantity control must address primary energy and land use, and it must set the target of a progressive reduction of greenhouse gas emissions, and, implicitly, of resource use, by some 80% worldwide by 2050! For individual citizens and companies, this would involve a massive price incentive in favor of more efficiency, more renewable resources and more sufficiency. The best solution would be a two-stage certificate-trading system, on the one hand between countries at the global level, and on the other involving primary energy companies and land users at the national/continental level, which would, however, differ drastically from the existing emissions-trading system, having a broader base, stricter goals and no loopholes. The main reasons that a global quantity-control solution will be necessary to address sustainability problems are the global nature of those problems, the danger of displacement effects and the threatening race to the bottom in terms of standards (ibid., 6E III 1–2).

Quantity control for resources and/or the climate would make sense for a number of reasons, including aspects of social distribution, if the small yields it would achieve in the West and the larger yields it would achieve in the South were to be used as an eco-bonus per capita of the population. In this way, it would be possible to address both the long-term fatal social effects of climate change and resource depletion, and, at the same time, the struggle against poverty in developing countries. Moreover, the model would favor the building of administrative, educational and welfare-state institutions in the developing countries, and would contribute to cutting population growth – which, like demographic change in general, is generally viewed too much as a cause and too little as the effect of problems (ibid., 1A, 6E III 3), and is a key precondition for many additional positive developments. Moreover, it would ensure the permanent availability of affordable energy, and prevent a global race to the bottom in social policy, which would ultimately be damaging for all. Finally, by supporting innovation, it would spark a number of additional socially desirable ancillary effects, such as job creation. In addition, there are good arguments for having per capita emissions rights – or per capita use rights for certain resources – distributed not only in an egalitarian manner, but rather, contrary to the current consumption situation, in a manner even slightly distorted in favor of developing countries, in order to enable further certificate sales to the North, and thus to create the above-mentioned increased eco-bonus for the South. On the other hand, a complete equalization based on all historic emissions cannot be justified (ibid., 6E III 3).

Sustainability quantity control could be initiated in the EU alone, without being established globally, if it were supplemented by marginal compensation mechanisms for imports and exports. Displacement effects for emissions or resource use could thus be avoided, and pressure would then be exerted upon other countries to participate in a quantity-control system. Moreover, such a measure would demonstrate the economic viability of effective sustainability policy, so that ultimately, a path could be opened for future agreements at the global level (ibid., 6E IV).

A central issue is that of the supplements – for other resources and/or other instruments – even such a quantity-control model would need. Such an approach with regard to fossil fuels and land use would also indirectly remove considerable pressure from other important assets, such as biodiversity and bodies of water, due to the expected rollback of conventional agriculture. For example, in the case of the resource phosphorus, which is essential for life, a supplementary further quantity-control instrument would be conceivable. Here, as in the cases of bioenergy in land use (ibid., 6E V 1–3), or in the area of building heating, a well-conceived climate quantity-control program could of course ultimately largely cover the requirements for regulation (ibid., 6E V 4). For some resources, supplemental additional quantity-control measures under administrative law, in place of certificates or taxes, might be possible, particularly if such measures were to be strictly applied on an overall basis, with quality goals, i.e. if they were to function like a certificates market, with a "cap" element, but no "trade" element (for an elucidation with reference to EU water policy, see ibid., 6E VI 2). And quantity-control approaches are also conceivable for entirely different sustainability issues with no classical connection to resources, such as national debt or financial policy (ibid., 6E V 5).

In any case, a number of supplemental administrative legal bans in the area of sustainability, particularly regarding biodiversity or such technologies as nuclear power, are important, as is the abolition of many non-sustainable subsidy programs (ibid., 6E VI 1). Moreover, in the areas of climate and energy policy, a staggered renewable energy subsidy, albeit different in major ways from the current German version (ibid., 6E V 1), and planning and subsidy support for the expansion of power lines and energy storage facilities, is necessary. The same is true for informal instruments. Other essential flanking measures for a gradually emerging postgrowth society, such as basic income and a further developed educational system, are also being discussed (ibid., 6E VI 3).

All this also has priority over basic economic rights, both under German and under European law, and in the latter area, also over specific guarantees of freedom, such as the freedom of traffic in goods and the EU State Aid Law. Such considerations complete the ethical and legal derivation regarding the new interpretation of freedom, and regarding the theory of the balanced consideration of interests (ibid., 6F I, III). Moreover, such approaches as corporate social responsibility and self-regulation are fundamentally not advantageous, but rather problematical (ibid., 6F II).

Sustainability, globalization free world trade, and the future of postnational international law

A global sustainability policy would have to be able to win a contest against unfettered transnational corporate business. In addition to the general problems of a governance which primarily depends on voluntary corporate responsibility (CSR) and competition (ibid., 6B), it is particularly cross-border free trade that shows the most typical social and ecological defects. The attempts to prove the contrary and to postulate the productivity of a "competition between countries," and worldwide unlimited free trade no longer reflects the latest state of economic research. In that respect, the balance sheet of the WTO to date is ambivalent, even if its legal establishment and its ability to implement policy make that organization potentially interesting as a nucleus of a global policy level – a "global EU." In any case, a categorical rejection of market economic systems is not convincing (ibid., 7A).

The current minimal state of global institutionalization is however only questionably compatible in ethical and human rights terms with the justification for the establishment of a universal, global and intertemporally oriented liberal democracy. Stronger global institutions are necessary, which would (a) operate continuously; (b) be able to make decisions by majority vote; (c) have effective implementation mechanisms; (d) be based on more strongly formalized participatory structures; and (e) in the medium-term, move cautiously toward the establishment of the parliamentarization of international decision-making in the area of human rights. Also necessary – parallel to the democratization of nation-states at the global level – is a long-term reinterpretation of the relations between international law, European law and national law, with a shift in the priority relationship to the benefit of the higher legal levels, and the gradual overcoming of the concept of the nation-states as "the lords of treaties." All that would open the way to the integration of climate and resource protection law into the WTO, as a "little global EU" (ibid., 7B).

Under international trade law today, it would already be possible for several countries, such as the EU in alliance with a few others, to take the lead in pushing sustainability and climate and resource policy, including the control of imports and exports by means of the border-adjustment mechanism – a surcharge on the former and a discount for the latter, to account for resource costs. Possibly, it would not even technically violate the mandates in favor of free trade, but it would at least be possible to interpret Article XX of the GATT accordingly, if one were to view it from a globalistic, human rights-based perspective oriented toward the actual – and not merely the economic – goals of the WTO (ibid., 7C).

Notes

1 Thus, the subsumption of norms always also requires facts – which does not, however, mean that such a statement of fact as "X was killed and Y was the perpetrator" can serve as justification for the normative interdiction against killing.
2 The distinction between definition and content, as well as between normative justification and descriptive declaration in the discussion of the Rawlsian theory of justice, is continued in Sanden 2008, pp. 435 and 455–56. (incl. "define"; Fn. 57; p. 435 "explanation").
3 For a number of reasons, sustainability indicators are, even without an orientation based on "pillar logic," not a convincing alternative to the ethical/legal framework developed herein of the "target space," which is based on the theory of necessity and of balanced consideration of interests, supplemented by certain cost-benefit elements. This conclusively determines the norms regarding what can be stated regarding sustainability. By the same token, the focus on attempts to interpret the explicit term "sustainability" in laws is hardly useful (Ekardt 2011, 1C II, 5C II 1, 5C III).
4 Much less discussed to date, however, is the fact that resource use in the industrial countries, too, will need to be cut by about three-quarters during the coming decades if a permanent and globally maintainable level is to be achieved. Cf. Wuppertal Institute 2009, p. 104.
5 This is often simply affirmed; e.g. Oberthür 2008, pp. 49ff. (here, mild criticism is perceptible, but no overall accounting is attempted), or Lindenthal 2009.
6 Cf. here Ekardt 2011, 1B I and other sources, compiling the scattered documentary information of the IPCC, (originally IPCC 2007), and natural-scientific research. Of course, the natural sciences cannot provide a normative goal, but can only express the necessity for certain targets which must be achieved. Certain threatening developments, such as resource wars, are assessed as being negative from a legal/ethical/political perspective.
7 Explicitly on the human rights side of climate change and sustainability, Ekardt 2011, 4, 5, 6 III 3; 6F; see too at the UN level, the report the OHCHR 2009.

Bibliography

Ekardt, Felix (2011). *Theorie der Nachhaltigkeit: Rechtliche, ethische und politische Zugänge – Am Beispiel von Klimawandel, Ressourcenknappheit und Welthandel*. Baden-Baden: Nomos.
IPCC (2007). *Climate Change 2007. Mitigation of Climate Change*. Accessed September 9, 2014 via: www.ipcc.int.
Lindenthal, Alexandra (2009). *Leadership im Klimaschutz. Die Rolle der EU in der internationalen Klimapolitik*. Frankfurt: Campus.
Oberthür, Sebastian (2008). Die Vorreiterrolle der EU in der internationalen Klimapolitik – Erfolge und Herausforderungen. In: Varwick, Johannes (Ed.). *Globale Umweltpolitik*. Schwalbach: Wochenschau-Verlag, 49ff.
OHCHR (2009). *Human Rights and Climate Change*. UN Doc. A/HRC/10/61 of January 15, 2009. Accessed September 14, 2014 via: http://www.refworld.org/docid/498811532.html.
Sanden, Joachim (2008). Überlegungen zur Generationengerechtigkeit aus der Umweltperspektive. *Zeitschrift für Umweltpolitik und Umweltrecht*, 3, 435ff.
Stern, Nicholas (2006). *Stern Review Final Report*. Accessed September 14, 2014 via: www.hm-treasury.gov.uk/stern_review_report.htm
Wuppertal Institute (2009). *Zukunftsfähiges Deutschland in einer globalisierten Welt*. 3rd Edition. Frankfurt/Main: S. Fischer.

7 Theories of "sustainability" and the sustainability of theories

For alternatives to the mainstream, and against simple solutions

Fred Luks

> Even the notion of being able to solve problems is theoretically inappropriate.
> *Stefan Hermann Siemer*

Big questions and fast theories

In a marathon race, the seconds gained by starting out too fast mean minutes lost at the end. The same may be true of sustainability theories: moving too fast at the outset will mean an ultimate loss. Indeed, this should be especially true of a field like "sustainability," for theories of "sustainability" necessarily involve thinking beyond the current day, otherwise they are not sustainable. Not every bit of would-be discourse that gets run through the sustainability roost is deserving of theoretical reflection, however. Obviously, Schumpeter's "pre-analytical vision" is a major factor in deciding which issues are to receive attention. Obviously too, that pre-analytical vision – and not only when espoused by economists – is essentially shaped by faith in, as opposed to knowledge of, the necessity and possibility of endlessly continuing growth.

Theoretical work around or for "sustainability" – in other words, sustainability-theoretical work – means approaching the world with a certain interest – questioning, seeking, thinking and learning. That interest generally refers to literally existential issues. For many, no less than "saving the world" is at stake. Or, to put it only a little more modestly: the object of sustainability theories is to examine how a good life might be possible today and in the future, and which economic, social and ecological factors will play a role in it. This essay is about the questions which, in my view, are central to this effort, or should be:[1] What could an attractive alternative construct to the dominant growth-and-efficiency paradigm look like? What will the future role of resiliency be – that quality which currently seems to be the hottest candidate for sharpening and vitalizing the discourse on "sustainability?" And, last but not least: What is to be done in light of the danger of a certain kind of "populism of simple solutions," which seems to be increasingly in evidence in the sustainability discourse?

Generosity as an alternative construct to efficiency

The view that it might be possible to continue growth indefinitely by means of innovation and efficiency so dominates the sustainability discourse that sustainability theories cannot ignore it. If we don't wish to abandon the goal of "(greater) economic growth," and at the same time want "sustainability," there will be no alternative to de-linking economic efficiency from consumption of the environment. Such de-linkage will be inconceivable without innovation. If we want "sustainable" development and growth in a finite world, we will not be able to do without de-linkage, without innovation, and without efficiency. The permanent combination of reduced or stable consumption of nature on the one hand and simultaneously growing production of value on the other is in any case only conceivable by means of the de-linkage of these two quanta. No de-linkage means no "sustainability." Or no growth.

One point that is often overlooked here is that this strategy of taking the technological path has its limits, and requires – even today, and yet more tomorrow – supplementation or even at least partial substitution by a path which Paech (2005) calls "cultural," involving generosity, sufficiency and exnovation. Sufficiency, here, means a rethinking of goals, for the possibility of an "enough." "Exnovation" means the abolition of undesired things – as the necessary supplement to the introduction of the new to the world by means of innovation. If we do not believe in a generations-long – ultimately eternal – de-linkage, we have to get out of the loop of scarcity – growth – more scarcity – more growth – still more scarcity – and so forth. Efficiency will not save the world.

The fundamental problem of non-"sustainable" developments is the endless loop of more production and more desire without measure, no timeline and no endpoint, none of which is changed by improved efficiency. If the world is to become "more sustainable," we will have to find a way out of this loop. This issue should therefore be central in the landscape of sustainability theories. Economic history since the industrial revolution is to a very great extent a history in which scarcity, efficiency and growth have occupied the main roles. The endless loop is kept running by the fact that a gap is continually being created and continually having to be closed. Again: there is no end in sight, no timeline which, once we have passed it, anything will be different. What we see is the logic of unhampered increase, acceleration and expansion. (The word "we" appears a dozen times or more in this text: it means quite simply, you and I, but, too, the community of sustainability research, and beyond that, those people who are affected by non-"sustainability." In other words, many people.)

At the core of this situation is an unfulfilled promise – or several of them – or, in other words, what is at issue is hope, possibilities. There is a chasm, a gap consisting of wanting to close the emptiness and to never be able to do so, for reasons of logic. That longing is connected with the incredible technological possibilities for the consumption of nature: and that is the core of the issue which the model of "sustainable" development in a finite world addresses, and which, after forty years of discourse on growth, still needs to be dealt with in the context of sustainability theory. If this problem is not addressed, it will remain with us – and the hopeless struggle against scarcity will continue to generate new scarcities. Even during the early phase of the modern sustainability discourse, in 1994, the German Advisory Council on the Environment (SRU 1994) pointed out that the economic process has the effect of aggravating scarcity:

> In accordance with the technological/rational means available to it, the modern economy is able to develop and produce new, hitherto unknown commodities with which it not only responds to existing requirements, but also constantly develops these further. In that respect, it is oriented not only toward meeting, but also toward creating needs. It not only overcomes scarcity, it also continually creates it anew.
>
> (p. 44)

In other words, growth can never "overcome" scarcity, so that the result is a "vicious circle of growing productivity and growing needs" (Leiss 1978, p. 10).

The growth process itself leads to ever-new desires. Growth goes hand-in-hand with new products and technologies, and these in turn change society and its standards of assessment. The growing supply of goods pushes the level of what is considered "normal prosperity" upwards, resulting in new shortages which in turn generate new growth processes. With the aid of science and technology, the goal is to use ever more "natural resources" – materials, energy and space – for these processes. Thus, in a finite world, an increasing shortage of the "ecological" factors which are needed to counteract the scarcity of goods emerges.

The process of the "continual production of scarcity," as Gerschlager (1996, p. 48) puts it, is due in part to the fact that

> all economic activity involves a never-ending struggle against supposed scarcities. Each increase in production is in turn the point of departure for a new experience of scarcity and higher level of production. This process then continues. As long as the positive feedback of desire and economic production is not broken, each satisfied need will bring forth another in its wake, so that the productive alleviation of scarcity is at the same time the production of scarcity.
>
> (ibid.)

The fact that growth leads to more growth by creating needs is also a central argument in John Kenneth Galbraith's (1971) famous book *The Affluent Society*. He emphasizes that the urgency of desires cannot justify the urgency of production, if production produces the very desires that it satisfies. Seen in that light, production only fills a gap which it has itself created. It is sometimes understandable that from the point of view of system theory, scarcity is "a paradoxical problem." As Luhmann (1994, p. 179) has put it: "Access creates what it seeks to eliminate. It seeks to secure for itself an adequate quantity, and thus creates scarcity, which only then makes it reasonable to secure a sufficient quantity."

Of course, society cannot avoid this and other paradoxes of the combating and creating of scarcity by means of efficiency strategies. Sustainability theories should seize upon this, and seek alternatives. An alternative image to efficiency could be generosity: generosity toward nature (the possibility of non-use), toward others (rethinking such concepts as needs and performance), and, very generally, toward technical and other possibilities. To refrain from doing something that is possible, even if it promises profit or expansion – that appears to us an at least somewhat weird thought. But it is precisely such thoughts that sustainability theories will need in a world full of problems and uneconomic growth. The latter – which according to Daly (1991) means growth the added value of which is less than the damage it causes – might become more clearly visible if we would make generosity the object of the considerations of sustainability theory. If not only the scarcity of resources, but also the abundance of many "things" relevant to the quality of life were to enter into our awareness, it would certainly permit sustainability theories to gain in power. For that reason, generosity is an alternative image to the dominant perspective of efficiency.

I stress: an alternative image. For no single alternative will move the practice and theory of "sustainability" forward; only many different ones can do that, as I will discuss below. Generosity seems to be worthy of special emphasis because it could become one of the few attractive alternatives to a fixation on efficiency. Certainly, generosity means something different today than it did to Aristotle or to Adam Smith. For Aristotle (1985), generosity or munificence is the ideal mean between excess profligacy or deficient miserliness. Thus, generosity is as far removed from miserliness as it is from profligacy – even if Aristotle considered the latter less unseemly than the former. In an age dominated by an almost panicky obsession with efficiency, this ideal mean has shifted. What we today see as economically rational, and hence efficient, is much closer to miserliness than it is to the ideal mean of generosity. Miserliness in the guise of efficiency is not good. To regain the mean would mean less miserliness, but a somewhat more relaxed attitude toward profligacy – which might then no longer be considered profligacy. Again: what we today often see as good and right must be considered miserliness toward our fellow humans and toward our environment. The striving for efficiency in its extreme form is nothing other than miserliness. That means that what we consider profligacy to be today is much closer to the ideal mean than economists and sustainability researchers have hitherto placed it. We need generosity, and we need sustainability-theoretical work on the question of what that means concretely.

Resiliency as the salvation of saving the world through "sustainability"?

Efficiency eliminates things from the world which we should not completely eliminate if we are interested in saving it. Ecologically, economically and also socially, we need resources available to act as buffers against "disturbances." Resiliency, as we have come to realize, is of great value for running an economy "sustainably." This is particularly true from an ecological point of view, but it is true, too, even from an economic point of view, as the economic situation since September 15, 2008, has demonstrated impressively. A view of the current range of discourses strongly suggests that resiliency is to become "the next big thing" in the sustainability discourse. And that would be a good thing. Why? Because the critical force of the discourse is being threatened by plastic phraseology, hot air and randomness. "Sustainability" today can mean virtually anything, and hence ultimately nothing at all – that is one reason why I keep setting it in quotes. Resiliency may be a concept that could fill the gap that is appearing here.

If resiliency – the capacity of systems and individuals to withstand disturbances and burdens – is to receive its proper priority of place, we will need redundancy. The existence of redundancy – in other words, of resources and elements which are not used and are hence in this respect superfluous – is fundamental to resilient structures. Here is an important cause of some of the incompatibility between ecological and economic goals. From an economist's point of view, and, too, from the perspective of the dominant society, a "security buffer" such as that outlined here is considered inefficient, and hence as profligacy, or more succinctly: viewed through the lens that is usually used today, the attempt to approach "sustainability" by means of redundancy and slack means nothing more than profligacy or waste, since it means permitting the under-utilization of possibly utilizable resources.

Ecology can teach us that nature does not react in a stable, linear and straight-forward manner to our interventions into it, but rather in a very nonlinear manner and with great leaps, and then sometimes with a certain amount of slowness which causes us not to notice that things are going wrong. The fact that the word "ecological balance" is a purely anthropocentric concept goes without saying in this respect. Concepts such as threshold effects, chaos and positive feedback can be seen as warning signs with regard to the consequences that the use of materials and energy and space have. What is needed in nature is a redundancy of structures and potentials which can provide a cushioning effect when subjected to burdens. What is needed in the economy is the realization that the consumption of nature to the maximum extent is dangerous and must therefore be avoided. That may mean, for example, that available resources not be completely exploited, that we not try to run the economy as close as possible to the – presumed – ecological load limits, that we literally leave more space. And then we will realize that we won't get any further without value judgments. That is obviously a key issue for ambitious sustainability: we must decide which nature we want and what we want to protect and how careful we want to be and what priority of place effi-ciency is to have.

This can be illustrated by using Daly's (1991) famous metaphor, which reminds us that a ship can still sink even if its load has been optimally stacked – simply because that load is too great. However, the decision to be made here is further-reaching and deeper, as Sachs (1994, p. 18) puts it:

> . . . once the crew has decided not to sink itself by continually piling on more cargo, they have two possibilities. Either they can try to load the ship to the

limits of its possibilities regardless of the weather, the tides or the swell. For this purpose, they could equip the ship with a satellite-based system for monitoring the sea, install sensors and monitoring instruments in the hold and on deck, hire personnel capable of thinking systemically, and continually restructure the cabins and the superstructure so that the ship will always be running exactly at the limits of its carrying capacity. Or the crew might lose interest in always operating at the limits of capacity, and orient themselves and the ship in accordance with their good sense and their philosophy of life, so that they would only have to worry about the load limits as a marginal factor. Then, the entire operation would not have to be tailored to optimal utilization, nor would the self-monitoring cybernetic equipment have to be installed.

And that is precisely the point: to leave a sufficient gap between what is considered possible in terms of load and what is in fact being used. Obviously, this gap will itself be based on uncertain knowledge. Problems of knowledge, of risk minimization and of a combination of both will result in the demand to leave some slack, and – watch out, the argumentative circle is closing! – to limit efficiency. The point is, if we want resiliency, and hence redundancy, and hence slack, we want to assign efficiency to a different position than that which it has today. We cannot run an economy on the basis of efficiency and of redundancy at the same time. Efficiency is the absence of redundancy; redundancy is, by definition, inefficient. Redundancy has something to do with generosity.

It may be soothing to some to recall that slack is indeed an honorable concept in business administration. It is certainly seen as sensible for reasons of safety, etc., to have more at hand than one needs, something that is to remain unused. If efficiency and expansion are everything, while safety and quality mean little, things can go wrong – very wrong, as we know today. We know that from the economy, and we will very probably get to know it in a very unpleasant way from the climate. Engineers have for some time used this principle. Every design of a bridge, an aircraft or other technological device which harbors dangers includes safety buffers. Normally, a bridge can carry much more than the authorized load. The fact that passenger planes do not drop from the sky like stones as soon as one engine fails is thanks to this form of excess safety. That is, if you ask me, all very comforting – and very inefficient.

Excess – or, to put it differently, the underuse of existing potentials – has yet other advantages. If you don't fill up your time to the limits, you may be able to think, consider and wait. And that is true, too, of the economy. Ever more rapid progress and innovation cycles have their costs, both for consumers and for producers. We all know that taking detours will improve your familiarity with a place. That is true, too, of the debate around "sustainability." There are things that one should just not do. But there are some things that need to be tried out before we decide for or against doing them. "Sustainable" development is also a seeking and learning process. And that also means that we learn by seeking – and change things through thought processes which, after all, require time. And last but not least, slack is not only ecologically sensible and also something to be considered from a business perspective, but also macro-economically relevant. We need not only complexity, but also simplicity – albeit not too much, as I will show in the last section.

Not only ecosystems and economic systems can be differently resilient in terms of burdens: Leggewie and Welzer (2009) describe how societal and communal forms of organization are capable of creating varying degrees of resiliency. For example, extreme divisions of labor and technology structures are, they say, extremely vulnerable, while systems based on mutuality and the association of citizens are comparatively resilient. If we always operate at the limits of capacities, that will always involve, too, serious risks which, once we stray from the course of expansion, will immediately lead to negative chain reactions. The economic crisis has shown this very impressively.

The much discussed "2°C limit" needs to be put in perspective in this context. There is little doubt as to the political-practical-rhetorical suitability of its implementation. Very probably, there will be disastrous consequences if anthropogenic climate warming is not limited to 2°C. However, this goal is actually based on an assumption, and, in view of the probable dangers, waiting for its rock-solid scientific certification would probably have to be considered a more or less insane "strategy." The fact that it is only "assumed" is part of the problem, and cannot be eliminated by more research, more discourse or more money. We may regret that, but we would be well-advised to accept it – and to act accordingly. Obviously, to act (or not to act), on the basis of research and discourse, and with the use of money. Once again: we also need efficiency, but to seek to base the compatibility of human society with nature solely on the hope of endless increases in efficiency is just plain Russian roulette: risky, with an uncertain result, and irresponsible from a societal point of view. What would be responsible would be a position which explicitly stated those uncertainties – and replaced the promise of ever more for all with appropriate communications regarding the complex array of problems we face, the solutions to which simply are not "simple."

The populism of simple solutions is a challenge for sustainability theories

Societal resiliency is created by redundancy and diversity, not by efficiency and uniformity. To bet the bank on a single card is an extremely risky strategy, with respect to concepts of "sustainability," as elsewhere. Here too, sustainability theories have an important function. They can teach us that simple solutions to complex problems cannot, given the state of affairs, provide a sustainable contribution to "sustainability." To deal with "sustainability" theoretically thus means more than simply to question dominant concepts and to develop alternatives.

Certainly, "sustainability" requires alternative images to the dominant paradigms, such as growth, efficiency and innovation. However, what sustainability theories can also achieve is a critical view of these alternatives. If a certain populism of simple solutions begins to spread within the sustainability discourse, the existence of sustainability theories will prove to be absolutely indispensable for ensuring that "sustainability" can continue productively. What any theory of "sustainability" can and must teach us is that there are no simple solutions. That is of course true, too, for such concepts as generosity and resiliency, which should be considered as contributions to learning processes toward "sustainability," not as the ultimate solutions to complex socioeconomic and ecological problem complexes.

Currently, there is of course a certain bullish atmosphere for "big solutions," which should be encountered with critical skepticism. Whether efficiency or sufficiency, the Common Welfare Economy or the Great Transformation, microcredits or ecological tax reform, the cradle-to-cradle or the post-growth economy, innovation or exnovation, generosity or resiliency – in all cases, the theoretical debate should include the questioning of such concepts, regardless of how normatively attractive they may appear to us – including to me. If, for instance, we are promised that all we have to do is switch from "evil capitalism" to a "Common Welfare Economy," and everything will be all right, that should set off the sustainability-theory alarm bells to a degree that they would even be heard outside the academic community. Maybe sustainability theory needs a section on populism research.

In view of new concepts, sustainability theories also have a number of paradoxical functions: they should concern themselves actively – and also beyond the mainstream – with new concepts of "sustainability," pay attention to them, and feed them into the public discourse. On the other hand, theories of "sustainability" should not uncritically embrace "great ideas" for saving the world, but rather should analyze what the contribution of such ideas might be, and where the limits of such approaches are. Accelerate here, maybe put on the brakes there – the decision as to which strategies are appropriate is itself an object of research.

Some simple solutions are theoretically unambitious, some may be politically dangerous, some are both. Whether and to what extent the societal utility or uselessness of concepts of "sustainability" should have any part whatever in the sustainability theories is one of the questions which these theories will not be able to avoid. Concepts such as "Mode 2," "transdisciplinarity," and especially "post-normal science" are representative of the concern for questions of the political utility, the normativity, the model function and the rhetorical dimension of scientific statements – issues which sustainability theories will have to address.

Precisely because the populism of simple solutions is apparently becoming ever more important, we will not be able to avoid the rhetorical dimension of the object of our interest. We need good theory – but also the capacity to recount a convincing narrative of change. The power of conviction of theory-based narratives certainly increases whenever they are able to dock onto political, economic and other societal practices. Probably at least as important as this is the ability to connect our plausibility, entertainment value (!), convincing images and metaphors – and, last but not least, humor, which is one of the scarcest resources in the sustainability discourse. Wolfgang Sachs (1995) who, better than most, is able to tell stories based on theories, once wrote of "counting and recounting," adding that "sustainability" required both. Yes, we need measurements, weights, number-crunching and model building. But we also need good, reliable, humorous and enthusiastic narratives if the society-changing force of sustainability theory is not to lose its breath too soon.

Note

1 Parts of this essay have already appeared in similar form in the books *Endlich im Endlichen* (2010) and *Lost in Transformation?* (2011). A deeper and broader exposition of my own thoughts appears in *Irgendwas ist immer* (2012) and the forthcoming book *Öko-Populismus*, all published by Metropolis. I would like to thank Stefan H. Siemer for his critical remarks. Any shortcomings, opinions and peculiarities are my responsibility alone. This text is dedicated to Wolfgang Sachs.

References

Aristotle (1985): *Nikomachische Ethik* (edited by Günter Bien, based on the translation by Eugen Rolfes). Hamburg: Felix Meiner.

Daly, H. E. (1991): Elements of Environmental Macroeconomics. In: R. Costanza (Ed.): *Ecological Economics. The Science and Management of Sustainability* (pp. 32–46). New York/Oxford: Columbia University Press.

Galbraith, J. K. (1971): *The Affluent Society*. Second Edition, Revised. Boston: Houghton Mifflin.

Gerschlager, C. (1996): *Konturen der Entgrenzung. Die Ökonomie des Neuen im Denken von Thomas Hobbes, Francis Bacon und Joseph Alois Schumpeter*. Marburg: Metropolis.

Leggewie, C., & Welzer, H. (2009): *Das Ende der Welt, wie wir sie kannten*. Frankfurt a.M.: Fischer.

Leiss, W. (1978): *The Limits to Satisfaction: On Needs and Commodities*. London: Marion Boyars.

Luhmann, N. (1994): *Die Wirtschaft der Gesellschaft*. Frankfurt a.M.: Suhrkamp.

Paech, N. (2005): *Nachhaltiges Wirtschaften jenseits von Innovationsorientierung und Wachstum*. Marburg: Metropolis.

Sachs, W. (1994): Ökologischer Wohlstand statt Wachstumsträume. In: *Toblacher Gespräche 1994. Ökologischer Wohlstand statt Wachstumsträume* (pp. 18–20). Toblach/Bozen: Toblacher Gespräche / Ökoinstitut Südtirol.

Sachs, W. (1995): Zählen oder Erzählen: natur- und geisteswissenschaftliche Argumente in der Studie "Zukunftsfähiges Deutschland." In: *Wechselwirkung*, 76, 20–25.

SRU (Rat von Sachverständigen für Umweltfragen) (1994): *Umweltgutachten 1994. Für eine dauerhaft-umweltgerechte Entwicklung*. Bonn: Deutscher Bundestag.

8   Sustainability and the challenge of complex systems

Joachim H. Spangenberg

Introduction: Models of sustainable development

The point of departure for the sustainability debate is the definition of the World Commission on Environment and Development (the "Brundtland Commission"), which is, however, usually quoted incompletely (WCED 1987, p. 43). The complete definition reads as follows:

> Sustainable development is development that meets the needs of the present without compromising the ability of future generations to meet their own needs. It contains within it two key concepts:
>
> * the concept of "needs," in particular the essential needs of the world's poor, to which overriding priority should be given; and
> * the idea of limitations imposed by the state of technology and social organization on the environment's ability to meet present and future needs.

Two basic dimensions are thus defined: (i) the social dimension of human needs; and (ii) the environmental dimension; the imperative is to preserve the ability to provide ecosystem services. The reference to technology and social organization addresses a further, institutional dimension of sustainable development (Spangenberg et al. 2002); what is missing from the definition, however, is an economic dimension (Kopfmüller et al. 2001). Economic growth, a central issue in the WCED report, is thus viewed by the Commission not as a goal for its own sake, but rather as a means for achieving the key aim of satisfying needs while recognizing the ecological limits established and shaped by society. The "three-legged stool" model (in German the *Drei-Säulen-Modell,* or three-pillar model) was therefore based from the outset on a category error: the confusion of means and ends. Nonetheless, it has become a common metaphor, suggesting the independence of the three pillars, or legs; the fourth, the institutional dimension, has generally been neglected.

An improvement on this model is provided by the "Sustainability Triangle" metaphor. It repeats the same category error, but no longer implies the independence of the three dimensions, and emphasizes the interconnections among them – which are essential for the formulation of sustainability policies. Even more helpful is the "Prism of Sustainability," which includes the institutional dimension as well, thereby providing a structure which represents a comprehensive description of sustainable development (Spangenberg 2002). For such a description, it is necessary to develop ontologies and computer-based models capable of adequately reproducing the dynamics of a four-dimensional interactive system. Of course, the purpose of using models is to simplify concepts in order to facilitate comprehension; however, if the model used does not adequately reflect the real dynamics involved, it can lead to ineffective or even counterproductive problem-solving proposals, as Ackerman et al. (2009) demonstrated with reference to the results of the economic Integrated Assessment Models (IAMs) of climate change, and the proposals they generated for climate policy. This is the risk of oversimplification inherent to any model choice.

For this reason, the main part of this paper consists of a description of a complexity gradient of natural and social systems which permits an evaluation of the suitability of various models for representing the systems' dynamics. For systems as complex as nature, society or the economy the available models have proven, almost without exception, to be insufficiently complex. Cybernetic systems theory offers a more adequate approach; an overview of the systems-theoretical sustainability concept using orientor (or orientation) theory (Bossel 1998) thus constitutes the second part of this paper. For economics in particular, the analysis shows that the complexity of real economies by far exceeds that of the neoclassical ontology and the computer models based upon it. Such models are suitable as instruments of analysis only in special cases, as they are lacking the capability to represent the dynamic processes shaping the properties and behaviors of evolving dynamic systems.

Systems and their complexity

In general, systems are not obviously recognizable, clearly self-defined units. Both describing something as a system, and the definition of the system boundaries are subjective processes which are strongly influenced by the knowledge and interest of the systems analyst; being defined as a system is what determines a system, not objective facts of its existence as such (Funtowicz/Ravetz 1993). Anything can be defined as a system if it can be described as consisting of system elements interconnected by a system structure and system rules. It is a characteristic of systems that they produce results which cannot be attributed to any single one of their elements.

Systems are almost always hierarchically organized, since such a structure optimizes the efficiency of resource use; a supra-, meta- or overall system contains one or more sectoral or sub-systems. The principle of hierarchical organization requires that each system or sub-system has a certain degree of autonomy, and sustainability demands that it be viable in its specific system environment. The overall or meta-system, in turn, is only viable if all essential systemic elements are viable, and hence sustainable. This can be seen, for example, in the assessment of "planetary boundaries": disregarding any one boundary lowers the sustainability thresholds of the remaining boundaries, thereby aggravating problems for all the other elements (Rockstrøm et al. 2009). These system elements can in turn themselves be viewed as systems, i.e. as sub-systems of the system being observed (Odum 1989). The system boundaries define the spatial, temporal or functional dividing lines between systems and their respective environment, and hence their identities (Bossel 1999). The boundaries thus defined are the functional loci of the input and output of a system.

The repertoire of possible behavior and reaction modes of a system, their predictability and occasionally their probability, can be deduced from the system rules defining the options for action of any system. One possible result is unpredictability of a system's behavior; another is that a system could tend towards a dynamic equilibrium. If such an equilibrium exists, the target point of the system development is called the attractor if it can be unequivocally determined and is constant. If it oscillates within a clearly defined range, that range is called the attractor zone. A rule of thumb is that the shorter the period of observation selected, the less probable it is that non-sustainable developments will become apparent (Wilkinson/Cary 2002), and the more probable it is that the "laws" deduced from the empirical data will progressively deviate from real developments.

Levels of system complexity

Luhmann (1980) defined the complexity of a system as the number of its elements and their possible interactions. According to this definition, rules which exclude, *a priori*, a number of otherwise possible interactions, necessarily reduce complexity. Thus, the less the behavior of a system is determined by fixed system rules, the more complex that system will be. With each additional rule, the explanatory model will become more deterministic, while its complexity is reduced.

System rules can be formulated in various ways. The structure used in this paper, based on Allen (1998; 2001), was chosen because it allows existing types of economics ontologies and models, as well as the economy itself, to be directly classified with reference to their respective degree of complexity. In this way the suitability or non-suitability of economics' ontologies and models for the explanation of the real-world economy and its sustainability can be directly determined (Spangenberg 2005a).

Following this schema, a system can be characterized by how many of five cumulative assumptions regarding its final determinacy and the behavior of its components have been made; with each additional assumption, a higher degree of determinacy arises. The level of complexity is assessed by starting with a maximally determined system in which all five basic assumptions apply, and then eliminating one rule at a time, at each step describing the properties of the class of models which thus emerges by comparing it with usual model classes or conceptualizations, and with empirical findings. According to Allen (2001), the five

basic assumptions, each of which builds upon the previous ones, and which constitute the system rules in the respective system observed, are as follows (Spangenberg 2005a; 2005b):

1   It is possible to define an indisputable boundary between the part of the
    world which is to be described, and the rest of it. In other words, it is possible
    to clearly delineate the "system" from its "environment."
2   Classification rules are available for all components of the system; the result-
    ing taxonomy is instrumental for distinguishing the components and makes
    it possible to analytically – or frequently even intuitively – understand the
    processes that unfold between them.
3   The active subunits or system elements are either all identical, and thus also
    identical with the average, or the range of their behavior forms a normal
    distribution around the average at any point in time.
4   The individual behavior of these subunits can be described by means of aver-
    age interaction parameters.
5   There is a stationary state, or state of equilibrium, toward which the system
    tends, which permits fixed relationships between the various system vari-
    ables to be defined.

Depending on how many of these assumptions are made, different interpretation frameworks for describing reality emerge, with the order of the assumptions predetermined by their inherent logic. Systems are thus characterized by
the degree of freedom of action offered by their respective level of complexity,
which also determines how well empirically observed facts can be explained by
the model.

Five rules: Equilibrium models, no development

A system in which all five assumptions apply represents the "final state" a system can reach if it is not subject to any qualitative changes. Since rules 1 to 4
preclude this, the system is clearly oriented towards the attractor range in which
it is located at the time of observation. The corresponding models and theories
assume that all actions and reactions occur simultaneously, with each variable
calculated as a function of the others. They are by definition either static equilibrium models which assume the state of equilibrium as the point of departure and
analyze the effects of small deviations; or else they are models oriented toward a
cyclical or chaotic attractor, i.e. toward an attractor zone.

   The equilibrium models of the neoclassical economic tradition are based on
the assumption of declining marginal utility and marginal productivity, which
are in turn based upon the assumption of incremental change (marginality) and
complete substitutability (Christensen 1989). They thus correspond to the type
of system in which all five rules apply. Since it is moreover assumed that all actors
have access to all information, and that all transactions are carried out simultaneously, an attractor emerges which is unambiguously determinable, point-shaped

and constant (every attractor is constant provided it is observed only at any arbitrarily chosen but fixed point in time). However, this excludes from consideration those cases, which are also possible in equilibrium models, in which the attractor has predictable cycles or chaotic variations with fixed ranges of oscillation and a constant average.

Equilibrium models with constant attractors have the advantage that their results are clearly predictable: they are characterized by a stationary state determined by fixed relationships of relevant quanta and a simultaneously solved system of differential equations. They thus provide the possibility of making decisions which are rational within the framework given by the model, and undertaking optimizations. For this purpose, clearly determinable situations before and after an economic or political action can be compared with one another, which is for example the basis of cost-benefit analyses, or of rational choice theory.

This type of model is problematic in two respects: First, from a system-theoretical point of view, it must be determined whether rules 1 to 5 also apply to the given subject of the model, the real economy. This applies particularly to rule 5, the assumption of equilibrium, which ultimately states that during the establishment of equilibrium, no new disturbance will arise, keeping the system from its hypothetical state of equilibrium. For this purpose, nonlinear effects, such as those generated by positive feedbacks, must be excluded. In particular, the learning capability of actors, enabling them to change their behavior in real time in response to the perceived situation and its anticipated development, is not permissible in such equilibrium models and can consequently not be explained by them. Such behaviour can change the attractor, i.e. the target equilibrium of the system, beyond the stochastic oscillations or incremental shifts (which the neoclassical models can deal with; see Schumpeter 1928). A second level of theoretical criticism challenges the assumptions not in their formulation as system rules, but rather in their formulation as fundamental assumptions of economics.

All in all, such simple models are incapable of adequately depicting socioeconomic processes in general and sustainability processes in particular. Their oversimplified assumptions view the future as a structurally unchanged continuation of the present, and hence make it impossible to interpret the real progress of processes of change in the model. They are not suitable for depicting sustainable economic development, which includes structural changes.

Four rules: Nonlinear dynamic models, determined development

Nonlinear dynamic models are the result of positing rules 1 through 4 as applicable, but not rule 5 on the existence of equilibrium. In such models, also known as "system dynamics models," the development always follows the most probable path, and because of the uniform interaction between the system elements, that path is also the only one which is ultimately realized. Other options theoretically available to the system do not become relevant, since rule 4, while it does allow for variations and fluctuations, at the same time stipulates that the average forms of interaction correctly describe system behavior, and are hence dominant.

The identical interaction parameters lead to the continual repetition of the same interactions (iteration); they are realized in economics by such assumptions as the construct of the *homo economicus* as a standardized asocial utility maximizer, and the exclusive observation of the exchange of goods in markets based on their price relationships, with fixed, exogenously set preferences. These are unchangeable, which means that learning processes and changes in behavior are excluded, and presumes either descendants who are identical in this respect, or immortal unlearning individuals. Under these assumptions, even fluctuations such as price and quantity variations do not lead to any deviation from the most probable path of development. The resulting models, with such elements as steady production and consumption functions, are dynamic; they provide a mechanical description of change. In contrast to equilibrium models, in which the model already determines the result, dynamic models can develop towards different final states. The model determines the type of development and the number of possible endpoints, while the starting conditions unalterably determine the location of the attractor basin of the model run and thus the equilibrium to which it will converge. In system-dynamic models, under rules 1 to 4, such an attractor need not represent an unchanging state; it can change cyclically – and in extreme cases even chaotically. Such processes, resulting from no longer assuming a constant equilibrium, are described, e.g. by Schumpeter (1928), as short- and medium-term innovation cycles.

Again, we have to ask whether systems of this type are appropriate for reflecting the complexity of the real world economy, and whether they are suitable as models for economic sustainability processes. Neither is the case, for system-dynamic models, too, are still largely determined, and thus not in a position to switch from one target to another; possible developments are limited to paths within the basin of a predefined attractor. With knowledge of the initial conditions, the development of the system is thus predictable. The cause of this predictability is rule 4, which demands a standardized interaction of system elements. Thus, for example, it is impossible to grasp the impact of social interactions, which occur parallel to economic interactions and which tend to change the standardized forms of interaction. Overall, the question remains as to whether the interaction of all individuals can be adequately described with average parameters: sociologists had hoped to be able to do so during the 1950s and 1960s, a hypothesis they now vehemently reject.

The system thus remains mechanistic; it cannot depict the learning effects which arise directly in human systems, and via the processes of evolution in natural systems, nor the changes in behavior and structure that they bring about. The system follows a substantial rationality built upon predictability and reversibility. It thus fails to reflect the real dynamics of ecological and economic processes.

Three rules: Self-organizing systems, stochastic development

Self-organizing systems are distinguished from nonlinear dynamic models in that the assumption of uniform interaction among the elements is dropped. However, the assumption that all system elements or subsystems are either identical, or that their behavior is distributed following a normal distribution around the average, remains. The narrower case, i.e. the assumption of identical actors, presumes that the actors in an economy are homogenous groups, and therefore – as in the fundamental approach of microeconomics (in contrast to psychology) – can be represented by a "representative agent" with behavior identical to that of all agents he represents (for instance consumers, entrepreneurs and other functional groups). This assumption of identity is not an arbitrary simplification which can be abandoned whenever needed, but is necessary for neoclassical theory to be able to build a bridge between micro- and macroeconomics, by defining demand and consumption functions of representative agents at the macroeconomic level (Keen 2001). Group-specific modes of behavior, familiar from consumer research, are thus excluded; even such factors as higher income or higher education do not imply that different (e.g. higher-value) goods are purchased; the demand structure remains unchanged. The system is to a large extent determined.

In the second case, not all preferences remain identical; nonetheless, the economic actors can be represented by a single representative agent, since his behavior reflects the mean value of all individual actors, and their behavior follows a normal distribution. In spite of these limitations, the system produces a variety of new behavioral options from the random oscillations of non-learning, homogenous actors no longer tied to an identical and thus average behavior. The possibility of non-average behavior of individual agents permits the realization of improbable behavior variants; while the limits of the attractor basins remain valid for the mean value of behavior, they become permeable to individuals due to their random oscillations. All existing development paths or trajectories can thus be exhausted, albeit with a much lower probability than converging towards the main attractor basin. Since the direction of system development can switch between various attractors (including cyclical and chaotic attractors), the trajectories and the final equilibrium states are no longer established *a priori*; even knowledge of the system and the initial conditions does not permit any prediction of the results: development paths can only be described *ex post*. This type of systems is referred to as "self-organizing systems"; they are characterized by the formation of new structures and modes of behavior on the basis of uncontrolled random decisions which have not been shaped by learning processes. The interaction of the system elements leads to new, so-called *emergent properties;* overall, the system behaves in a more organized and orderly manner than the rules which determine the behavior of the elements would prescribe (Richter/Rost 2002). Self-organization is a non-deterministic, out-of-equilibrium phenomenon. Its central mechanism is the automatic reinforcement of some of the available options for action or development; which ones depends in part upon internal system properties, but in part also on the availability of resources beyond the subsistence level. The combination of a spectrum of permissible interactions with their iteration thus leads to specific development paths in historical time, shaped randomly and through influences of the system environment: even initially identical systems develop different "biographies." Self-organization is a characteristic internal to the system, but the direction it takes is influenced by the system environment (Odum 1988). Self-organization can be seen as a passive adaptation to changing external conditions, but not as an active or even an anticipatory activity. While the individual agents are, as a result of the rules, incapable of learning, the system as a whole is capable of adaptation. For this reason self-organizing systems which react to the conditions of the system environment are also called complex adaptive systems; their properties have been studied by e.g. artificial-life researchers (Richter/Rost 2002) using simulations and other tools. Their capacity to re-create real-world processes in formal models has been considerably expanded in recent years in the context of climate research; with regard to ecological systems however, it is still limited to relatively simple systems.

The insights provided from the analysis and interpretation of self-organizing systems go far beyond those system-dynamic models can offer. Nonetheless, compared to most biological and socioeconomic systems and ecosystems, they are still remote from reality, as neither homogeneity of actors nor a normal distribution of behaviors around the average has been empirically observed. Self-organizing systems do develop, but in a random, not a teleological manner. Since feedback mechanisms are a major factor in the economy as well as in society, these systems still remain an insufficiently complex form of description. Concepts, proposals and prognoses formulated on this basis should therefore be handled with care, particularly because they do at first glance seem to take into account essential properties of ecological and socioeconomic systems (self-organization and development capability).

Two rules: Evolving complex systems, learning development

In dropping rule 3 we eliminate the assumption that the spectrum of behavior of active subunits (such as consumers, companies, etc.) will at any given time follow a normal distribution around the average; the scope of possible behavior modes becomes dynamic, and is not limited *a priori*. Agents can change their behavior spontaneously through learning or as a result of local processes in the system.

Due to the variability of behavior modes thus enabled, evolution occurs not only at the system level, but also at that of the micro-actors themselves. As a result of their capacity to change their behavior depending on the respective (local) state in the system, an internal selection dynamic emerges which can lead to seemingly teleological adaptations of the entire system, even in the case of non-goal-oriented micro-actors such as organisms and populations of animals and plants, as a result of the positive feedback effects of success-and-imitation strategies. New behaviors are tried, successful behavior is rewarded and imitated, and unsuccessful behavior suppressed. Successful behavior – successful given a certain state of the system environment – will thus solidify into evolutionarily stable strategies (Maynard-Smith 1974; Maynatd-Smith/Parker 1976; Dawkins 1978). By means of such mechanisms, the system components react to the state of the system and its partly externally influenced dynamics; this, in turn, influences the structure and state of the system in an iterative feedback process. Accordingly, a complex evolving system is one in which the internal structure of its constituent elements changes over time, and in which feedbacks emerge which change the structures at the system level, so that the initial context of the elements – and hence their behavior – is changed. These interactive effects give rise to an evolutionary development (Allen 1998).

In anthropogenic systems, this evolutionary process is intentionally directed and accelerated when agents react anticipatively to expected changes, and thus, with varying degrees of reflection and intention, not only influence the behavior of the system as a whole, but also the effect of the system on its environment. The more the evolutionary processes of trial and error are replaced – or at least influenced – by anticipatory solutions to problems, the more effective and efficient the system's reaction and adaptation capability will become (Hornung 1985), and the more it will contribute to shaping societal orientations, *leitbilder* and norms.

These processes spark a dynamic which leads to the continuous further development of the behavior of actors and systems, which in turn leads to changes in the state of the system and of its environment, and forces new adaptations. From this, a process of co-evolution of the economy, society and the environment emerges, based on the non-conscious and hence slow, yet targeted, adaptation of ecosystems, and, for human systems, on the rapid combination of adaptation and learning processes in economy and society (Spangenberg 1998; Norgaard 2002). Real world economies, ecosystems and societies are evolving systems. In all cases, behavioral innovations of actors towards explorative non-average modes of action are essential for the reaction dynamics of the entire system. These emerge from the individual characters of individuals as system elements, but also from the behavior-shaping mechanisms which, over time, convey knowledge, experience, techniques and heuristics to individuals.

Macroeconomics, in essence, analyzes the interaction of system components on the aggregate level. Once freed from the restrictive, reality-denying assumptions of microeconomics (focused on market exchange analysis), it permits the description of processes of system development in which the systems, their environments and their subunits (elements, subsystems) undergo a co-evolutionary, non-mechanical, joint learning process. For a description of economic developments to withstand the test of reality, it must have an evolutionary orientation, particularly with regard to the sustainability of the economy, and such an evolutionary view of the economy (or evolutionary economics) must necessarily include the co-evolution of economic, social and ecological systems (Costanza et al. 2001). A co-evolutionary economics cannot build upon the methods of substantial rationality, but rather requires a transition to a procedural rationality which describes irreversible, open-ended development processes, emphasizing processes of discourse and social consensus, rather than prognoses (Faucheux/Froger 1995).[1]

One rule: Undetermined systems

If we also abandon the second rule in Allen's (2001) structure, what remains are systems distinguished from their environment (i.e. system borders exist and can be described) in which no statement can be made regarding the interaction of their components. No specific systemic properties or behavioral characteristics can be derived; the resulting models are too general to be usable as instruments for exploring real-world systems. For the analysis of natural and social systems, we have now, after dropping a number of restrictive assumptions (rules 2 to 5) and thus progressively improving both the complexity and the reality fit of the model, surpassed the point of useful generalization.

The properties of evolving systems

Economies, like societies and ecosystems, are complex, evolving systems. Although there is to date no universal theory of such systems, several of their general characteristics are rather well known (see e.g. Holling et al. 1998; Rees 2002). Each such system can be described as a *dissipative structure* (Prigogine 1988), i.e. a result of structure formation processes far removed from equilibrium and stabilized by the continuous throughput of resources (usable energy, materials and information), which they use for their self-organized structure formation and the maintenance of adaptability. Since systems with a high degree of order represent a low level of entropy, this permanent input of low-entropy resources from the system's environment and their transformation into high entropy-waste is, according to the laws of thermodynamics, a necessary and irreversible process. Industrial economic activity uses societal/institutional structures and human labor to transform low-entropy resources such as ores or fossil fuels into products, services and social structures, plus high-entropy heat, wastes, exhaust gases and sewage, and in this way produces jobs, income, consumption opportunities and entropy (Georgescu-Roegen 1971; Daly 1996). This exploitation of the results of geological, biological and social evolution, in the context of a socio-institutional framework of conditions shaped by this very process, is the physical basis of industrial economic activity, its functional precondition, and hence, too, a limit to its development.

The more general statement that environmental problems are essentially societal phenomena can thus be made more concrete, since they are both primarily societally generated and defined, and their negative impacts affect economy and society as much as they affect the environment. For this reason, a systemic understanding of the interdependencies of environment, society and economy is necessary in order to find adequate answers to ecological problems (Kraemer 2008).

Evolving complex systems which, according to the system rules, consist of heterogeneous elements, and demonstrate heterogeneous patterns of existence and activity, have a number of typical properties (Beckenbach 1998; Spangenberg 2005a):

•   They are usually hierarchically structured, in that each system is part of a meta-system which defines the framework conditions for the lower level; systems at different levels form nested hierarchies (Simon 1974), or "panarchies" (Holling et al. 1998).

- The system processes are marked by nonlinear cause–effect relationships, such as threshold-value phenomena causing tipping points, and by other discontinuities, delays and network effects generated by mutually overlapping positive and negative feedback loops. As a result, even marginal parameters changes can trigger drastic effects at the system level which have an impact upon the super-ordinate levels of the panarchy. The behavior of the meta-system cannot be determined by bottom-up aggregation of processes at sub-ordinate levels (Körner 2002).

- The newly emerging structures within developing systems allow for a wide variety of simultaneously existing possible stable states; as a result of external effects or internal developments, the system may depart from the attractor basin of a stable equilibrium, and then either shift to another stable condition or manifest chaotic behavior, from which in turn various, in some cases stable, path-dependent developments can emerge (Prigogine/Stengers 1984).

- Evolutionary system development is only possible if the active subunits (e.g. companies or consumers) are not identical in their behavior, and the spectrum of their behavior does not follow a normal distribution. The lack of applicability of system rules 3 to 5 is a condition for system evolution in general and the capacity for sustainable development in particular. The opposite assumption is, as already mentioned, of decisive importance for neoclassical microeconomics, since without it, an aggregation of individual demand functions would not be possible, and hence no macro-level economic demand function could be derived from individual demand curves.

- The flexible adaptability of evolving systems is based on the functional diversity of their structures, and constitutes a form of systemic efficiency which is clearly different from the efficiency concepts of standard economics (Rammel/van den Berg 2003). If policy is shaped according to the latter criteria, the result will be a reduction of functional diversity in favor of a narrowly conceived and only transitorily valid definition of efficiency, and hence a reduction of the resilience and the long-term effectiveness of the system.

Systems in variable environments cannot be both static and stable (a static economy cannot exist over the long term in a dynamic environment); their viability is secured by the capacity to adapt to change. Such evolving systems are hardly ever in a state of equilibrium, and both their temporal dynamics and the heterogeneous spatial distribution of equilibria and attractor zones result in a situation in which what may be a stable equilibrium at one moment may be an unstable one – or none at all – at a different time or place. The systems are either subject to cyclical development processes, or they stabilize at the supra-system level, as a result of the continued succession of system crises at the subordinate levels providing the dynamics, while the overall integrity of the systems remains intact (Odum 1989). Schumpeter's (1928) concept of economic dynamics fits well with this systemic characteristic.

The fallacy of misplaced precision

The process of system development emerges from the interaction of systems and subsystems; it is characterized by nonlinearity and random dependence. While processes of system development are optimization processes due to the selection effects, they do not necessarily lead to an equilibrium, due to the continuous changes in the system and its environment. Instead of unequivocal, system-wide and permanently valid optima, what emerges is a large number of solutions which are, at a certain point of time and under the respective system state and environment conditions, adequately suitable. Such a development is different from the mechanistic and deterministic optimization concepts of standard economics, in that the local relative optima are not constant, neither regarding their localization nor their character as optima: the future is open and uncertain. Random oscillations or innovations may lead to spontaneous changes in the nature, location and timing of points of possible equilibria (attractors) – something that economists should be aware of, since Schumpeter. If an optimum of system fitness is achieved in an evolutionary process, the validity of that optimum will only be relative or local and of limited duration, i.e. the closest of a number of attractors accessible to the system at that particular moment. It will be approximated as selection processes eliminate the solutions not adequately adapted to the situation, while a large number of suitable, and hence relatively optimal solutions develop further (evolutionary optima are not homogeneous). Absolute optima and stable equilibria cannot be defined in an evolving system without introducing additional system rules, thus changing the character of the system. The resulting system would be more calculable, but no longer evolving, and hence not potentially sustainable.

In connection with threshold values, randomly driven development and innovation processes generate discontinuities typical of thermodynamic systems (Prigogine 1988; Funtowicz et al. 1998). "Stable situations" are the result of dynamic processes dependent on numerous factors interacting at various levels, whose mutual relations may change over time. The innovations emerging within this process change the structure of the system irreversibly. The results are path-dependent development processes in historical time. They run the risk of becoming trapped in inferior solution situations (lock-ins), which can be prevented by securing diversity (the "insurance hypothesis": the preservation of suitable, but momentarily suboptimal solutions, or "excess baggage" as a precautionary measure), and functional redundancy (what is redundant in a certain situation will not necessarily remain so over time; in that sense, redundancy is an element of diversity). These are empirically observable phenomena which cannot be explained by the concept of reversible processes, clearly defined optima and permanent system equilibria of neoclassical growth theory or of environmental economics (Rammel/van den Bergh 2003, Spangenberg 2005a). Their analysis makes it possible to comprehend more clearly the dynamics of structural change and adaptation to external forces, which are relevant within the context of sustainable development (Funtowicz/Ravetz 1994).

The properties of evolving systems as observed in a certain context are specific to that context (*ceteris* is never *paribus*), and their analysis is never completely objective: already in the definition of system boundaries and, in empirical research, in the definition of the properties to be analyzed and the timeframe of observation, subjective decisions are inevitable, which affects the results of the analysis (van der Sluijs 2002). The assumption that the *ex post* analysis of parameter development time series will lead to valid conclusions regarding future system structures and processes, and thus to reliable *ex ante* prognoses, is erroneous in evolving systems; a predictive analysis is not possible, and uncertainty cannot be eliminated (Spangenberg 2005b). Econometric time series analyses have only limited explanatory power for future developments. As a result, clear, prognosis-based policy recommendations, which seemingly shift the burden of identifying the best decision from politicians to economists promising "optimal solutions," do not work in reality. Responsibilities cannot be delegated – each decision taken, always under uncertainty, remains the responsibility of the respective decision maker, if only for the choice of advice s/he endorses. Economists' recommendations – and the policies based upon them or otherwise developed on the basis of economic theories – assume that the respective probabilities of various policy options and their impacts can be quantified, and hence that the unambiguously best solutions can be identified. The risk is that the inevitably mistaken prognoses (OECD 2013), when taken as the basis for action, will lead to mistaken measures at the expense of current and future generations, as uncertainties, risks and irreversibility are not sufficiently taken into account.

The standard models in neoclassic economics and its derivatives like environmental and resource economics have been developed based on assumptions which are not compatible with the observable real world, including the complexity of evolving systems. In particular, the standard economic models are several levels more deterministic than the observable economy itself; they assume rules 3 to 5, or at least elements thereof, to be applicable. The sustainability discourse in economics is all too often an attempt to describe systems, their evolution and their interactions in the language of neoclassical economics, although their complexity by far exceeds the capabilities of such language. The charge of a lack of complexity is particularly applicable if not only the economic system, but also its interactions with other economies, with society and with the environment, are the object of analysis (Spangenberg 2007).

Sustainability and orientor/orientation theory

To date no theory exists which would allow the systematic analysis of the sustainability of evolving systems, at the system level. Orientor theory (in Hornung 1985, "orientation theory") was developed by Bossel and his associates in order to find, at a relatively high level of abstraction, universally valid answers to the questions of how scenarios, policies and development paths in evolving systems and in a dynamic system environment could be evaluated, and how sustainable strategies and management approaches could be identified. Orientor theory analyzes

the minimum survival conditions for evolving systems in a dynamic environment, using the long-term persistence of the system with intact (but evolving)
system functions as an operationalization of sustainable system development. In
this way the theory permits identifying sustainable system conditions, i.e. permanently sustainable arrangements of a dynamic co-evolution of the system and its
environment.

This approach is selected as the basis for further analysis for two reasons. First,
it refers specifically to evolving systems; it does not oversimplify. Secondly, it is
the best-known theoretical approach for formulating general sustainability criteria for such systems, and for applying them interpretively to various systems (e.g.
Müller/Jørgensen 2000, for ecological systems, and Spangenberg 2005a; 2005b,
for economic systems).

Orientor theory describes a set of properties valid for all evolving systems,
enabling them to adequately respond to changes in the respective system environment and thus to remain viable. If these internal system properties are present, the system can be considered sustainable, not absolutely, but within the
limits of the system environment changes analyzed. Which properties those are
depends not only on the system itself, but also on its environment: every system
must react to the conditions and dynamics of its environment, and vice versa:
that is the essence of evolution. Orientor theory classifies the large number of
environmental parameters into six categories, or basic properties, of system environments; the system properties responding to and/or induced by them are the
orientors.

The basic properties of possible system environments are distinct and complete, i.e. none of the stated properties can be expressed in terms of any combination of other properties, and together they provide an exhaustive characterization
of those characteristics of system environments which are of relevance for the
future flourishing of the system (Hornung 1985). The six basic properties of system environments are (Bossel 1998; Spangenberg 2005b):

1   The normal state of the environment: the current state oscillates around it
    at a certain maximum distance;
2   Scarcity of resources vital for the system: materials, energy and information
    are not directly available where and when they are needed;
3   Diversity: many qualitatively very different processes and patterns of envi-
    ronmental variables are permanently or recurrently present;
4   Variability: the state of the environment deviates from the normal state such
    that it may diverge significantly from it for limited periods of time;
5   Change: the normal state of the environment changes, i.e. another state
    becomes normal, gradually over the course of time, or abruptly; and
6   Other actor systems: the environment includes other actor systems, the
    behavior of which is of subjective significance to the system observed.

As these basic system environment properties are distinct and complete,
every system's environment can be exhaustively described by a six-digit vector

containing their specifications as qualitative and quantitative data. Each of these environmental properties corresponds to an orientor, i.e. a basic property of the system, which, if present, will allow the system to react to the respective basic properties of the environment, ensuring its continued existence. These six basic orientors of systems are:

1   Existence (and reproduction)
2   Effectiveness
3   Freedom of action
4   Security
5   Adaptability
6   Coexistence.

This set of orientors is, like the set of environmental properties, complete – covering all essential aspects of the system – and distinct. The respective specifications of the orientors thus characterize a system comprehensively, but not unambiguously (different systems with the same orientor specifications may exist).

The formulations of basic environmental properties and orientors have been theoretically deduced (Bossel 1998); both have been shown to constitute exhaustive, systemically derived system descriptions. Empirically, the suitability, i.e. the applicability and explanatory power, of this system has been confirmed in a cluster analysis of approximately 200 existing value systems (Hornung 1985). The orientor system has thus been theoretically and empirically shown to constitute an abstract evaluation grid which can be applied to evolving systems of all kinds.

A central statement of orientor theory is that *the long-term existence of any system, and hence its sustainability, is seriously threatened whenever the fulfillment of only one of the orientors falls below a certain minimum* (Rockstrøm et al. 2009 have argued in a similar vein with respect to the Earth System).

In hierarchically structured systems or panarchies, the same criterion applies for all evolving subsystems, since without their permanent functionality, the sustainability of the entire system would be endangered (Bossel 1996a). Continued system functionality is achieved only by those actor systems which can not only sufficiently realize their own interests, but also, simultaneously, take into account those of the actor systems in their system environment. Sustained existence requires coexistence (orientor no. 6) with other actor systems (property no. 6) upon whose viability a system depends; this corresponds to the ecological, social, economic and institutional sustainability conditions of each of the subsystems. For instance, if the speed of change in one system leads to rapid changes of its state and thus of coexisting systems' environmental conditions this could impose stress on the other systems by challenging their adaptability (Settele/Spangenberg 2013).

The independence of basic orientors does not mean that the fulfillment of each orientor is independent from that of the others. External influences can simultaneously have positive and negative effects on one or several orientors, the short- and long-term effects possibly differing. For instance, new technologies in the economic subsystem can both destroy jobs (security, coexistence with the social subsystem) and create new ones (adaptability). The devaluation of established stocks of knowledge by the introduction of technological innovation reduces freedom of action, but at the same time tends to increase the effectiveness of the system, particularly in combination with the development of new intellectual capacities (Spangenberg 2001).

The specifics of anthropogenic systems

When applying natural science concepts to anthropogenic systems, not only the dependence of socioeconomic systems on natural ones via the physical side of the economy and society must be taken into account, but also the impacts of society and economy (and their interactions) on the environment. Even more important are the fundamental differences between both classes of systems: economic and social systems differ from merely biological-chemical-physical systems regarding their level of complexity, and in that learning actors intentionally orient them towards implicitly or explicitly defined ends – they are *teleological systems*. The actors are able to reflect upon the future impacts of their past and current decisions, actions and objectives, and to adapt the *telos* accordingly. They, and through them the systems, are anticipatory (which neither precludes errors, mistaken perceptions, assessments and decisions, nor erroneous interpretations such as interpreting macro-level phenomena as generalizations of micro-level ones: the meta-system is not a generalization of any of its subsystems). They can also learn from past and present mistakes through conscious and unconscious adaptation, sometimes imposed, but goal-oriented, and can change objectives and measures planned or taken. Thus they are both reflective and reflexive (Beck 1996). They cannot only adapt to changing system states and properties of the system environment, but within certain limits, they can also shape them; in this sense they are self-conscious (Falconi-Benitez/Ramos-Martin 2002). This flexibility, based on the capabilities of the system elements, i.e. reflecting human beings, distinguishes anthropogenic systems from bio-geogenic ones: whereas the latter can only passively adapt to changing system environments, the former can do so proactively, reacting not only to already manifest but also to expected changes.

Orientor theory takes this into account by introducing additional orientors for anthropogenic systems. In addition to the six externally induced orientors, there are three additional ones which represent a reaction to the internal properties of the system itself (the second and third in particular covering individuals described as [sub]systems):

- If systems are *capable of self-reproduction*, the maintenance of this capability constitutes a new orientor (in evolving systems, this orientor will in time merge with the existence orientor, as indicated above);
- If the system is *sensitive*, it attempts to avoid palpable stresses; Bossel has called this the "psychological needs" of the system; and

- If a system *makes value-based choices* between options with different consequences, this implies an orientor "responsibility."

Social systems with conscious actors develop a sense of meaning, most clearly evident in their justifications of the meaningfulness and desirability of their sustained existence. Such justifications range from religious motivations (the preservation of creation, the will of God, as for H. Daly 2001: "Sustainability means using [available] resources in order to best serve God, [. . .] by caring for Creation, protecting it, and learning from it"), through fundamental ethical convictions, such as justice-related goals (Rawls 1971) or ethical responsibility (Jonas 1979), all the way to utilitarian worldviews (e.g. Bentham and Mill) and the system-theoretical argumentation of Bossel (1996, p. 202): "The objective function of all living and evolving systems resulting from the process of evolution."

This assignment of meaning is also the foundation for various forms of dealing with evolving systems, and with the results expected from them, which are based on various pre-analytical visions. The following are the most important pre-analytical visions or world views (comprising an ontology including an anthropology, an axiology and an epistemology, Spangenberg 2014). The first two are fairly common, e.g. in economics, but only the third is adequate to the management of complex systems towards sustainability goals (ideal types, from Schütz 2000):

- *The assumption that self-organization is a goal in and of itself*, and leads *a priori* to optimum results; hence, interventions in the process should be minimized (Hayek 1972; Luhmann 1982). This implies minimizing societal or political interventions into individual decision-making, which is seen as independent, unquestionable, and of top priority. In particular, the use of such interventions for the purpose of pursuing super-ordinate system goals is strictly rejected. This view is unrealistic in two respects: first, it assumes autonomous, i.e. a-social individuals, whose decision-making is not influenced by societal processes. Second, it ignores the fact that any system must support measures which preserve the functionalities of the (meta-)system as a whole, given the mutual dependency in nested systems, even if that runs counter to particular short-term interests of an individual subsystem. Since in this world view it is assumed that the system *per se* produces optimal results, the optimality criteria are beyond question; they are seen as predefined components of the system.
- *The definition of a generally binding and supposedly "neutral" standard of values*, externally imposed and independent of the interests of the actors, allowing the identification of a clearly optimal solution. This can be based on the stipulations of outside parties provided with, for example, spiritual authority, on the results of democratic voting, or on market processes (Bossel 1996b). However, since in a comprehensive system markets and voting are part of the system, and any "outside party" is necessarily either a part of the system, or connected to it as part of the nested meta-system, and hence motivated by

interests intrinsic to that system, this world view implies a shift of power to authorities, parties or price-determining institutions such as markets, experts or government agencies, excluding the representatives of other value systems from the decision-making process (Luhmann 1982).

- *Institutionalization of decision-making processes based on multidimensional criteria* and sets of indicators (Munda 1995; Bossel 1999). This world view assumes that none of the value standards represented in a system will *a priori* be "correct," and hence binding; even scientific "proof" of a certain position is affected by the subjectivity of the actors involved. All decisions are based on incomplete information; they are never only technical selection procedures. The solution must be sought in negotiation processes involving the "extended peer community," with a procedure considered fair by all participants (Rawls 1971). A new understanding of research ("mode 2 science," "uncertainty science," "sustainability science," "post-normal science," etc.) is needed, replacing the illusion of value neutrality without falling victim to the arbitrariness of social constructivism.

However, problem-adequate discourses are complicated by the process dynamics and the time lags between cause and effect inherent to complex systems (delay elements are typical constituents of complex systems). More generally, identifying causes is difficult, as the typical risks of modernity (Beck 1986) are characterized by unclear causalities, delays of effects and spatial disconnection of cause and effect (the "hypothetical risks" of Häfele 1974). The delaying effects of system inertia can make strong symmetrical system coupling appear temporarily as asymmetrical, suggesting a weak unilateral coupling, e.g. between the economy and the environment. In real-world terms this would imply that the damaging effects of the economy on the environment are quite limited (high absorption capacity, weak coupling), while the reverse impact of the environment on the economy is negligible ("agriculture accounts for 3% of GDP – so why worry about climate change impacts?" overlooking the need to eat), and thus that sustainability-oriented changes of the mode of production and consumption are not necessary. Another line of argumentation presumes a bilateral but also weak system coupling, leading to the conclusion that even significant damages to environmental systems will cause only minimal disturbances of the economic or social systems, which will be manageable by technological innovation without requiring structural changes of the socioeconomic system.

Conclusion and outlook

A comprehensive system-analytical sustainability analysis in nested systems is a recursive process, from the meta-system down to the level of detail demanded. The depth of analysis required depends on the research question: the goal of the analysis is not completeness – the number of possible recursive steps is infinite – but an appropriate resolution for answering the question.

Essential steps of the analysis are (Spangenberg 2005a; 2007):

- Interpretation of the orientors, deriving criteria specific to the object area;
- Interpretation of the criteria, derivation and selection of operational indicators, rather than obtaining indicators through aggregation, or the summation of incommensurable objects (i.e. which have no common denominator), as is typical in many bottom-up processes;
- A gradual increase in the diversity of other legitimate interpretations (reflecting the pluralism of cultures and interests in democratic societies [Söderbaum 2010]). In cases of divergent positions the rejection of the concept must be distinguished from diverging interpretations of a common base (in the latter case, the differences tend to be fewer, and the conflicts more intense).

Sustainability differs from other social theories not through a different subject area, but due to its different perspective (emphasizing interactive dimensions), and specific, non-negotiable basic values. These define sustainability as needs-orientation plus the acceptance of limits. Needs-orientation requires participation opportunities; the physical, legal, economic, social, intellectual, status-dependent, etc. possibility to take part in decision finding must be enforced in all four dimensions (which can also be described as subsystems) – the economy, society, the population, and the environment (Spangenberg 2005a).

These four dimensions, together with their respective orientations (which can be formulated as categorical imperatives) constitute the "Prism of Sustainability"; qualities count at least as much as quantities. As soon as sustainability norms are operationalized beyond the level of fundamental ethical principles, they can often be better described dialectically than normatively, requiring a political process to concretize them and a political discourse for their implementation. Sustainability policy is necessarily transdimensional, as every measure of environmental, social or economic politics has impacts on the other dimensions/subsystems, necessitating broad *ex ante* impact assessments (broadness implying for instance the use of social and gender criteria when evaluating environmental and economic policy). Multi-criteria analyses and discursive decision-making processes are necessary, as the dimensions and their elements are incommensurable: there is no optimal solution to be identified. Such an approach requires pluralism in the political and academic communities, as well as a continuous learning process, the possibility of and the readiness for self-correction. Differing interpretations, tensions and competing explanations are not only legitimate, but are forms of plurality to be supported, as they are a precondition for further sustainable development – sustainability requires diversity, not uniformity. Since societies and their values, goals and technologies are in a permanent process of change, a "sustainable society" cannot be a fixed state; rather, sustainability means the maintenance of system reproduction capabilities in a system environment whose future evolution and resulting states cannot be known. However, the simultaneous maintenance of the functional dynamics of all four dimensional subsystems, as well as that of the meta-system, largely ensures the functionality of the overall system, as shown for instance for the social and political sciences by Luhmann (1988) and Willke (1989), for ecology by Odum (1973) and Cruse (1981), and for the economic sciences by Daly (1996) and Messner (1996).

The concept of sustainability could build on earlier work, such as on the reversibility of technological innovations (today also called "exnovation"), or on the necessity of error-friendly social, economic and technological systems (von Weizsäcker/von Weizsäcker 1998), today discussed as "resilience," which partially excludes the social actors; unfortunately, their potential to contribute to the sustainability discourse has thus far scarcely been realized. In the scientific community, "sustainability science" has been established as a new discipline cutting across the established ones, in many cases in the teeth of their embittered resistance (Spangenberg 2011), not least due to its methodology choice emphasizing participatory and multi-criteria decision-making in situations of fundamental change, and in the context of uncertainty ("Where facts are uncertain, stakes are high, values disputed and decisions urgent" [Funtowicz/Ravetz 1994]). However, its findings have not (yet) played a significant role in political decision-making – a fate it shares with other cross-disciplinary research approaches such as sustainable consumption research (Røpke 1999; Shove 2004), and feminist research, especially in the area of precautionary and reproductive economics (cf. Biesecker/Hofmeister 2007).

In this section, only a few of the challenges for an adequate description of complex evolving systems and the analysis of their sustainability could be described, and a few hints for overcoming these obstacles could be provided. Integrating the system dynamics approach with other sustainability assessment methods and procedures may pave the way for a more comprehensive understanding of the systems to be managed, and thus for more coherent and effective sustainable development policies.

Note

1 However, these forms of social evaluation are, in the context of sustainability, tied to the normative conceptual limits of decision-making, which are in turn the result of social processes in the complex evolving system that is society. The necessary discursive search for solutions corresponds to the character of the systems, but also to the complexity of goals such as sustainability, justice or freedom (Sen 2000).

Literature

Ackerman, F., DeCanio, S. J., Howarth, R. B., Sheeran, K. (2009). Limitations of integrated assessment models of climate change. *Climate Change* 95, 297–315.

Allen, P. M. (1998). Evolutionary complex systems and sustainable development. In: J.C.J.M. v. d. Bergh, M. W. Hofkes (eds.). *Theory and Implementation of Economic Models for Sustainable Development*. Dordrecht: Kluwer Academic Publishers, 67–100.

Allen, P. M. (2001). The dynamics of knowledge and ignorance: Learning the new systems science. In: H.M.W. Matthies, J. Kriz (eds.). *Integrative Systems Approaches to Natural and Social Dynamics*. Berlin: Springer, 3–30.

Beck, U. (1986). *Risikogesellschaft*. Frankfurt/Main: Suhrkamp.

Beck, U. (1996). Das Zeitalter der Nebenfolgen und die Politisierung der Moderne. In: U. Beck, A. Giddens, S. Lash (eds.). *Reflexive Modernisierung – Eine Kontroverse*. Frankfurt/Main: Suhrkamp, 19–112.

Beckenbach, F. (1998). Paradigmatische neuorientierung. *Ökologisches Wirtschaften* 1998(3–4): Spezial 1–3.

Biesecker, A., Hofmeister, S. (2007). *Reprodutionsökonomie*. Munich: Ökom.

Bossel, H. (1996a). *20/20 Vision. Explorations of Sustainable Futures*. Kassel: Center for Environmental Systems Research.

Bossel, H. (1996b). Deriving indicators of sustainable development. *Environmental Modelling and Assessment* 1(4), 193–218.

Bossel, H. (1998). *Earth at a Crossroads – Paths to a Sustainable Future*. Cambridge: Cambridge University Press.

Bossel, H. (1999). *Indicators for Sustainable development: Theory, Method, Applications*. Winnipeg: IISD International Institute for Sustainable Development.

Christensen, P. P. (1989). Historical roots for ecological economics – Biophysical versus allocative approaches. *Ecological Economics* 1(1), 17–36.

Cruse, H. (1981). *Biologische Kybernetik, Einführung in die lineare und nichtlineare Systemtheorie*. Weinhein: Verlag Chemie.

Daly, H. E. (1991). *Steady-State Economics*. Second edition with new essays. Covelo/ Washington, D.C.: Island Press.

Daly, H. E. (1996). *Beyond Growth. The Economics of Sustainable Development*. Boston: Beacon Press.

Dawkins, R. (1978). *The Selfish Gene*. Oxford: Oxford University Press.

Falconi-Benitez, F., Ramos-Martin, J. (2002). *Integrated assessment of development trajectories: the two sides of the bifurcation of economic development*. 7th biannual ISEE conference, Sousse/Tunesien.

Faucheux, S., Froger, G. (1995). Decision-making under environmental uncertainty. *Ecological Economics* 15(1), 29–42.

Funtowicz, S. O., Ravetz, J. R. (1993). Science for the post-normal age. *Futures* 25(7), 735–755.

Funtowicz, S. O., Ravetz, J. R. (1994). The worth of a songbird: Ecological economics as a post-normal science. *Ecological Economics* 10, 197–207.

Funtowicz, S. O., Ravetz, J. R., O'Connor, M. (1998). Challenges in the utilisation of science for sustainable development. *International Journal of Sustainable Development* 1(1), 2–10.

Georgescu-Roegen, N. (1971). *The Entropy Law and the Economic Process*. Cambridge: Harvard University Press.

Häfele, W. (1974). Hypotheticality and the new challenges. The pathfinder role of nuclear energy. *Minerva* 1974(3), 303–322.

Hayek, F. A. (1972). Die Theorie komplexer Phänomene. In: W. Mohr (ed.). *Vorträge und Aufsätze*. Tübingen: Walter Eucken Institut, 7–38.

Holling, C. S., Gunderson, L. H., Peterson, G. (1998). Comparing complex systems. A four phase adaptive cycle approach. *Ökologisches Wirtschaften* 1998(3–4). Spezial 5–6.

Hornung, B. R. (1985). *Grundlagen einer problemfunktionalistischen Systemtheorie gesellschaftlicher Entwicklung. Sozialwissenschaftliche Theoriekonstruktion mit qualitativen, computergestützten Verfahren*. Frankfurt: Peter Lang.

Jonas, H. (1979). *Das Prinzip Verantwortung*. Frankfurt/Main: Insel.

Keen, S. (2001). *Debunking Economics. The Naked Emperor of the Social Sciences*. Annandale: Pluto Press Australia.

Kopfmüller, J., Brandl, V., Jörissen, J., Paetau, M., Banse, G., Coenen, R., Grunwald, A. (2001). *Nachhaltige Entwicklung integrativ betrachtet*. Berlin: Edition Sigma.

Körner, C. (2002). Umweltforschung zwischen exakter Kuriosität und verschwommener Realität. *GAIA* 11(1), 48.

Kraemer, K. (2008). *Die soziale Konstitution der Umwelt*. Wiesbaden: VS Verlag.

Luhmann, N. (1980). Komplexität. In: E. Grochla (ed.). *Handwörterbuch der Organisation*. Stuttgart: Poeschel.

Luhmann, N. (1982). Autopoiesis, Handlung und kommunikative Verständigung. *Zeitschrift für Soziologie* 11, 366–379.

Luhmann, N. (1988). *Soziale Systeme. Grundriß einer allgemeinen Theorie*. Frankfurt: Suhrkamp.

Maynard-Smith, J. (1974). The theory of games and the evolution of animal conflict. *Journal of Theoretical Biology* 47, 209–221.

Maynard-Smith, J., Parker, G. A. (1976). The logic of asymmetric contests. *Animal Behaviour* 24, 159–175.

Messner, D., Eßer, K., Hillebrand, W., Meyer-Stamer, J. (1996). *Systemic Competitiveness – New Governance Patterns for Industrial Development*. London: Frank Cass.

Müller, F., Jørgensen, S. E. (2000). Ecological Orientors: A Path to Environmental Applications of Ecosystem Theories. In: S. E. Jørgensen, F. Müller (eds.). *Handbook of Ecosystem Theories and Management*. Boca Raton: CRC Publishers, 561–575.

Munda, G. (1995). *Multicriteria Evaluation in a Fuzzy Environment*. Heidelberg: Physica.

Norgaard, R. B. (2002). Optimists, pessimists, and science. *BioScience* 52(3), 287–292.

Odum, H. T. (1989). Self-organization, transformity, and information. *Science* 242, 1132–1139.

Odum, E. P. (1973). *Fundamentals of Ecology*, 3. ed. Cambridge: Harvard University Press.

OECD (2013). OECD forecasts during and after the financial crisis: a post mortem. *OECD Economics Department Policy Note, No. 23*. Paris: OECD.

Prigogine, I. (1988). Die physikalisch-chemischen Wurzeln des Lebens. In: H. Meier (ed.). *Die Herausforderung der Evolutionsbiologie*. Munich: Piper.

Prigogine, I., Stengers, I. (1984). *Order Out of Chaos: Man's New Dialogue with Nature*. London: Heinemann/Boulder.

Rammel, C., v. d. Bergh, J.C.J.M. (2003). Evolutionary policies for sustainable development: Adaptive flexibility and risk minimising. *Ecological Economics* 47(2), 121–133.

Rawls, J. (1971). *A Theory of Justice*. Cambridge: Harvard University Press.

Rees, W. E. (2002). Nachhaltigkeit: Ökonomischer Mythos und ökologische Realität. *Natur & Kultur* 3(1), 3–34.

Richter, K., Rost, J-M. (2002). *Komplexe Systeme*. Frankfurt: S. Fischer.

Rockstrøm, J., Steffen, W., Noone, K., Persson, Å., Chapin, F. S., Lambin, E. F. . . . Foley, J. A. (2009). A safe operating space for humanity. *Nature* 461(7263), 472–475.

Røpke, I. (1999). The dynamics of willingness to consume. *Ecological Economics* 28(3), 399–420.

Schumpeter, J. A. (1928). The instability of capitalism. *The Economic Journal* 38, 361–386.

Schütz, J. (2000). Sustainability, systems and meaning. *Environmental Values* 9, 373–382.

Sen, A. (2000). *Ökonomie für den Menschen*. Munich/Vienna: Carl Hanser.

Settele, J., Spangenberg, J. H. (2013). The age of man: Outpacing evolution. *Science* 340, 1287.

Shove, E. (2004). Changing human behaviour and lifestyle: A challenge for sustainable consumption? In: L. A. Reisch, I. Røpke (eds.). *The Ecological Economics of Consumption*. Cheltenham: E. Elgar, 111–130.

Simon, H. A. (1974). The organization of complex systems. In: H. H. Pattee (ed.). *Hierarchy theory: the challenge of complex systems*. New York: George Braziller.

Söderbaum, P. (2010). *Sustainability Economics*. London: Earthscan.

Spangenberg, J. H. (1998). Systeme zwischen Evolution, Trägheit und technischer Beschleunigung. In A. Renner, F. Hinterberger (eds.). *Zukunftsfähigkeit und Neoliberalismus*. Baden-Baden: Nomos Verlag, 299–319.

Spangenberg, J. H. (2001). Investing in sustainable development. *International Journal of Sustainable Development* 4(2), 184–201.

Spangenberg, J. H. (2002). Environmental space and the prism of sustainability: frameworks for indicators measuring sustainable devolopment. *Ecological Indicators* 2(4), 295–309.

Spangenberg, J. H. (2005a). *Die ökonomische Nachhaltigkeit der Wirtschaft. Theorien, Kriterien und Indikatoren*. Berlin: Edition Sigma.

Spangenberg, J. H. (2005b). Economic sustainability of the economy: Concepts and indicators. *International Journal of Sustainable Development* 8(1/2), 47–64.

Spangenberg, J. H. (2007). Precisely incorrect. *Alternatives Journal* 33(2/3), 32–36.

Spangenberg J. H. (2011). Sustainability science: A review, an analysis and some empirical lessons. *Environmental Conservation* 38(3), 275–287.

Spangenberg, J. H. (2014). The world we see shapes the world we create. How the underlying worldviews lead to different recommendations from environmental and ecological economics – The green economy example. *International Journal of Sustainable Development*, in press.

Spangenberg, J. H., Pfahl, S., Deller, K. (2002). Towards indicators for institutional sustainability: Lessons from an analysis of Agenda 21. *Ecological Indicators* 2(1–2), 61–77.

van der Sluijs, J., (ed.) (2002). *Management of Uncertainty in Science for Sustainability*. Utrecht: Copernicus Institute, Utrecht University.

von Weizsäcker, E. U., von Weizsäcker, C. (1998). Information, evolution and "error-friendliness". *Biological Cybernetics* 79(6), 501–506.

WCED World Commission on Environment and Development (1987). *Our Common Future*. Oxford: Oxford University Press.

Wilkinson, R., Cary, J. (2002). Sustainability as an evolutionary process. *International Journal of Sustainable Development* 5(4), 381–391.

Willke, H. (1989). *Systemtheorie entwickelter Gesellschaften*. Weinheim: Verlag Chemie.

9 Sustainable development

A global model – universal and contextual

Jürgen Kopfmüller

Introduction

The function of models is to provide fundamental goal orientation for the formulation of development processes. They are used today in numerous contexts – in the operations of corporations, institutions and administrations, and in such policy areas as transportation, education and spatial planning. They are developed in complex processes, and should, to the extent possible, have an integrating effect extending beyond the actors and participants directly involved. Accordingly, societal models are created and become effective in the larger context of societies. They are institutionalized or legally standardized in various forms, be it in constitutional provisions or legal codes, such as the German Civil Code, or in the form of semi-institutionalized concepts of basic societal orientation, such as justice, or the social market economy.

The concept of sustainable development has been discussed for more than twenty years as a comprehensive and global approach to development, and attempts have been made to implement it through concrete action. It emerged as a basically political reaction to the increasing environmental and development processes which appeared in aggravated form during the second half of the twentieth century. Today, there are few who question its position as a development model for science, government, business and civil society. Nevertheless, there are still significant controversies regarding the concrete definition of its goal orientation, and the implementation of its goals.

For some time, sustainability debates have been carried out primarily at the level of practical implementation, and less at the conceptual or even theoretical level. At the same time, a certain deficit as regards the theoretical foundation for the justification, specification and implementation of the model is evident (cf. e.g. Schulz et al. 2008; Grunwald 2004). Theories serve the purpose of systematic observation and description of segments of reality, so that prognoses and recommendations for action may be derived from them. Basically, they consist of assumptions, fundamental statements/hypotheses, measurement concepts for empirical review, and final results in the form of the verification or refutation of hypotheses. Without a doubt, the central issue of the justification and especially the scope – the subjects and addressees – of the sustainability model, and above all the question as to the universality and the realization of that model, will require such a theoretical grounding.

In this paper, I will address the question of what constitutes the global dimension of this model, and to what extent it has, or can claim, universal validity. I will reflect upon the possibilities and limits of the universal validity of models, using the example of the human rights issue, and of the debate surrounding it. Based on that, and on the practice of existing international regimes, I will attempt to show how the model of sustainability might be operationalized through an appropriate linkage between universal and specific, context-referenced orientations.

The global dimension of the sustainable development model

The idea of sustainable development has over the past two decades developed into a formative concept for the academic community, policy-making circles and society as a whole, to the extent that relevant papers, documents and proclamations can hardly be imagined anymore without it. At least at that level, it has become one of the essential models for human development. Based on such seminal documents as the Brundtland Commission Report, the Rio Declaration or the Agenda 21, as well as a large number of other international documents and debates, three fundamental constituent elements of the model have crystallized (cf. Kopfmüller et al. 2001): first, the postulate of inter-generational and intra-generational justice, in other words, fairness between successive generations as well as within generations; second, a global perspective which seeks development paths for all human beings worldwide; and third, an anthropocentric approach, which, while placing humans at the center, sees the conservation of nature as being part of the well-understood self-interest of humankind. The fundamental idea is the simultaneous striving for the preservation of the natural foundations of life, as well as the assurance of "a life worthy of human beings" for all people living today, and for those who will live in the future.

Without a doubt, societal development as well as social and political action necessarily always occur simultaneously at the individual, the family, the local, the regional, the national and the global levels. Since the mid-twentieth century, however, these processes are increasingly transcending national boundaries, and exhibiting a global dimension. This is true of the exchange of goods and services, of the use of production factors (particularly of capital), of information, of knowledge, of science and research, of lifestyles, and also of the phenomena of environmental destruction, unequal distribution of goods and resources, unemployment and poverty.

In this regard, the term "global" must be understood in two ways: in the sense of "ubiquitous," i.e. that phenomena are basically occurring worldwide; and in the sense of "globally linked," in other words, that cause-and-effect contexts transcend the boundaries of countries and continents in the development and the description of social, economic and ecological systems and their interactions. This global perspective has from the outset determined the model of sustainability and the debates surrounding it.

Three facets in particular have characterized and justified the global dimension of the model (cf. Kopfmüller et al. 2001). First, there is the ethical aspect, which was also present in the Brundtland Commission Report. There, sustainable development is described as a "global ethic for human survival and well-being" (Hauff 1987, p. 302), which is to serve as a model for global change and human progress. Based on that, various initiatives arose during the 1990s, with the goal of defining fundamental principles for a global development ethic (cf. Kopfmüller 2011). A second facet is the increasingly global character – in the above-mentioned senses – of many development problems, such as climate change, water-resource shortage and pollution, and poverty, to name only a few, and the contexts in which they arise. Finally, the global dimension can also be seen in the fact that for the solution to global problems, strategies must at least in part be developed and implemented on the basis of global coordination and a global division of labor.

The implementation of inter-generational and intra-generational fairness demands, first and foremost, the consistent application of three basic principles of action, which also have global dimensions: the principles of responsibility, of fair distribution, and of cooperation. Responsibility is basically seen as the responsibility both of the global community and of each individual to ensure a life worthy of human beings for future generations, as described by Hans Jonas (1979), and for all human beings living today. The distribution of societal resources, such as income, natural goods, education, etc., of opportunities, such as access to the resources or information, and of risks, and also of the advantages and burdens inherent in such contexts as the implementation of political measures, is both a key point of departure and the result of societal processes of development. A distribution ensuring fair opportunities is both ethically justifiable and necessary in order to avoid the problems which arise as a result of unfair distribution.

Global cooperation between institutions, governments etc. are, after all, necessary in order to ensure the realization of both principles at the global level. One of the central goals formulated in the Rio Declaration and in the Agenda 21 was that of "a new quality of global cooperation," in order to reduce or avoid global conflicts over distribution. Such cooperation would have to be oriented toward the principles of equal rights of participants, and the dismantlement of the institutional and other privileges of the rich, and the discrimination against poorer countries, including the provision of sufficient aid by the rich for the needy – a corrective measure, as it were, in case of insufficient implementation of the first two components.

From globality to universality?

The global dimension with the stated facets thus has essential significance for the definition and implementation of the model of sustainability. However, does "global" also mean that this model can claim universal applicability as a goal orientation for human development, in other words, is there a "global ethic" of life for all human beings, and if so, in what form? These are questions that must be, and are being raised, and which have not been satisfactorily answered to date.

The term "universal" or "universality" means a general, comprehensive and immutable validity of phenomena, statements or elements of factual knowledge, unlimited in time and space. In ethics for instance, it refers to the general validity of concepts, convictions or values; in the law, to the global validity of legal relationships.

As for the concept of justice, which is, after all, at the core of the idea of sustainability, both moral-philosophical democracy theory and Christian social ethics generally assume the fundamental justifiability of universal standards of justice. The essential precondition for that is stated as being the assurance of a formal procedure of discourse, a search for consensus, or a vote among equal participants regarding agreements or institutions (cf. e.g. Pogge 2001). The major point of discussion is then the question of which material criteria of justice are to be used in a particular case, and what, for example, such a goal as "ensuring a life worthy of human beings for all" means exactly (Heidbrink 2000).

However, in view of worldwide social and cultural diversity on the one hand and increasing technologization, differentiation, and ever more complex development processes of social systems on the other, the doubts regarding particularly the definability of universal models and also of their implementability, for example through the acceptance of "global responsibility," often prevail. A look at the debates and activities to date on sustainability in the political and academic spheres would tend to enhance these doubts. Beyond the quasi-global consensus, which encompasses, at a very general level, the oft-quoted core definitions of the Brundtland Commission Report (Hauff 1987, p. 46), and the key ideas of the Rio Declaration and the Agenda 21 of 1992,[1] there are still a number of approaches involving differing fundamental conceptions, goals, measurement and implementation of sustainability (Grunwald/Kopfmüller 2012).

Sustainability-related activity occurs primarily at the national level, mostly based on sustainability strategies and, at the regional and local levels, in the context of strategies or Agenda 21 initiatives. While concrete sustainability goals are indeed often defined there, they tend to differ from each other regionally in terms of their thematic focus and concretization, and moreover generally lack any legally or politically binding character. They thus often have only very limited guiding character for everyday policy decisions. Reality is thus just as far away from deserving the label "sustainability policy" as it is from any international uniformity or even standardization. Moreover, controversy still persists between those who do not see sustainable development as a rigid program, but rather as a permanently open societal process of searching, dialogue and learning (Enquete Commission 1998), and hence generally reject efforts toward universality, and those who emphasize the necessity of at least globally coordinated goals (Grunwald/Kopfmüller 2012).

At the supranational level, the question arises as to whether development goals, or the key sustainability goal of the assurance of "a life worthy of human beings," should be defined uniformly, or to what extent they should be defined differently, for example for various regions, of course in special ways. In spite of the fundamental difficulties outlined, various initiatives which have grown up since the 1990s have pursued the goal of ensuring that such fundamental values as freedom, equality, nonviolence, tolerance or the preservation of nature be recognized and practiced as basic principles of global and enforceable development ethics. One example is the Commission on Global Governance (1995), which demands "a global civic ethics" consisting of common principles and values as the basis for cooperation between various societies and cultures, and which drafts proposals to that end. The same is true for the UNESCO's Universal Ethics Project (Kim 1999), and the Global Ethic Foundation (Küng 1991). These initiatives have certainly sparked discussions, albeit to date with only limited international visibility and few concrete results.

The UN's Millennium Goals (UN 2000) are among the few examples to date of the formulation of global development goals. With their stipulations for the issue complexes of poverty, hunger, infant and maternal mortality, elementary education and access to water, they described the minimum existential requirements for a life worthy of human beings, and thus link up to some of the sustainability issues being discussed internationally. As the orientations agreed upon by the international community, they have without a doubt achieved considerable visibility and significance for international development policy and cooperation (Gehne 2011; Holtz 2010). However, they do face critical questions regarding their lack of key issues, their blind eye for the major causes of global economic and structural problems, and the regional uniformity of their target values, which are seen as implicitly disadvantageous to the poorest countries. More than anything however, they too lack any legal binding character or enforceability in case of the non-achievement of goals. This is certainly a key reason why the current assessment to the effect that the goals have been achieved only in part and in a few countries (UN 2010) has hardly gotten any response from policymakers or in the public, although it has been published in international studies.

Human rights and sustainable development: Universality vs. contextuality

In the debates both around human sustainable development, or development in general, and on the issue of universality, human rights certainly are of key significance.

Human rights and sustainable development

Discussions regarding sustainable development do not take place in isolation, but rather within existing standards, contexts and frameworks. Here, human rights, which have for decades been a basic orientation for human development with a firm legal foundation and with recognition by most countries, play a very important role for the sustainability model. They include all civil, political and other fundamental rights of human beings, as stated in the Universal Declaration of Human Rights of the United Nations in 1948, and in various other human rights agreements concluded since that time (Koenig 2005). By confirming them in their national constitutions – in Germany, Article 1, Section 2 of the Constitution – countries assume the obligation to formulate and implement human rights and actionable rights. Their fundamental conception and their internal commonality are often described with the terms universalism, freedom and equality (Bielefeldt 2008).

Based upon and oriented toward the principle of human dignity (Bielefeldt 2008), human rights should on the one hand primarily provide protection from excesses by the state against personal development and the exercise of democratic rights by individuals, and on the other, ensure the satisfaction of the basic needs of people. The distinction is often made between so-called first-generation rights, which include civil, political and freedom rights, such as the inviolability of the person, the right to freedom of movement, the right of property, etc.; second-generation rights, including economic, social and cultural rights, such as the right to adequate food, education, jobs and social security; and third-generation rights, meaning the rights both of the individual and the collective, to development, peace, an intact environment and a just share of natural resources.

Human rights are fundamentally based on the same vision as the concept of human development, in the center of which is the realization of the so-called fundamental freedoms of humankind: freedom from discrimination, want, injustice, and threats to personal security, as well as freedom of participation, the realization of individual potential, and decent work without exploitation (UNDP 2000, p. 40).

The relationship between sustainable human development and human rights is thus close and multifaceted. Although the sustainability discourse does not view the protection of human rights in their totality as a specific sustainability demand, human rights do constitute a substantive basic pillar for sustainable development if a holistic or integrated concept of sustainability is taken as the point of departure. This is due on the one hand to their far-reaching thematic links, and on the other to the fact that they are an indispensable prerequisite, due to their positive legal foundation and the fact that they enable individuals to design safe, dignified and self-determined lives. Accordingly, human rights and sustainable development can be viewed as mutually conditioning and reinforcing elements (see e.g. UNDP 1998).

Universality versus contextuality

While Articles 3 through 30 of the Universal Declaration of Human Rights of 1948 specify the rights and also the duties of the individual, the Preamble of the first two articles describe the legitimate scope of their applicability (cf. UNDP 2000, pp. 18ff). Accordingly, there evidently exists the demand that all human beings have a claim to equal rights simply on the basis of the fact that they are human beings, and that these rights are universal, inalienable and indivisible (Menke/Pollmann 2007; Gosepath/Lohmann 1998). The claim to universality is thus both quantitative: *all people* have rights; and qualitative: all people have substantially the *same* rights.

Nonetheless, the questions as to the extent to which human rights do in fact apply universally, de jure and/or de facto, and to which plurality, diversity and/

or contextuality are decisive, has, as it were, from the outset remained the object of academic and political controversy (cf. e.g. Nooke et al. 2008; Dudy 2002; Hamm/Nuscheler 1995).

The key arguments for universal applicability are:

(a) The ideas of equality and indivisibility are seen as a world ethic grounded in "natural law," in the tradition of the human rights declarations of the eighteenth century – the Virginia Bill of Rights in 1776, and the French Declaration of the Rights of Man and the Citizen of 1789.

(b) The Universal Declaration of Human Rights (UDHR), and especially the Covenants on Civil and Political Rights and on Economic Social and Cultural Rights adopted by the UN General Assembly in 1966, which came into force in 1976 after having been ratified by 90% of the countries (Donnelly 2007), and having been adopted into their national constitutions.

(c) Based on the social philosophical approach of ethical universalism (Birnbacher/Schicha 1996), the claim to universality is seen as compatible with cultural or religious diversity.

(d) The universal claim to applicability is recognized, regardless of the certainly existing deficits in the practice of the implementation of rights.

(e) Finally, the mere demand for the universality of rights is seen as an important support for those struggling for human rights, or at least for the implementation of a "hard core" of them.

The key counter-arguments are:

(a) The cultural/relativistic view, according to which the human rights which emerged in Europe in the spirit of the Enlightenment can be fully applicable only there, since, like other standards and values, they cannot be viewed independently of the cultural context.

(b) The demand for universality is in conflict to the human right to cultural difference, as expressed in varying interpretations in Asia, Africa and the Islamic nations.

(c) The Declaration, and especially the Covenants, are diplomatic compromise formulations with no factual legal effectiveness.

(d) The claim to universality is interpreted as a hegemonic/imperialistic act on the part of the rich countries, directed especially against the poor countries, or by the Western countries against oriental cultures.

(e) Finally, the really existing deficits are raised, particularly the insufficient implementation of material law, the constellations of power and interest which prevent implementation, and also the factual hierarchization between the three generations of rights.

In view of this continuing controversy, the idea of "relative universality" (cf. Donnelly 2007; Honecker 2002; Tetzlaff 1998; Hamm/Nuscheler 1995), or "moderate universalism" (Nathan 2001) has for some time been discussed as an approach to a solution. The point of departure here is that on the one hand, strict universalism is difficult to justify and implement empirically, politically or even ethically, in view of global realities, while it is on the other hand untenable for fundamental theoretical reasons (cf. e.g. Sukopp 2005), and because the fundamental idea of human rights would thus be badly damaged, which no one in the debate really intends. The idea is therefore to use as a point of departure a defined minimum standard of human rights, which would at least morally apply regardless of cultural, religious or other particularities. Beyond these, varying interpretations and implementations could be admissible.

To date, no concrete proposals for the formulation of such an approach yet exists. Two fundamental options are at least conceivable: first, the establishment of minimum standards for certain rules, i.e. a hierarchization of rights, ranging from those with universal validity, such as the rights to life, limb and liberty, to those with possible "contextuality." This would, among other things, counter the criticism against a political trend toward an unattainable "right to everything." Such weighting is already being applied de facto in a range of variations, although there is to date no systematic framework for handling it. One thing that would, however, have to be considered in this context is that it would at least open the door to establishing a class of "legitimate" violations of human rights.

Another option, favored by this author, would involve the establishment of minimum standards for all rights, which would then constitute, in each case, their non-contextual core elements, to then be defined, and which would be delimited from the contextual elements of those rights, and, if appropriate, balanced against them. For such differentiation, it would be necessary to evaluate the various elements and facets of each right with regard to its relevance, and to ascertain appropriate "quanta" of its fulfillment, which would permit a practicable differentiation between potentially contextual and non-contextual elements. For example, the question should be raised – and answered – as to what constitutes the alienable core element of such a right as that to property, or to freedom of movement, and what degree of serious restriction or violation of such rights would have to be established, in which contexts. Examples would include appropriation of property as eminent domain, or national regulations on immigration and work permit for foreigners, etc.; appropriate indicators for the concretization, measurement and evaluation of all these factors would have to be defined.

In view of the controversies existing at the theoretical and political levels, the compromise approach outlined above pursues the goal of describing a solution which might be acceptable to at least the moderate proponents of both the universalist and the relativist positions, and which might be implementable in practice.

Universality and contextuality in the operationalization of the sustainability model

More or less analogously to the issue of human rights, the model of sustainability, as mentioned above, also raises the question as to what constitutes the universal and the contextual elements, and how such a differentiation could be operationalized and implemented in practical activity. Here, a general opera-tionalization plan for the model can be established which would encompass the core elements, fundamental ideas/values, principles/rules, indicators and strate-gies for action. This plan may be concretized for specific sustainability relevant issues.

In the following, I would like to outline the general procedure by reference to the example of the issue of climate protection and governance of greenhouse gas emissions, assigning to the particular elements their respective places in a spectrum ranging from universality to contextuality, as shown graphically in Fig-ure 9.1. This issue has been selected for illustrative purposes particularly because a relatively highly developed global regime already exists here, which has been implemented in practice, and can therefore serve the purposes of orientation – a decisive prerequisite for an appropriate handling of global issues, as is character-istic of the sustainability context.

"Climate justice" has become a key basic point of orientation in the debates around the climate-change issue (Posner/Weisbach 2010). The central idea here is, first, that the emissions of the greenhouse gasses which are causing global warming and climate change must be greatly reduced, and especially that they must be apportioned more fairly – according to the "contraction and conver-gence" principle. Moreover, the globally very unequal distribution of the effects of climate change, which particularly impact the poorest countries, must be

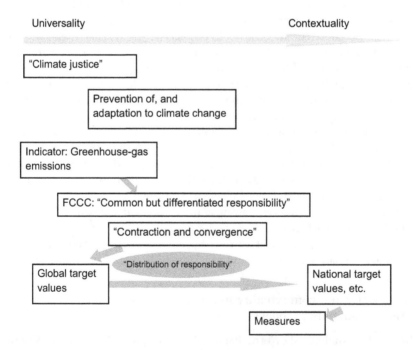

Figure 9.1 Universality and contextuality with regard to the issue of climate protection
Source: Author.

cushioned or compensated for. There is a de facto global consensus regarding the fundamental appropriateness of this goal, even though that consensus may not extend to all the details of its implementation. For this reason, the term global justice can be classified as generally "universally valid."

The prevention and reduction of climate-change-causing emissions, as well as the adaptation to climate changes which can no longer be avoided, are the two fundamental and globally applicable action alternatives of climate policy. At the same time, there are in some cases very significant regional differences, particularly as regards the concrete goals of the two alternatives and their weighting in concrete action. For this reason, this has been placed further to the right of the spectrum in the figure. There is moreover a far-reaching consensus that the quality of greenhouse gas emissions is an appropriate indicator of the measurement and evaluation of climate change and climate policy.

The determination of target values for this and other indicators, and the implementation of measures for achieving these goals, are therefore the decisive steps in climate policy. In the global perspective, fundamental orientations for the differentiation of goals according to countries or groups of countries, and for the global distribution of financial and other burdens of climate policy are needed. In Principle 7 of the Rio Declaration of 1992, and also in Article 3.1 of the UN Climate Framework Convention adopted that same year, the principle of "common, but differentiated responsibilities" was established for this purpose, and has status under international law (UN General Assembly 1992). The regional distribution of contributions to solutions to the problem is here on the one hand assigned in accordance with responsibility for present – i.e. historically accumulated – emissions, and on the other, according to the financial capabilities of nations. From this orientation toward criteria of fairness and justice, there is a clear prioritization of responsibility for the industrial countries over the developing countries as regards the distribution of future emissions-reduction burdens.

Based on both scientific and sociopolitical considerations, the UN Conference of the Parties (COP) in Cancun established the global goal of limiting global warming to 2°C, and global emissions to a corresponding quantity, over the next decades. On this basis, context-specific obligations for emissions reductions were formulated according to the stated fairness criteria – especially the assumption of an equal "emissions budget" of two tons of CO_2 in 2050 per human being, which would apply primarily to the industrial countries, and, in the future, for other countries as well. This represents the point of departure for measures oriented both toward national and regional contexts and conditions, and towards global coordination.

The fundamental idea is thus that for any issue or problem area, a globally valid – universal – goal should be established, which could then be further concretized and also differentiated; these changes would then be integrated into the overall system. They would involve substantive aspects, and particularly regional differences corresponding to the particular cultural, economic, geographic or other context conditions, and especially taking into account fairness and justice criteria – a key point in the sustainability context.

Conclusion and perspectives

This example shows clearly that the issue which is fundamental to this paper, the localization of the sustainability model between universality and contextuality, must be seen in a differentiated manner, depending upon the stage of operationalization in which we find ourselves. The message is therefore not "either-or," but "both" – as much universality as possible; as much contextuality as necessary. There can thus be no absolute or uniform answer to the question; rather, a different picture for each of the various fields will have to emerge, consisting of both universal and contextual elements.

Nonetheless – or else precisely for this reason – what remains are at least as many questions as answers as to how sustainability can be conceived and implemented in this continuum – or area of conflict – between the two absolute extremes. Some of these questions, and possibly associated requirements for further research, are outlined below:

• First of all, it is necessary to ascertain whether the international community would even agree to operationalize the most vital sustainability issues, selected according to certain key aspects, analogously to the climate issue. After all, despite all the shortcomings in the process of implementation and the results of the Climate Change Convention which certainly exist, there are good reasons to assume a basic transferability of this approach to other fields. Whether this will actually occur will depend to a considerable degree on the value that is assigned to the sustainability model in general, and to the development of such issue-specific regimes.

• What are, from a global perspective, the "key" sustainability issues, and how might a decision regarding them be brought about? From my point of view, two issues are near the top of any such ranking: biodiversity and national debt. Biodiversity is of key importance not only for the functioning of ecosystems as resources for health-related and other purposes, but also due to the fact that there was already an international convention adopted on the issue in 1992, as well as national strategies in some countries. The issue of public debt is of crucial importance because it directly affects inter-generational justice in terms of the permissible financial burden upon future generations, because the capacity of the state to act as an indispensable guarantee for the core elements of the general interest of the people is thereby significantly restricted, as experience has shown, and because a close link is emerging to the situation on the financial markets, and hence to a key factor which affects economic activity, including sustainable economics.

• Another topic could be that of a global resource-management system. The issue to be addressed here would be how to deal with especially scarce or strategic resources and how to take better account of the interests of the source countries, which are often developing nations, particularly through bilateral or multilateral resource partnerships, or compensation for diminished exports in case of reduced resource use in the "north." The topic of education, too, would be of similar significance. Here, it would be possible to link up to the numerous activities undertaken in the framework of the UN Decade of Education for Sustainable Development (2005–2014), with the goal of enabling a minimum level of basic education for all people, as a prerequisite for sustainable development, and appropriately incorporating the sustainability issue as a subject in all phases and stages of education.

- What might regimes on these issues look like? To what extent are analogies to the global-warming regime possible? Which additional elements might be necessary? To what extent will new institutions have to be created, or existing ones restructured?

- The question as to the extent to which the adoption of fundamental values into positive law, as has been done in the case of human rights, can be transferred to the issue of sustainability, could be examined. To date, the model of sustainability has only been incorporated into the legal system to a very small extent and very un-systematically, both at the international and at the national levels; certainly, this is true in the case of Germany. Moreover, where it has been adopted, it has usually been established in line with its simple definition of "permanence," and hence not in accordance with the idea of the model (cf. e.g. Gehne 2011; Grunwald/Kopfmüller 2007).

- What might the minimum requirements be that would be universally valid for all people in the above-discussed and other areas, and how might they correspond to possible contextual elements? How might common solutions be found here which could become part of a global regime?

- One key foundation for this would be better knowledge of existing differing definitions, interpretations, feedbacks and action-oriented strategic focuses, especially in culturally different regions, and their justifications, preconditions, and assessments regarding stability over time. In addition to the currently existing knowledge, which is generally spotty, very comprehensive, systematic surveys and comparisons, as well as initial indications regarding existing or conceivable areas of consensus, are needed.

When addressing these issues and topics more closely, theoretical aspects will in many cases be of significance, explicitly or implicitly. In other cases, steps toward implementation or institutionalization will be primary. Hence, at least from the point of view of the author and the issues addressed here, the goal will not so much be the development of a – or *the* – theory of sustainability, but rather the appropriate consideration of theoretical elements in addressing issues, formulating new ones when necessary, or revising them.

The key to the realization of a global sustainability policy in the form outlined here will be the creation of appropriate forms, structures and orientations, in and with which processes of dialogue, learning and negotiation will be possible, and in which the international community, the academic community, governments and civil society will appropriately institutionalize and implement what one might call a "global community of solidarity."

Note

1 See http://www.un.org/esa/dsd/agenda21/?utm_source=OldRedirect&utm_medium=
redirect&utm_content=dsd&utm_campaign=OldRedirect

Bibliography

Bell, L., Nathan, A., Peleg, I. (eds.) (2001). *Negotiating Culture and Human Rights*. New York.
Bielefeldt, H. (2008). *Menschenwürde. Der Grund der Menschenrechte*. Study by the German Institute for Human Rights. Berlin.
Binswanger, H., Ekardt, F., Grothe, A., Hasenclever, W., Hauchler, I., Jänicke, M. . . . Scherhorn, G. (eds.) (2011). *Jahrbuch nachhaltige Ökonomie 2011/2012. Im Brennpunkt: Wachstum*. Marburg.
Birnbacher, D., Schicha, C. (1996). Vorsorge statt Nachhaltigkeit – Ethische Grundlagen der Zukunftsverantwortung. In: Kastenholz, H., Erdmann, K., Wolf, M. (eds.). *Nachhaltige Entwicklung. Zukunftschancen für Mensch und Umwelt*. Berlin, 141–156.
BMU – German Federal Ministry of the Environment (ed.) (1992). *Konferenz der Vereinten Nationen für Umwelt und Entwicklung im Juni 1992 in Rio de Janeiro* (German version of the Rio documents). Bonn.
Commission on Global Governance (1995). *Our Global Neighbourhood*. Oxford.
Donnelly, J. (2007). The Relative Universality of Human Rights. In: *Human Rights Quarterly*, Vol. 29, No. 2, 281–306.
Dudy, P. (2002). *Menschenrechte zwischen Universalität und Partikularität. Eine interdisziplinäre Studie zur Idee der Weltinnenpolitik*. Münster.
Enquete Commission (1998). *The concept of sustainability: From vision to reality*. Bundestag Publication No. 13/11200. Bonn.
Gehne, K. (2011). *Nachhaltige Entwicklung als Rechtsprinzip*. Tübingen.
Gosepath, S., Lohmann, G. (ed.) (1998). *Philosophie der Menschenrechte*. Frankfurt.
Grunwald, A. (2004). Die gesellschaftliche Wahrnehmung von Nachhaltigkeitsproblemen und die Rolle der Wissenschaften. In: Ipsen, D., Schmidt, J. (eds.). *Dynamiken der Nachhaltigkeit*. Marburg, 313–341.
Grunwald, A., Kopfmüller (2007). Die Nachhaltigkeitsprüfung. Kernelement einer angemessenen Umsetzung des Nachhaltigkeitsleitbilds. In: *Politik und Recht*. FZKA Report No. 7349. Karlsruhe.
Grunwald, A., Kopfmüller, J. (2012). *Nachhaltigkeit. Eine Einführung*. 2nd ed. Frankfurt.
Hamm, B., Nuscheler, F. (1995). *Zur Universalität der Menschenrechte. Report des Instituts für Entwicklung und Frieden* (INEF). No. 11/1995. Duisburg.
Hauff, V. (ed.) (1987). *Unsere gemeinsame Zukunft* (German version of the Brundtland Commission Report). Greven.
Heidbrink, L. (2000). Grundprobleme der gegenwärtigen Verantwortungsdiskussion. In: *Information Philosophie*, No. 3, 18–31.
Holtz, U. (2010). Die Millenniumsentwicklungsziele – Eine gemischte Bilanz. In: *Aus Politik und Zeitgeschichte*, No. 10, March 8, 3–8.
Honecker, M. (2002). *Wege evangelischer Ethik. Positionen und Kontexte*. Freiburg.
Ipsen, D., Schmidt, J. (eds.). *Dynamiken der Nachhaltigkeit*. Marburg.
Jonas, H. (1979). *Das Prinzip Verantwortung. Versuch einer Ethik für die technologische Zivilisation*. Frankfurt.
Kim, Y. (1999). *A Common Framework for the Ethics of the 21st Century*. Paris.
Koenig, M. (2005). *Menschenrechte*. Frankfurt.

Kopfmüller, J. (ed.) (2006). *Ein Konzept auf dem Prüfstand. Das integrative Konzept nachhaltiger Entwicklung in der Forschungspraxis*. Berlin.

Kopfmüller, J. (2011). Die globale Dimension der nachhaltigen Entwicklung: Definition – Herausforderungen – Umsetzung. In: Binswanger, H., Ekardt, F., Grothe, A., Hasenclever, W., Hauchler, I., Jänicke, M. . . . Scherhorn, G. (eds.) (2011). *Jahrbuch nachhaltige Ökonomie 2011/2012. Im Brennpunkt: Wachstum*. Marburg: Metropolis, 289–310.

Kopfmüller, J., Brandl, V., Jörissen, J., Paetau, M., Banse, G., Coenen, R., Grunwald, A. (2001). *Nachhaltige Entwicklung integrativ betrachtet. Konstitutive Elemente, Regeln, Indikatoren*. Berlin.

Küng, H. (1991). *Projekt Weltethos*. Munich.

Menke, C., Pollmann, A. (2007). *Philosophie der Menschenrechte*. Hamburg.

Nathan, A. (2001): Universalism: A Particularistic Account. In: Bell, L., Nathan, A., Peleg, I. (eds.) (2001). *Negotiating Culture and Human Rights*. New York, 349–368.

Nooke, G., Lohmann, G., Wahlers, G. (eds.) (2008). *Gelten Menschenrechte universal? Begründungen und Infragestellungen*. Freiburg.

Pogge, T. (ed.) (2001). *Global Justice*. Oxford.

Posner, E., Weisbach, D. (2010). *Climate Change Justice*. Princeton.

Schultz, J., Brand, F., Kopfmüller, J., Ott, K. (2008). Building a "Theory of Sustainable Development": Two Salient Conceptions within the German Discourse. In: *International Journal for Environment and Sustainable Development*. Vol. 7, No. 4, 465–482.

Sukopp, T. (2005). Wider den radikalen Kulturrelativismus – Universalismus, Kontextualismus und Kompatibilismus. In: *Aufklärung und Kritik*. Vol. 12, No. 2, 136–154.

Tetzlaff, R. (1998). Modernisierung und Menschenrechte aus politikwissenschaftlicher Sicht: Zur Begründung einer relativen Universalität der Menschenrechte. In: *Jahrbuch für christliche Sozialwissenschaften* Vol. 39, 54–82.

UN (2000). *Millennium Development Goals*. Accessed via: www.un.org/millenniumgoals/

UN – United Nations (2010). *Global Monitoring Report 2010: The MDGs after the Crisis*. New York.

UN General Assembly (1992). *Report of the United Nations Conference on Environment and Development* (Rio de Janeiro, 3–14 June, 1992). Accessed via: www.un.org/documents/ga/conf151/aconf15126–1annex1.htm

UNDP – United Nations Development Programme (1998). *Integrating Human Rights with Sustainable Human Development*. UNDP Policy Document. New York.

UNDP (2000). *Human Development Report 2000. Human Rights and Human Development*. New York.

10 The non-identity problem

An irrefutable argument against representation of future generations?

Jörg Chet Tremmel

Introduction: The blind spot within sustainability theories

Intergenerational justice is a central normative foundation of virtually all sustainability concepts. During the past decades, intergenerational ethics has become firmly established as a branch of ethics, and there is now extensive literature on theories of intergenerational justice.[1] Within political philosophy, there is a growing library on the representation of future generations that provides the interested reader with more and more proposals for institutions to fulfill this task.[2] If the term "institutions" is broadly defined, it encompasses organisations, laws, norms and all other sorts of societal arrangements. Such a broad concept enables us to identify all classifications of institutions in a multi-level model. On the first level we can distinguish:

1   Constitutional and other legal clauses: Some constitutions mention *expressis verbis* the "rights" of future generations: Norway (Art. 110b); Japan (Art. 11); Iran (Art. 50); Bolivia (Art. 7); and Malawi (Art. 13). Others contain language that relates to ecological or financial sustainability such as the "protection of the natural basis of life" in 20a of the constitutional law of the Federal Republic of Germany or the "debt brake" in article 126 of the Swiss constitution.[3]

2   Codes of conduct, self-commitments, acting morally: One strand of the literature argues that present people (and especially present members of parliament) should impartially consider the interests of future generations rather than ensuring representation of future generations.[4] It is questionable if this will ever happen to the necessary extent. Nevertheless, it might be acknowledged that such moral behavior by present elected representatives happens to a certain extent and thus is an "institution" that benefits future generations.

3   Organisations with a specific mandate for the representation of future generations (e.g. the Commission for Future Generations in Israel, the Ombudsman for Future Generations in Hungary or the Parliamentary Advisory Council for Sustainable Development in Germany).

On a second level, institutions can be categorized according to the policy fields they treat. Those dealing with all areas of policy making must be distinguished from those which deal with only a few selected policy fields. In the case of the latter, the policy areas in question are usually environmental or finance policy. However, other policy fields are also conceivable (e.g. pension, health, education or labour policy.) A fully fledged "future branch" of government would have to deal with all policy fields without any restrictions.

On a third level, institutions can be distinguished according to their regional scope: They can be established at the international, supranational (as EU law or a new EU institution), national or a subnational/regional level.

This multi-level approach is heuristically well-suited to exploring the "uncharted territory" in the "universe of cases" of institutions to represent future generations. The exact design, the projected impact, their scope – these questions will keep political theorists and philosophers busy for years.

But haven't we overlooked something? This new research agenda outlined above implicitly assumes that there are obligations towards future generations in the first place. But this is contested. Especially the non-identity problem has often been viewed as a serious challenge to theories of intergenerational justice and models of representation of future generations. Viewed strictly, any single irrefutable "no-obligation" argument would necessarily and with one blow spell the end to any account of the representation of future generations.

The aim of this chapter is to discuss the challenge the non-identity problem (NIP) poses to theories of intergenerational justice – theories which postulate that the present generation has duties towards future generations.

The non-identity problem

In the literature, a particular intergenerational ethical problem has been discussed since the end of the 1970s[5] under such headings as "the non-identity problem" (Parfit, 1987, p. 359) or "the future-individual paradox" (Kavka, 1982, p. 186). It has been viewed as such a serious challenge to the justification of *any* obligation towards future generations that the debate over the *extent* of such obligations, which began during the 1970s with a number of remarkable collections of essays (Bayles, 1976; Sikora & Barry, 1978; Partridge, 1980), has ebbed.[6] Mulgan (2002) has noted that the "non-identity challenge" is to this day "plaguing present Western theories of generational justice" (p. 8). By the same token, Wolf (2009) states, "The non-identity problem calls into question whether distant future persons might claim rights against members of the present generation. . . . For this reason, some theorists have more or less abandoned the idea of intergenerational justice altogether" (p. 96). Parfit (1987), too, sees the significance of the non-identity problem as very great, claiming:

> We may be able to remember a time when we were concerned about effects on future generations, but had overlooked the Non-Identity Problem. We

may have thought that a policy like depletion would be against the interest of future people. When we saw that this was false, did we become less concerned about effects on future generations?

(p. 367)[7]

Parfit's statement can be interpreted to the effect that intellectually gifted people cannot deny the validity of the NIP. And indeed, for a time, it did achieve the status of a kind of paradigm in the Kuhnian sense among philosophers (Kuhn, 1963). They stopped discussing the rights or wrongs of it, and were concerned only about researching issues within the paradigm itself (Cohen, 2009).[8]

The NIP can be formulated as follows: The present actions of members of the currently living generation determine not only what the conditions of life of future people will be, but also which people will exist (Kavka 1978, p. 192). If the NIP is a valid argument, actions in the present change the contents of the telephone book of the future, hence leading to "disappearing victims" and "disappearing beneficiaries" (Partridge, 2007, p. 3). If there were *certain* future persons who simply did *not yet* exist, there would be no NIP; the reason that there is a puzzle, however, is that *certain* persons will *never* exist if we behave in a particular way.

In this context, the terms "same-people choices" and "different-people choices" have become established (Parfit, 1987, p. 356). Decisions in the framework of an ethic which is valid in the near term, spatially and temporally (the "neighborhood ethic"), generally change neither the number nor the identity of those affected by an action, and are hence "same-people choices." But if the identity of future persons is affected, we are in the realm of "different-people choices." The latter occur whenever our decisions determine who is to reproduce with whom and, consequently, which individuals are to be born and populate the future (Page, 2007, p. 133). The NIP theoreticians further distinguish between "different-people/same-number choices," and "different-people/different-number choices," depending on whether the number of people, too, would change.

Parfit (1987) has established a "time-dependence claim" (TDC), which he initially formulates as follows:

> TDC1: If any person had not been conceived when he was in fact conceived, it is *in fact* true that he would never have existed.
>
> (p. 351; emphasis in original)

Since Parfit seeks to make his argument as strong as possible, he takes the female menstrual cycle into account. If the combination of the egg and sperm cells were to occur a few minutes, hours or days earlier or later, it is almost 100% certain that a different sperm cell would be involved, because every second, a man's genetic endowment, consisting of some 200 million gametes, is constituted anew (Partridge, 2007, p. 3). In the case of the female egg cell, however, the same cell may be involved regardless of whether the insemination occurs a little earlier or a little later. Hence, Parfit (1987) formulates a second version:

"TDC2: If any particular person had not been conceived within a month of the time when he was in fact conceived, he would in fact never have existed."

(p. 352)

Parfit rightly takes the fact into account that the identity of a person is at least partially constituted by his or her DNA. Mulgan (2002) reformulates Parfit's idea, and calls it the "genetic dependence claim": "If any particular person had not been created from the particular genetic material from which they were in fact created, they would never have existed" (p. 6).

In this context, the debate about "wrongful life" is interesting.[9] This refers to cases in which it is against the interests of children to be born in certain circumstances. The standard example is the case of a doctor who has been approached by a couple wishing to have a child. Because of a mild hereditary disease in the family, the hopeful parents decide in favour of in vitro fertilization in connection with pre-implantation genetic diagnosis (PGD), in order to ensure that the disease will not be transferred to the child. Of four embryos fertilized outside the womb, three bear the genetic defect, and one does not. The doctor then erroneously selects one of the embryos with the defect, which is then implanted into the woman and carried to term by her. When the parents notice after the birth of their child that it does in fact carry the hereditary disease, they sue the doctor for damages. Under the "genetic-dependence claim," the doctor has in fact inflicted harm upon the parents, but not upon the child itself, for if the mother had, as the parents desired, received the healthy embryo, they would not have conceived the now existing child, but instead a different, non-identical one. Hence, the child has no grounds to complain. In this example, it is assumed that the child, in spite of its hereditary disease, will be able to lead a "life worth living," in any case a better one than none at all. The question as to whether there is such a thing as a life which is "not worth living" is difficult to answer.[10] In the following, we will assume that there are such lives, for instance if a newborn child were to be born with a hereditary disease which would lead to its death after a few months, and which is known to cause great pain. If the "genetic-dependence claim" is valid, the paradoxical condition arises that any person with a life better than one "not worth living" could never be harmed by any action which was causal for his or her existence. When speaking of harm, it is usual to compare the existing situation of a certain person with the situation which would prevail if the harmful action had not taken place. If the former situation is worse than the latter, the conclusion to be drawn is that the person has suffered harm. Parfit (1987) refers to a "two-state requirement" (p. 487); Meyer (2003), more accurately, refers to the "better-or-worse-for-the-same-person" condition (p. 6). "Non-existence" cannot be considered the situation of a person. In such a "non-identity context," the usual concept of damages and payment for damages is inapplicable: "We can no longer say that the persons harmed are worse off than they otherwise would have been. Had the harmful action not occurred, the persons in question would never have come into existence," Laslett and Fishkin

(1992, p. 4) conclude. American courts have used the non-identity argument to dismiss wrongful-life suits (Wolf, 2009, p. 96).

So what does all this have to do with generational justice? (2008, p. 460) illustrates the connection by describing the situation of a father who drives to work every day with his car, thus harming the environment. If his daughter were to someday reproach him for this, he could respond that the point in time of his return home to his wife from work in the evening also affected the point in time of their sexual intercourse. If he had instead used his bicycle, he might have caused less harm to the environment, but then his daughter, the one who is now reproaching him, would never have been born. Presumably, a different sperm cell would have fertilized a different egg cell, so that instead of Individual X, Individual Y would have been born. According to the proponents of the non-identity argument, it is not possible to cause harm to future individuals (or to the generations they form), provided their life is worth living.

Consider the following example: If Generation 1 were to ensure that its entire electric power supply were to be generated by nuclear power, so that Generation 2 then inherited huge amounts of radioactive waste, and let us, for the sake of the extreme argument, assume one major nuclear accident per year, the members of Generation 2 would nonetheless be unjustified in making any accusations against Generation 1, for without the massive resettlement measures undertaken for the inhabitants of the contaminated regions, the members of Generation 2 would never have been born. For had the nuclear-power policy carried out by Generation 1 not been implemented, different sets of parents would have met, married and reproduced, so that Generation 2a would have emerged, which would have been non-identical to Generation 2.

The important step taken by Parfit, Kavka and later an entire generation of theoreticians of the non-identity paradigm was to use the NIP not only for reproductive decisions, but also for decisions on policy and on individual life which have only a very indirect connection with reproductive decisions (Roberts and Wassermann, 2009, p. xvii). Only at this point does the NIP become a problem for theories of generational justice and the related research questions, especially in environmental or financial policy. In order to clearly identify this step, which is rarely identified as such in the relevant literature, I will in the following refer to the "non-identity problem as a problem for theories of generational justice" (NIPPTG) when I criticize not the validity of the non-identity argument *per se*, but the expansion of its scope of application.

Several unconvincing objections against the non-identity problem

As mentioned, the non-identity argument has gained great importance among philosophers. Let us now examine whether it is really an insurmountable hurdle and a nightmare for all theories of generational justice. The following arguments are in any case *not* suitable to refute it:

First objection: "People are more than their DNA"

One could raise the objection that the non-identity argument focuses only on the genetic structure of the human being, but not his or her socialization. Without here recapitulating the "nature versus nurture" debate, it is incontestable that no person's personality is entirely defined by his or her genetic code. However, the proponents of the non-identity argument need not claim that. For their argument, it is enough that genes are *one factor* in making a person what he or she is. Let us assume that a mother aborts a baby and a year later carries another one to term. Even if we were to assume that the child who has now been born would undergo the exact same education and socialization as the one who had been aborted would have, they are still two different personalities. Almost certainly, they would not have the same appearance, the same size, and perhaps not even the same sex.

Wolf (2009) has been concerned with the gene-code-identity nexus, and notes that it is conceivable that a person's identity does not change even if his or her gene code were to change *after* birth:

> If a person were given a genetic therapy that changed the DNA in each of his cells, but left others of his characteristics unchanged, we would not regard him as having become a different person. Genetic therapy of this sort would not, for example, imply that the resultant individual no longer owned property that was owned by the person who chose to undergo the procedure, or that the person who left the operation would not be contractually bound to pay for it (since a different person had chosen to undergo it!).
>
> (p. 100)

The question of identity is certainly a thorny one. Wolf's argument is in my view too weak to refute the entire non-identity problem, as the identities of established persons cannot be compared with the identities of unborn ones. In other words, if a couple were to have 200 million children and each sperm cell were to fertilize an egg, no child would be completely identical in appearance with any of his or her sisters or brothers. Each would, for example, have a different number and arrangement of birthmarks.[11] If we define "identity" narrowly – and distinct from "personality" – each of these potential children would have a different identity.[12]

Second objection: "We have moral responsibilities towards future people, even if their identities are indeterminate to us"

Inflicting harm on someone is not necessarily dependent upon knowing this person's identity.[13] Let us assume that someone hides a bear trap, which snaps closed with a trigger mechanism, near a children's playground in a forest. Here, too, the intention is that some child be injured. The fact that the victim's identity at the time the trap is set has not yet been determined makes the deed no less evil.

Particularly when someone hurts others "at random," the crime appears to us to be particularly heinous.

If we break a bottle at the beach, we have an obligation to pick up the pieces and throw them in the rubbish bin, not in order to protect any *certain* person from injury, but to ensure that *no one* will be injured (Partridge, 2007, p. 6). The principle of morality demands to fulfill obligations towards individuals by description and not denotatively; that is due to shared general qualities and relations rather than qualities that distinguish persons as individuals like their genetic codes or personalities (Partridge, 2007, p. 6). The "children on the forest playground," and the "barefoot people walking on the beach" – all these are empty set identities, not identifiable identities of particular persons. And nonetheless, persons identifiable by name, such as you and I, have moral obligations towards them. In brief, the argument of indeterminacy in no way releases anyone from the duty to take into account, in our actions here and now, the interests of future generations, consisting of personalities yet to be determined.[14]

Unfortunately, that does not help us refute the non-identity problem. For this NIP is based on dependence, not on indeterminacy. Above, the behavior of a person who hides a bear trap next to a playground was branded as immoral. Would we also do so if this heinous behavior were the necessary condition for the existence of the child who steps into the trap and is wounded?[15] In my view, the answer would necessarily be no. Hence, our good arguments against the indeterminacy argument do not hold against the dependence argument and thus cannot obviate the non-identity problem.

Third objection: "The snowball effect of the non-identity problem is minimal"

Do all decisions really lead, directly or indirectly, to nonidentical individuals in the second generation? According to Parfit (1987), "Very many" do (p. 356).[16] How many is a question we will address below. Parfit (1987) points to the snowball effect created by government measures:

> Suppose that we are choosing between two social or economic policies. And suppose that, on one of the two policies, the standard of living would be slightly higher over the next century. . . . It is not true that, whatever policy we choose, the same particular people will exist in the further future. Given the effects of two such policies on the details of lives, it would increasingly over time be true that, on the different policies, people married different people. And, even in the same marriages, the children would increasingly over time be conceived at different times.

> (pp. 361ff.)

This statement implies that a government policy can alter the "genetic shuffle" of future meetings, reproductive encounters, and births in a way that the earth is soon repopulated by different individuals. But how decisively can government policy really mix up the gene pool of future generations within a limited period of time? Indisputably, the overlap between that generation which actually came into being and the one that would have come into being had this policy not been in effect would initially be very high, and over the course of time become smaller. It seems fair to say that the NIP would be refuted if an action harmful to posterity would for a long time result in a relatively large overlap between the people actually born and those potentially born, i.e. if the snowball effect of the NIP were minimal. But to know exactly how great this effect is, we have to calculate:

Example 1

Let us take an environmental policy decision of the last century which has been seen by many as inimical to the world of the future: the decision to build nuclear power plants for the purpose of providing a significant share of our energy requirements. For a concrete country, e.g. Germany, for how many people did that policy decision change the point in time at which they met their partners and conceived children? For hardly any, at first glance, except for nuclear industry workers themselves. However, let us for the sake of the snowball-effect argument assume that as a result of direct and indirect effects, a quarter of the population had changed their plans with regard to procreation as a result of the policy decision to build nuclear power plants. According to such a scenario, it would have lasted 180 years before the German population would have consisted entirely of different individuals (assuming generations of thirty years).[17]

Within this period of time, the non-identity argument would not be fully applicable. Is a time span of 180 years long or short? Certainly not long enough to obviate the NIP. Unfortunately, the snowball effect of non-identity has a greater effect when the policy of the first generation is more inimical to the world of the future.

Example 2

Let's assume that Generation 1 has built many nuclear power plants with poor safety features. The next generation, Generation 2, then suffers one major accident with massive radiation pollution every year. Virtually the entire population would thus have been affected by resettlement. For some 90% of the population, the point in time at which Generation 2 conceives its children would have changed.

After almost ninety years, there would only be one single individual unaffected by this change.[18] A policy threatening such harm to future generations would thus change the marriage decisions of considerably more people than was the case in Example 1. And the argument can be made stronger by referring to even more drastic cases that would influence the lives and marriages of almost everybody. There are thus enough examples under which the overlap between

Generation 1, i.e. those born after a certain measure has been taken, and Generation 1a, i.e. those who would have been born had it not been taken, will fairly rapidly approach zero.

By way of an intermediate summary, we can state that the three above cited counterarguments – and others[19] – do not succeed in refuting the NIPPTG.

Convincing objections against the "non-identity problem as a problem for theories of generational justice"

The "reincarnation-may-be-possible" argument

This argument is directed not only against the NIPPTG, but fundamentally against the NIP. The NIP is based on a very specific concept of the soul or of consciousness, stating that each soul and each consciousness is tied to a very definite body and can only exist together with that body. This "body-equals-person" concept is a typical Western, specifically Protestant view.[20] Hindus, Buddhists, Jains and Confucians, as well as adherents of other religions, believe that a person can be born into a new body after death. Their belief is that every person existing today has been born countless times prior to his or her present life, and that this process will continue in the future. When a new body is formed, no new person is created; rather, the identity of an already existing person is taken into a new body. Eastern religions and the philosophical traditions based upon them thus uphold a concept which is incompatible with the "person-equals-body" concept.[21]

The non-identity argument is based on the premise that people are not reborn. If this premise becomes unstable, the whole non-identity paradigm, too, is weakened (Mulgan, 2002; Tremmel, 2006a). For over 5,000 years, people in various cultures around the world have been thinking about death and of what comes afterwards. Even in the Stone Age, they conducted ancestor worship. In ancient Egypt, Osiris was the judge of the dead. While Christians believe in heaven and hell, Hindus and Buddhists believe in reincarnation. What remains of these beliefs after 250 years of the Enlightenment and the natural-scientific demystification of the world? The question of what happens after death is still undecided. In case of "undecidable questions," neutrality is advisable. Nonetheless, an agnostic can, even in the realm of metaphysics, reject theories which are internally contradictory. Does the theory of reincarnation belong in that category, so that the advocates of the NIP are correct in categorically rejecting it?

The most important argument against reincarnation of the individual soul is the temporally limited nature of the ability to think: "If I am reborn in a new body, why don't I remember my previous life?" The reader would not be unjustified in asking. One answer might be: "Because when your body dies, all your nerve cells stop working, and there's no such thing as consciousness without the activity of nerve cells. For that reason, there's no such thing as reincarnation."[22] On the other hand, as Mulgan counters, reincarnation offers the best explanation for such everyday phenomena as remembrance, memory, birth, the limitation of life, and the apparently innate characteristics of newborn babies. Others consider reincarnation, in connection with the karma theory, as the only satisfactory explanation for the unjust suffering of innocent people (Mulgan, 2002, p. 8).

In conclusion, we can state that the theory of reincarnation is not internally contradictory or illogical.[23] Even if, like all matters of faith, it is not accessible to scientific methods of proof, it is nonetheless, no less than other religious beliefs, a "rational comprehensive doctrine" in the Rawlsian sense (Rawls, 1993, p. 59, 1999, pp. 573–615).

One important characteristic of political philosophy is neutrality in questions of religion. It would be ethnocentric and unscientific to proclaim the "person-equals-body" concept as the only correct one. By the same token, however, it would also be ethnocentric to proclaim the Eastern concept of identity as correct, and the Western one as wrong. Hence, the "reincarnation-may-be-possible" argument can in no sense refute the NIP. But it can limit its scope. For the future, we must therefore exclude all Eastern doctrines from consideration in the following discussion, and remain solely within the cosmos of Western thought, or, more precisely, in that of the "person-equals-body" idea. For here, too, there are incisive counterarguments to the non-identity thesis.

The "your-neighbor's-children" argument

In the above discussion, individual decisions ("Dad drives a car instead of riding a bike") and political programs (a generation's energy or war policy) have been discussed in a single breath. Now let us examine an argument which can only be used in the first category, but, there at least, succeeds in accomplishing a refutation of the NIP. Let us return to Gosseries's example, which suggested that a father could justify his environmentally harmful driving habits to his daughter by means of the non-identity argument. Gosseries (2008) reports the fictitious conversation between the father and his daughter as follows:

> Imagine then a father having to face his daughter. At seventeen, she has become a Green activist and asks him: "Why did you not choose to take your bike rather than your car? The atmosphere would be much cleaner today! And given your circumstances at that time, you had no special reason not to take your bike!" The father may want to answer: "True. Still, had I done so, you would not be here. Since your life in such a polluted environment is still worth living, why blame me? I certainly did you no harm. Which of your rights did I violate, then?" Some will find the father's answer at best misconstrued, at worst shocking. And still, the way out may not be as obvious at it seems.
>
> (p. 460)

But must the daughter now really fall silent? In my view, she could answer as follows:

> Very clever, Daddy. But have you ever stopped to think that our neighbor, Petra, who is also seventeen, also suffers from the exhaust from your car?

She's part of the next generation too, and I can't imagine that the fact that
you drove your car had anything to do with the point in time when she was
conceived. So your behavior is unfair to all members of the coming generation, maybe except to me.

Here, while the daughter does not question the validity of the NIP in her own
case, she correctly points out that it fails to constitute a challenge to complaints
raised by her generational peers. They are harmed by the pollution stemming
from the car. This is a refutation of NIP for *individual* (mis)deeds. But why does
the "your-neighbor's-children" argument lose its effectiveness with respect to *collective* actions, such as government policies? The reason is that in the example of
energy or war policy, it is not only the point in time of conception of one's own
children that is changed, but also that of the children of all one's neighbors. The
entire population as a collective – not only some individuals – is suffering from
an action harmful to posterity.

The "butterfly-effect" argument

While the "your-neighbor's-children" argument only limits the realm of applicability of the NIPPTG, the "butterfly-effect" argument seeks to disarm it altogether.
Let us take a second, closer look at the definition of the non-identity thesis:

> An action in the present is causal not only for the conditions of life of future
> human beings, but also for the fact of which people will exist. Such an action
> cannot harm a person, because without that action, that person would never
> have existed. Put differently: *Because of* a specific action by a present agent,
> a future individual came into existence.

The "butterfly-effect" argument then addresses the claim of causality, i.e. the
"because." In order for the non-identity problem to arise, it is, as pointed out
above, necessary that concrete actions or policies inimical to posterity have a
practical – and not merely a theoretical – effect on the points in time at which
marriages and conceptions take place. Let us use anecdotal evidence and ask some
couples with children which events were responsible for the fact that they met
in the first place. We could expect to receive such answers as, "Oh, we were in
the same dance course," or, "We happened to be sitting next to each other in the
bleachers at a football game." Such arrangements also seem to have a causal effect
on the "genetic shuffle" of future meetings, reproductive encounters and births.

   In the above example, we have referred to the construction of nuclear power
plants in Germany during the 1960s and '70s. According to the non-identity
concept, this had been causal for the non-identity of members of the ensuing
generations. The snowball effect has ensured that, after a certain period of time,
the German population is no longer genetically identical to the population
which would have existed had the government failed to pursue nuclear policies.
But precisely this alleged causality does not exist. Rather, the nuclear-power
policy was only one of countless aspects which affected the conjugal behavior of

the German population during the 1960s and '70s. During this period, the Germans experienced the postwar reconstruction, the consumer wave and the travel wave. With his sex education campaign, Oswald Kolle[24] changed what people did in their bedrooms; that was followed by the 1968 student uprising and the introduction of the contraceptive pill. Young people no longer met their future partners at tea dances, but rather, increasingly, at discos or on summer vacations. Moreover, the numbers of their sexual partners increased overall.

Can we say that the sexual revolution during the 1960s and '70s altered the "genetic shuffle" of meetings, reproductive encounters and births in a way that Germany was soon repopulated by different individuals? This would be just as right or wrong as to say that the government's nuclear policy mixed up the gene pool of a specific future generation of Germans. The non-identity thesis misinterprets the cause–effect relationship. In view of the countless decisions which all help determine which egg cell and which sperm cell will combine, it would be misleading to pick out one and make it causally responsible for the effect, in this case the conception and later birth of a child. In other words, the non-identity argument describes causalities which are not provable. This does not mean that they don't exist. Just as, under chaos theory, the flapping of the butterfly's wing in Asia could be responsible for causing a hurricane in the Caribbean, it is just as plausible that one of the countless events which will have occurred on the day on which a person was conceived would be a factor in determining that person's genetic code.[25] But it would be misleading to construct a mono-causal relationship from such a weak multi-causal context. The terms "necessary" and "sufficient" are inapplicable here, because they are part of a context of a limited – as a rule, single digit – number of influential variables. When we think about what "caused" something, we might hold variable A responsible for 50% of the effect, variable B for 30% and variable C for 19%. We know in the back of our mind that there is an undefinable number of additional variables that sum up to the last 1%, but we normally don't understand causality in that way. When a judge lists the causes of a car accident in his writ, for example, he will say that a slight drunkenness was 50% responsible, and a dispute in the car with the co-driver was to blame for the rest. He will not say. "Another cause is that no comet recently hit the area where the accident occurred and as a result the road was intact." But this statement would undoubtedly be "right." For if there had been such a comet impact, the accident would not have happened in this specific road.

Let us once again look at Gosseries's example, which suggests that the father might justify his environmentally harmful driving habits to his daughter by using the non-identity argument. This time, the daughter gives her father a different answer:

> Are you really trying to tell me that this behaviour of yours, which is harmful to succeeding generations, is responsible for the fact that I was conceived on March 14, 1996 at 8:11:43 p.m.? Okay, that may have been the reason that you were at home half an hour earlier than you would have been if you'd taken your bike. But on the day of my conception, if you were not caught in a traffic jam on the way home, and if you hadn't petted the cat on the way in, you would have also come through the door a few minutes earlier. And if you hadn't gone

to the refrigerator just before having sex with my mother, the point in time of my conception would also have been different. And anyway, the only reason you had to work so long since the beginning of 1996 was that the government had just passed a law lifting the restrictions on overtime work, which they had to do to meet the challenge of Chinese competition. All of these factors – and a billion other ones – are more responsible than your driving your car for the fact that I was conceived at exactly 8:11:43 p.m. So your car journey is not the reason and thus no excuse for the fact that you're polluting the atmosphere.

The "butterfly-effect" argument can not only be used against the claim that individual actions will lead to the non-identity of members of the ensuing generation but also against the claim that collective policies will have that effect. Hence, the NIP cannot be used to refute those who condemn the nuclear power policy for being intergenerationally unjust.

In this context, the exact formulation in Parfit's text is revealing. He wrote: "It is not true that regardless of which policies we choose, the same persons will exist in the remote future" (Parfit, 1987, p. 361). Note that Parfit did not write: "It is true that if alternative policies are chosen, different persons will exist in the remote future." Parfit had no greater chance of proving that a wasteful resource policy will cause different people to exist in the future than one might of proving that the flapping of a butterfly's wing had in fact engendered a hurricane on the other side of the world. Hence, he passes the burden of proof on to the opponents of the NIPPTG, demanding that they prove that a resource policy harmful to the future will not cause the existence of a different group of people in the future.

As my calculations showed for the snowball effect of the non-identity phenomenon, there is a big difference between the scenarios in which a generation builds twenty relatively safe nuclear power plants, as was the case in Germany, or 200 accident-prone ones, as we posited in our later scenario. But for the causality argument, this difference is relatively unimportant. Given the fact that 200 million male gametes exist at average at every second, this is comparable to the difference between the flapping of an eagle's wing, instead of a butterfly's.

Every combination of a certain egg and a certain sperm cell is the result of a countless number of actions and results with no obvious relationship to one another. It is thus impossible to associate certain specific political programs with certain specific effects upon concrete personal identities. The point in time of the combination of a certain egg and a certain sperm cell depends on the most insignificant conceivable events during the minutes before that occurrence. A yawn, a cough, a sneeze, a glance upward, a drink of this or that – all these are actions which can cause an individual with a different genetic code to be created. It has been said that the NIP is a problem for theories of intergenerational justice. Well, within the context of intergenerational justice theories, the most discussed policies are the expansion of public debt and the present rate of destruction of the natural environment. Such applications are not likely to uproot and resettle 99% of the population. No matter how much the proponents of the NIPPTG puff up their examples, they will never account for anything more than a miniscule factor in a network of billions of other miniscule factors.

The narrow range of applicability of the NIP

In Western thought – and again, we are remaining within its realm – there are indeed areas in which the non-identity thesis holds. This statement may surprise the reader, but remember that I, at the outset, distinguished between the NIP as such and the NIPPTG, the "non-identity problem as a problem for theories of generational justice." Now that I have sufficiently criticized that expansion of its scope of applicability, let me investigate the areas in which there is in fact a genetic non-identity, and a resulting "problem." These include cases from medical procreation clinics, for instance after a PGD, in which several embryos are selected and implanted, and the others disposed of. The major difference with respect to the NIPPTP context and the applications discussed above (e.g. environmental destruction, public debt) is that there, the egg cell has not yet been fertilized. As mentioned, of the 200 million sperm cells which a man ejaculates at one time, each could conceive a genetically different child. In the NIP cases involving PGD, however, the selection is made between only a handful of genetically different embryos. One of the 200 million sperm cells that could have fertilized the egg has in fact fertilized the egg. Here, the butterfly-effect argument does not apply.

It is surprising that on the one hand, Parfit considers the non-identity argument as applicable – and indeed, as applicable to a very broad range of cases – but on the other hand supports the "no-difference" view (Parfit, 1987, pp. 366–371); in other words, he claims that this makes no moral difference. For in reproductive medicine, which is for good reasons currently experiencing a vociferous ethical debate, the non-identity thesis is an important moral argument. If it is to be applicable to the situation such as public debt or environmental destruction, it should be of moral significance here as well. For this reason, the "no-difference" view is implausible.

Other arguments against the non-identity problem

The three arguments presented above ("reincarnation" argument; "your-neighbor's-children" argument; "butterfly-effect" argument) seem to me to be the strongest, but there are also others deserving of mention, such as Gosseries's "catching-up" argument and Meyer's new definitions of the concept of "harm."

Gosseries (2008) proposes a path that would in some cases circumvent the NIP, e.g. in the example he himself uses about the father who drove to work rather than taking his bike on the day he conceived his daughter:

> If we consider that the fulfillment of the obligation to bequeath a "clean" environment should be assessed at the end of each person's life (complete-life obligation), the following strategy can be envisaged. As long as the father's pro-car choice was a necessary condition for his daughter's existence, it remains unobjectionable. However, as soon as the daughter was conceived, all his subsequent polluting actions were no longer falling within the ambit of the non-identity context. Nor is there any reason to hold the view that given his pre-conceptional polluting behaviour, the father's obligation to

bequeath a clean environment should be attenuated accordingly. In principle, we should expect the father to catch up as soon as his daughter has
been conceived in order to be able, at the end of his life, to eventually meet
the requirements of his constitutional obligation. This "catch up" argument
relies on the existence of a generational overlap.

(p. 461)

As stated above, the normal use of the word "harm" involves a comparison
between the actual situation of a certain person and the situation which would
have prevailed had the harmful action not been carried out. Lukas Meyer's
"threshold-value concept" changes the definition of the term "harm" as follows:
"An action (or inaction) at time t1 harms someone only if the agent causes
(allows) the quality of life of the person harmed to fall below a threshold to be
specified" (Meyer, 2003). Meyer comprehensively *accepts* the NIP. His solution
is a second-order solution in order to circumvent the negative ramifications for
theories of intergenerational justice.[26] But as my intention is here to refute the
NIPPTG in the first place, I don't need to go further into the "threshold-value
concept," even if it is admittedly influential in the literature and has helped in
shaping the NIP as a paradigm.[27]

Conclusion

This chapter discussed the challenge the non-identity problem poses to theories
of sustainability and intergenerational justice – theories which postulate that the
present generation has duties towards future generations. After presenting the
NIP, several counterarguments were discussed. Some hold; others do not. But
those counterarguments that are valid are strong enough to refute the NIP as
a challenge to theories of intergenerational justice. It is thus no obstacle in the
search for the best institutions to represent future generations.

Notes

1 For an overview, see Gosseries and Meyer (2009); Tremmel (2009).
2 The number of proposals on how to represent future generations has become considerable. For further reading, see Kates (2011); Göpel and Arhelger (2011); Ekeli
(2005); Wood (2004); Barry (1999); Stein (1998); Doeleman and Sandler (1998);
Dobson (1996); Goodin (1996); Schlickeisen (1994); Kavka and Warren (1983); and
the second part of the *Handbook of Intergenerational Justice*, ed. Tremmel (2006b). The
research agenda of the ENRI network may serve as a further example.
3 Lists of these can be found in Tremmel (2006b, pp. 192–196); Brown-Weiss (1989).
4 For instance Jensen (2013); Beckman (2013) also denies the need for new institutions
that represent future generations on the premise that future generations are not bound
by the decisions made today.
5 First formulated by Schwartz (1978), Adams (1979) and Bayles (1980), then described
in greater detail by Kavka (1982), and developed most effectively by Parfit (1987). His
section on *Future Generations* (pp. 351–438) is to this day the point of reference for
most authors discussing the topic. More recent works include Gosseries (2002); Page
(2007, pp. 132–159) and the collection of essays by Roberts and Wassermann (2009).

6 The non-identity problem seems to be a veritable nightmare not only for all theories of generational justice which postulate duties toward future individuals but also for theories of historical justice involving issues of past injustices, such as slavery or land confiscation, and possible restitution claims in the present day. For reasons of space, we will not address this here.

7 Parfit (1987) supports the "no-difference view" (p. 367). However, his statement also makes clear that he has absolutely no doubts regarding the validity of the non-identity problem.

8 To some extent, this is also true for Meyer 2003, 2004, 2005.

9 Peters (2009); Nelson and Robertson (2001); Shiffrin (1999); Strasser (1999); Roberts (1998); Shapira (1998); Jackson (1996); Heyd (1992); Morreim (1988).

10 Parfit (1987, p. 358) believes that there is such a thing as a life not worth living.

11 The reason for that is the differing epigenetic manifestations of genetic material in various cellular phenotypes.

12 One could of course claim that our moral duty only extends to the *personalities* and not the *identities* of future human beings (cf. Grey, 1996), but that does not seem intuitively logical to me.

13 The following argument is carried out in the literature *partially* with the terms "person-affecting principle" and "impersonal principle." However, both terms are ambiguous, and hence prone to misunderstanding, as Wolf has shown (2009, p. 97). I have therefore consciously avoided using them. All arguments against the NIP that lead to total utilitarianism with ensuing problems like the "repugnant conclusion" are avoided here. It is just not necessary to mention them. There are enough arguments to refute the NIP within the realm of person-affecting theories.

14 So too Wolf (2009, pp. 105–110).

15 It should be noted that the analogy becomes invalid once an immoral person *kills* at random. The reason is that taking a life does not change the identity of a member of the next generation, but annihilates this identity altogether.

16 "Very many of our choices will in fact have some effect on both the identities and the number of future people" (Parfit, 1987, p. 356).

17 Given a population of 80 million in Germany, 60 million are initially unaffected. In the first round of marriages, each of those unaffected has a chance of 6/8 to meet a partner who is likewise unaffected. After the first generation, there will therefore be $6/8 \times 60$ million unaffected people. Expressed mathematically: Of the entire population V, the initial number of unaffected people (the 0th generation) is B0; then, after one generation, the number of still unaffected people will be $B_1 = (B_0/V) \times B_0 = (B_0)^2/V$. Since the second round of marriages will involve the same conditions, after two generations, the number of remaining unaffected people will be $B_2 = (B_1/V) \times B_1 = (B_0)^4/V^3$. After the nth generation, it will be $B_n = (B_0)^{(2^n)} / [V^{(2^n-1)}]$. Solving that for a (the number of generations) yields $n = \ln [\ln(B_n/V) / \ln(B_0/V)] / \ln 2$, or in this example:

$$n = \ln [\ln(1/80000000) / \ln(60000000/80000000)] / \ln 2; n = 5.983124.$$

Since one generation corresponds to 30 years, there would, after 5.983124 * 30 years (i.e. 179.49 years) be only one remaining unaffected person.

18 Precisely 89.47 years. n = 2.982416835 generations. B_0 = 8 million.

19 In the journal *Ethics* of July 1986, which is entirely dedicated to a discussion of Parfit's *Reasons and Persons*, Woodward (1986) raised additional objections to the non-identity problem. However, in the same issue, Parfit (1986) convincingly refuted them, so that I will not address them further here.

20 The term "Western concept" here should not be understood to be synonymous with "Christian concept," since Catholicism and Orthodoxy do recognize a body-soul dualism, and assume an immortal soul, which does not, however, reincarnate. Protestantism tends more toward monism in the sense of a "body-equals-person" concept. However, I cannot, for reasons of space, enter into a discussion of the theological details here.

142   *Jörg Chet Tremmel*

21 There are certain differences in the transmigration-of-souls concepts of these religions, which cannot be discussed here for reasons of space. Also, that which is reborn (the *atman*) does not necessarily correspond to Western concepts of self-consciousness. For the differences between the various Eastern religions and philosophical traditions, see Kim and Harrison (1999).
22 The Far Eastern philosophical tradition sees the soul as indivisible. The question: "Why don't I remember?" is, in the Far Eastern view, misplaced. It is not the individual that is reborn, but rather the migrating substance (Brahman, "omni-soul") which periodically takes on bodily form, and assumes a variety of – not always human – forms of existence. The issue is hence no longer the return of the consciousness, but rather the participation in the whole. For more, see O'Flaherty (1980).
23 Moreover, there are dissonances within the "body-equals-person" concept even in the West. A person born without a brain (anencephalus) is not considered a person, even though his body might be completely intact. Even in the West, someone who had part of his or her brain implanted would no longer unquestionably be seen as the same person as he or she had been prior to the operation.
24 A German-Dutch journalist/filmmaker whose work helped spark Germany's "sexual revolution" of the 1960s and 1970s.
25 The term "butterfly effect" was coined in 1963 by the meteorologist Edward N. Lorenz (Lorenz, 1963). In the context of a long-term weather prognosis, Lorenz investigated the behavior of heated liquids and gases with a simplified convection model, which he then characterized with three interconnected differential equations. He projected the numerical results into phase space, and obtained an infinitely long structure in three-dimensional space, which did not intersect itself and had the form of two butterfly wings. Interestingly, Lorenz stumbled upon the chaotic behavior of his model more or less by coincidence. In order to save computation time, he used the intermediate results of calculations he had already carried out, but only took three decimal places into account, even though his computer was operating with a precision of six decimal places. At the point of departure, the weather curves were so close that the deviation could indeed have resulted from the flapping of a butterfly's wing. However, that small "error" continued on and caused increasing deviations, until the old and the new weather curves were completely different.
26 For reasons of space, we cannot here examine whether the common definition of "harm" is unusable, and hence a new definition is necessary. At first glance, that does not appear to be the case.
27 See, for instance, the entry "Intergenerational Justice" in the *Stanford Encyclopedia of Philosophy*, written by Meyer (2003).

Bibliography

Adams, R. M. (1979). Existence, self-interest, and the problem of evil. *Nous, 13*(1), 53–65.
Barry, J. (1999). *Greening political theory*. London: Sage.
Bayles, M. D. (Ed.). (1976). *Ethics and population*. Cambridge, MA: Schankman.
Bayles, M. D. (1980). *Morality and population policy*. Tuscaloosa, AL: Alabama University Press.
Beckman, L. (2013). Democracy and future generations: Should the unborn have a voice? In J.-C. Merle (Ed.), *Spheres of global justice* (Vol. 2: Fair distribution – Global economic, social and intergenerational justice, pp. 775–788). Dordrecht: Springer.
Brown-Weiss, E. (1989). *In Fairness to Future Generations*. Tokio/New York: United Nations University/Transnational Publishers.
Cohen, A. I. (2009). Compensation for historic injustices: Completing the Boxill and Sher argument. *Philosophy and Public Affairs, 37*(1), 81–102.

Dobson, A. (1996). Representative democracy and the environment. In W. M. Lafferty & J. Meadowcroft (Eds.), *Democracy and the environment* (pp. 124–139). Cheltenham: Edward Elgar.

Doeleman, J., & Sandler, T. (1998). The intergenerational case of missing markets and missing voters. *Land Economics, 74*(1), 1–15.

Ekeli, K. S. (2005). Giving a voice to posterity: Deliberative democracy and representation of future people. *Journal of Agricultural and Environmental Ethics, 18*(5), 429–450.

Goodin, R. (1996). Enfranchising the earth, and its alternatives. *Political Studies, 44*(5), 835–849.

Göpel, M., & Arhelger, M. (2011). How to protect future generations' rights in European governance. *Intergenerational Justice Review, 10*(1), 3–10.

Gosseries, A. (2002). Intergenerational justice. In H. LaFollette (Ed.), *The Oxford handbook of practical ethics* (pp. 459–484). Oxford: Oxford University Press.

Gosseries, A. (2008). On future generations' future rights. *Journal for Political Philosophy, 16*(4), 446–474.

Gosseries, A., & Meyer, L. H. (Eds.). (2009). *Intergenerational justice*. Oxford: Oxford University Press.

Grey, W. (1996). Possible persons and the problem of posterity. *Environmental Values, 5*(2), 161–179.

Heyd, D. (1992). *Genethics*. Berkeley, CA: University of California Press.

Jackson, A. (1996). Wrongful life and wrongful birth. *Journal of Legal Medicine, 17*(3), 349–381.

Jensen, K. K. (2013). *Future generations in democracy: Representation or consideration*. Paper presented at the workshop "Representing Future Generations," 3–4 May 2013 in Munich, Germany.

Kates, M. (2011). *Justice, democracy, and future generations*. Paper presented at the APSA Annual Meeting 1–4 September 2011 in Seattle, USA.

Kavka, G. S. (1978). The futurity problem. In R. Sikora & B. Barry (Eds.), *Obligations to future generations* (pp. 186–203). Philadelphia, PA: Temple University Press.

Kavka, G. S. (1982). The paradox of future individuals. *Philosophy and Public Affairs, 11*(2), 93–112.

Kavka, G. S., & Warren, V. (1983). Political representation for future generations. In R. Elliot & A. Gare (Eds.), *Environmental philosophy: A collection of readings* (pp. 20–39). University Park, PA: Pennsylvania State University Press.

Kim, T.-C., & Harrison, R. (Eds.). (1999). *Self and future generations: An intercultural conversation*. Cambridge: White Horse Press.

Kuhn, T. S. (1963). *The structure of scientific revolutions*. Chicago, IL: University of Chicago Press.

Laslett, P., & Fishkin, J. S. (1992). Introduction: Processional justice. In P. Laslett & J. S. Fishkin (Eds.), *Self and future generations: An intercultural conversation* (pp. 1–23). New Haven, CT and London: Yale University Press.

Lorenz, E. N. (1963). Deterministic nonperiodic flow. *Journal of the Atmospheric Sciences, 20*(2), 130–141.

Meyer, L. H. (2003). Intergenerational justice. In E. N. Zalta (Ed.), *The Stanford encyclopedia of philosophy*. Retrieved 20 March 2007, from http://plato.stanford.edu/entries/justice-intergenerational

Meyer, L. H. (Ed.). (2004). *Justice in time: Responding to historical injustice*. Baden-Baden: Nomos.

Meyer, L. H. (2005). *Historische Gerechtigkeit*. Berlin and New York, NY: De Gruyter.

Morreim, E. H. (1988). The concept of harm reconceived: A different look at wrongful life. *Law and Philosophy, 7*(1), 3–33.

Mulgan, T. (2002). Neutrality, rebirth and intergenerational justice. *Journal of Applied Philosophy, 19*(1), 3–15.

Nelson, E., & Robertson, G. (2001). Liability for wrongful birth and wrongful life. *ISUMA, 2*(3), 102–105.

O'Flaherty, W. D. (Ed.). (1980). *Karma and rebirth in classical Indian traditions*. Berkeley, CA: University of California Press.

Page, E. (2007). *Climate change, justice, and future generations*. Cheltenham: Edward Elgar.

Parfit, D. (1986). Comments. *Ethics, 96*(4), 832–872.

Parfit, D. (1987). *Reasons and persons* (3rd rev. ed.). Oxford: Oxford University Press.

Partridge, E. (Ed.). (1980). *Responsibilities to future generations*. Buffalo, NY: Prometheus Books.

Partridge, E. (2007). *Should we seek a better future?* Retrieved 4 January 2008, from www.igc.org/gadfly/papers/swsabf.htm

Peters, P. G. (2009). Implications for the nonidentity problem for state regulation of reproductive liberty. In M. A. Roberts & D. T. Wassermann (Eds.), *Harming future persons: Ethics, genethics and the nonidentity problem* (pp. 317–331). Berlin and Heidelberg: Springer.

Rawls, J. (1993). *Political liberalism*. New York, NY: Columbia University Press.

Rawls, J. (1999). The idea of public reason revisited. In S. Freeman (Ed.), *John Rawls: Collected papers* (pp. 573–615). Cambridge, MA: Harvard University Press.

Roberts, M. A. (1998). *Child versus childmaker: Future persons and present duties in ethics and the law*. Lanham, MD: Rowman and Littlefield.

Roberts, M. A., & Wassermann, D. T. (Eds.). (2009). *Harming future persons: Ethics, genethics and the nonidentity problem*. Berlin and Heidelberg: Springer.

Schlickeisen, R. (1994). Protecting biodiversity for future generations: An argument for a constitutional amendment. *Tulane Environmental Law Review, 8*(1), 181–221.

Schwartz, T. (1978). Obligations to posterity. In R. Sikora & B. Barry (Eds.), *Obligations to future generations* (pp. 3–13). Philadelphia, PA: Temple University Press

Shapira, A. (1998). Wrongful life lawsuits for faulty genetic counselling: Should the impaired newborn be entitled to sue? *Journal of Medical Ethics, 24*(6), 369–375.

Shiffrin, S. V. (1999). Wrongful life, procreative responsibility and the significance of harm. *Legal Theory, 5*(2), 117–148.

Sikora, R., & Barry, B. (Eds.). (1978). *Obligations to future generations*. Philadelphia, PA: Temple University Press.

Stein, T. (1998). Does the constitutional and democratic system work? The ecological crisis as a challenge to the political order of constitutional democracy. *Constellations, 4*(3), 420–449.

Strasser, M. (1999). Wrongful life, wrongful birth, wrongful death and the right to refuse treatment: Can reasonable jurisdiction recognize all but one? *Missouri Law Review, 64*(1), 29–75.

Tremmel, J. (2006a). Einwände gegen Generationengerechtigkeit – Und ihre Widerlegung. *Intergenerational Justice Review/GenerationenGerechtigkeit!* (French–German bilingual edition), 6(1), 4–8 (in French 9–12).

Tremmel, J. (Ed.). (2006b). *Handbook of intergenerational justice*. Cheltenham: Edward Elgar.

Tremmel, J. (2009). *A theory of intergenerational justice*. London: Earthscan.

Wolf, C. (2009). Do future persons presently have alternate possible identities? In M. A. Roberts & D. T. Wassermann (Eds.), *Harming future persons: Ethics, genethics and the nonidentity problem* (pp. 93–114). Berlin and Heidelberg: Springer.

Wood, P. (2004). Intergenerational justice and curtailment on the discretionary powers of governments. *Environmental Ethics, 26*(4), 411–428.

Woodward, J. (1986). The Non-Identity Problem. *Ethics, 96*(4), 804–831.

11 The definition of society's relationship with nature on the basis of reproduction theory

A historical-systematic problem sketch

Michael Weingarten

Sustainability has tended to be viewed, on the basis of the historic model of for-estry, as a conception in which the conditions for the survival of human society are determined – even to this day. By contrast, the following sketch seeks to formulate the basic conditions under which the issue of sustainability might be transformed into a program of development theory. Formally, development can be defined as reproduction, non-identically extended. The implementation of this initially very formal definition can be oriented toward research programs initiated primarily by social geography, as a reconstruction of spatial structuring, particularly in everyday activity, and their confirmation over time as structures – which always means structures reproduced in activity. The underlying theory of activity has been systematically formulated in the dissertations of Claus Baumann and Jan Müller at the University of Stuttgart, and, with reference to climate change, in Karsten Gäbler's dissertation in social geography at the University of Jena.

Introduction

The theory of society's relationship to nature takes as the point of departure for the development of its approach the distinction between ecological, i.e. strictly life-scientific issues on the one hand, and issues of environmental science on the other, the latter being concerned with investigating the manner of the incorpo-ration of elements of nature into the reproduction of societal practice. It would, however, be a misunderstanding of this distinctive delimitation of the two disci-plines to assume that the same object were thus merely to be investigated from two different aspects or perspectives. Rather, it should be noted that ecology and environmental sciences are first and foremost different disciplines, each based on its own guiding purpose, and, in accordance with those purposes, its own objects of investigation. When deciding whether and how theoretical elements of the life sciences are to be – or can be – integrated into environmental sciences, very close reflection and even translation will be required. The same is true with regard to the reverse case: to what extent can social-scientific findings obtained in the context of environmental-scientific research, be incorporated into ecology – and to what extent should they be?

Whether such a translation from one disciplinary context to another makes any sense cannot be ascertained within the limits of the respective disciplines; what we rather need is a problem sketch preceding these disciplines, according to which the discipline-specific results and the procedures for obtaining them can be assessed and weighted. Precisely here, the development of a problem sketch, which can then, if necessary, be processed within the context of the disciplines, can be described as transdisciplinary research in the meaningful sense of the term, in which "cooperation leads to a permanent order of scientific systematics, which itself changes the orientation of the discipline and its object of study" (Mittelstraß 2001, p. 93). According to Mittelstraß, transdisciplinarity can then be described as follows:

> Transdisciplinarity is first of all an integrative, but not a holistic concept. It resolves isolations at a higher methodological level, but it is not grounded in any "holistic" pattern of interpretation and explanation. Secondly, transdisciplinarity eliminates bottlenecks within the historical context of the constitution of subjects and disciplines wherever they have lost their historical memory and dissipated their problem-solving power by becoming overly specialized; however, it does not lead to the formation of any new discipline, and can therefore not replace the existing subjects or disciplines. Thirdly, transdisciplinarity is a scientific principle of work and organization that transcends disciplines and their objects of study in a problem-oriented manner, but it is not a cross-scientific principle. . . . Fourthly and finally, transdisciplinarity is a principle of research and not a theoretical principle – or is so only secondarily, and only if the theories, too, pursue transdisciplinary research programs. It guides the perception of problem solution, but it does not get stuck in theoretical forms – either in a subject/discipline-related or a holistic framework.
>
> (Mittelstraß 2001, pp. 94–95)

Transdisciplinarity means a practical unity of knowledge, unlike classical concepts of the unity of science based on the methods and procedures of physics, or object-referenced holistic ideas, such as those at the root of Wilson's biologistic "unity of knowledge," the "Gaia" concept, or "deep ecology."

A historic memory

There are many indications that interest in natural history has, since the second half of the eighteenth century, been closely tied to problems of the justification of theories regarding the history of humankind, and/or the causes for the emergence of bourgeois society. Moreover, the discussions since the end of the eighteenth century show that the breeding of animals and plants, i.e. a certain practice structured around a means–ends relationship, moved ever more strongly into the focus of natural historians, since they expected to discover facts about the possible mechanisms of the transformation of living things. At the same time however, and this has to date received too little attention, it became clear that nature and society were intertwined in a *societal* relationship in the context of that practice.

Let us take as an example the work of Johann Gottfried Herder. He begins his *This Too a Philosophy of History for the Formation of Humanity* (1774) with a reference to many recent historical investigations:

> The more investigations bring to light about the most ancient world history, its migrations, languages, customs, inventions and traditions, the more likely become with every new discovery, the single origin of the whole species. One gets closer and closer to the fortunate climate where one human couple began spinning the thread – under the mildest influences of the creating prominence, and with the aid of a most facilitating fate all about, that was later drawn so far and wide with such confusions. . . .
>
> (Herder 1911, p. 121; Herder 2004, p. 3)

An unraveled ("spinning") thread, the teleological orientation of which toward a certain goal had become unclear through the permutations and confusions of human history – these formulations point not only to a predetermined goal of history ascribed to humankind; they at the same time point to the problem of where the capabilities of the first human beings, or rather the first human couple, their "inclinations, customs and institutions" were "root[ed] and ground[ed]" (ibid., p. 122/p. 5). If Herder attempts, in his execution, to represent the teleological development of humankind according to the model of an individual lifecycle, the question as to the origins of skills and inclinations of the first humans remains unanswered, and, in the context of this model, unanswerable – unless one wishes to take recourse in divine creation, as is certainly suggested by his metaphor-loaded description of the paradisiacal conditions of the lives of the first humans. It is precisely this problem that Herder will take as the main topic of his essay *Ideas for the Philosophy of History of Humanity*, which appeared ten years later, in which he attempts to develop a natural philosophical concept which was to demonstrate how every species (or, as he put it, *Gattung* – "genus," in modern German) had been born from the womb of mother nature, equipped by her with certain inclinations, capacities, and skills. While, after this creation, every living species was tied into a cycle of survival – e.g. through its instincts, the repertoire of behavior prescribed to it – the human being is presented as the "first emancipated being of nature," who has, however, only developed as a human being thanks to the emergence of human culture. Hence, while the human being is already human by nature, he or she must yet, by means of cultural development, yet attain that state which is by nature already given. Thus are the cycle and the teleological development brought together in a very odd concept.

In his review of Herder's philosophy of history, Immanuel Kant, while basically agreeing with the thesis of the first part, in which he saw history as the unfolding of those capabilities unique to human beings, nonetheless mocked Herder's natural-philosophical efforts. Unlike Herder, he was content to establish these capabilities as those which constitute human beings as human beings, by pronouncing in his first sentence his idea of a "Universal History for Cosmopolitan Purpose":[1]

> *All natural capacities of a creature are destined to evolve completely to their natural end.* Observation of both the outward form and inward structure of all animals confirms this of them. An organ that is of no use, an arrangement that does not achieve its purpose, are contradictions in the teleological theory of nature. If we give up this fundamental principle, we no longer have a lawful but an aimless course of nature, and blind chance takes the place of the guiding thread of reason.
>
> (Kant, 1968, vol. 11, p. 35)

The model implied by Herder, of development as a unity of reproduction and unfolding, is taken apart again by Kant, with natural preservation on the one hand and cultural, teleological unfolding on the other.

If we take a more precisely differentiated view of this discussion of human history, distinguishing, for instance, between social and cultural history on the one hand and economic development on the other, it appears that the cyclical model of reproduction postulated for nature as preservation can also be found in the emerging, self-shaping, conceived society. For the economists of the eighteenth century, particularly the physiocrats, were precisely confronted with on the one hand talking about development and emergence with reference to society, while on the other only being able, with their economic terminology, to fully describe self-preserving reproduction cycles.

> But at the same time, the essential difference between economy and history remains. For as far as Turgot, as an economist, was concerned, historical components only have the function of describing the emergence of bourgeois society. He investigated the process of emergence of an economic system which, once established, would thereafter maintain itself and remain identical to itself. The entire history of the world seemed to flow together to this condition, and there defined its ultimate fulfillment.
>
> (Rohbeck 1990, p. 71)

This ultimate prize, the designation of the fulfillment of the system as the ultimate condition, is based not only on the ideological and political foundations of the bourgeoisie as it established itself, but, more importantly, on reasons of theoretical conceptualization:

> But just as decisive is the problem of reproduction, which, for the first time, received an essential function in physiocratic theory. Since the physiocrats reduce the economic process to a cycle, and were therefore familiar only with simple reproduction, they were incapable of grasping economic growth occurring outside of reproduction in other than a purely quantitative form.

Hence, reproduction and expansion remained opposites; economists and theoreticians of history understand reproduction without extension, and extension beyond the reproduction of certain societies.

(ibid., p. 72)

This description of the aporia within physiocratic economic and social theory is the formulation of the task to be solved, which will permit the conceptual description of development: the establishment of a theory of extended reproduction. However, as long as philosophers, social theorists, and natural historians based concepts on the issue of the emergence of capabilities, inclinations and dispositions in living creatures, including human beings, the task of explanation could only keep being passed back and forth between human history and nature. Here, too, one might by way of example refer to Kant. While he does speak of the "means" by which things can be realized or developed, these means are exogenous to what is developing with the aid of these means; that which develops, develops not out of itself, not from the conditions to be found in its objective constitution, but is rather developed by something that exists outside of it, and separated from it.

In 1807, Alexander von Humboldt published his *Essay on the Geography of Plants*, which he had begun writing five years earlier, during his voyage which took him around South America all the way to Mexico. In this book, he attempted to show how plants can evolve divergently in interaction with the climatic factors under which they exist. These are not simply the causal factors which can effect modifications and certain paths of modification. Rather, developing upon the ideas of natural explorer Georg Forster, and particularly natural philosopher Friedrich Wilhelm Schelling, he rather wanted to show that this process of divergence was based upon the "never-ending struggle between the countervailing basic forces of matter." While it was true that "vegetable germ cells, according to the ancient myths of many peoples," first developed in one region, but then they "migrated to all regions of the world along pathways difficult to ascertain, and overcoming all differences of climate" (Humboldt 1960, p. 35; our translation). Thus, plants develop according to how they differentiate in interaction with their respective climatic conditions. The phenomenal, at first glance impressive, context of equilibrium between plants, animals, and their environment, which physical theology sought to explain as a result of the farsighted creative act of God, is, for Humboldt rather a dynamic process which, on the one hand, does regulate the process of the formation of divergence by means of climatic factors, toward a stable condition which permits preservation, but which on the other can then be overcome by the reproduction of the plants themselves, under these regulating conditions.

In the great concatenation of cause and effect, no material, no activity can be viewed in isolation. The balance which prevails amid the apparently contending elements emerges from the free play of dynamic forces, and a complete overview of nature, the ultimate goal of all physical study, can only be achieved by ensuring that no force and no formation is neglected, and that thus a broad field promising a rich yield will be prepared for the philosophy of nature.

(ibid., p. 55)

In this context, Humboldt also incorporates human beings and their agriculture. "Thus do people arbitrarily change the original distribution of plants, and gather around themselves the fruits of the most remote climates" (ibid., p. 41). "The restless labor of agrarian peoples" has, he said, torn usable plants "from their native soil, and forced him to inhabit all climates and all mountainous heights." Even if Humboldt believed that, as a result of this, "their original form" had not been notably changed, the careful reader might ask how the peasant was able to "force" the plants to such moves, and how he was able to use the variability of plants for his purposes, to cultivate wild forms and make certain demands of the cultivated forms.

The introduction of the concept of nature in the theory of society's relationship with nature

The approaches outlined above can be termed attempts to raise the issue of the difference and the connection between nature and society in the context of nature itself – where that connection can only be described in natural-scientific terms. The conceptual model upon which all these approaches are based can be described as a cyclical model, in which the initial conditions of a natural or other process are always approximately identically reproduced by the process itself. Thus, this is a model for the preservation of a condition which, while it incorporates the possibility of degeneration, excludes the issue of development.[2]

Society's relationship to nature are exemplified as the object of environmental research distinct from the above-described cyclical concept, and rather continuing in the tradition of the considerations initiated in terms of natural theory by Humboldt, and of social theory by the physiocrats and the Scottish political economists such as Ferguson and Smith, and systematically developed further by Marx. The term "society's relationship to nature" refers to the distinction between the natural and the social within society, undertaken for certain ends. If, initially, the concept of "nature" referred to a general entity which covered both itself and its opposite, society, then society, here, is the general entity which covers both the natural and the social; or, in other words: the concept of "society" contains the difference between the natural and the social as an internal distinction.[3] This object is introduced into the process of reflection upon societal activity, and here in particular, upon the objective means by which the ends of that activity may be achieved in cooperation with other actors. However, in order to avoid a sociologistical reduction of the reflection on society's relationship with nature, in other words, to avoid raising the issue of that relationship not only in the context of the risks and ancillary effects of technological *activity*, a concept of nature must be introduced in the process of reflection on the object of the environmental sciences (i.e. society's relationship with nature in its material dimensions) which can function as a – symbolically structured – means of understanding those aspects of society's relationship with nature which need to be criticized, changed or, on the other hand, preserved. The introduction of the concept of nature as a concept of reflection indicates that this use of the term "nature" does not refer simply to an object existing prior to human activity, but rather to an aspect of comprehension-oriented discourse about a societal relationship with nature which has been structured by activity. Only when these aspects – the definition of the object of the theory of society's relationship with nature, of the societal relationship with nature structured by activity and reproduced as a structure, the symbolic dimension of the discourse about nature, and the determination of the relationship between the two – have been fulfilled, will we be justified in speaking of a "critical theory of society's relationship with nature."[4]

However, this "critical theory of society's relationship with nature" should not be seen simply as a mere continuation of the now classical critical theory of Horkheimer and Adorno. Rather, it has to take the systematic deficit of this work of theory as its point of reference: That means that it must provide a real conceptual definition of the means by which the mediation between the "subject" – society – and the "object" – nature – can be achieved. Within the classical tradition of critical theory, therefore, especially with regard to the symbolic dimension of the discourse about nature, it would be more useful to continue on the path of Walter Benjamin,[5] who at the same time reflects about the difference between the domination of nature and a (societal) relationship with nature, particularly with regard to the example of experiences in World War I:

> Human hordes, gases, electrical forces were unleashed in a free-for-all, high-frequency shocks ripped through the landscape, new stars appeared in the sky, the airy heights and the ocean depths thrummed with propellers, and everywhere sacrificial shafts were sunk in the earth. This mighty struggle for the cosmos was for the first time fought out on a planetary scale, very much in the spirit of technology. However, since the ruling class's greed for profit meant to atone for its intention thus, technology betrayed mankind and turned the marriage bed into a sea of blood. Control of nature, the imperialists teach us, is the purpose of all technology. But who would ever trust a thrasher who stated that control of children by grown-ups was the purpose of education? Education, surely, is the essential ordering of the relationship between the generations – in other words, if one wishes to speak of control, control of generational relations, not of children? So technology, too, is not about controlling nature: controlling the relationship between nature and humanity.
>
> (Benjamin 2009, p. 114)

The control of a thing or an object implies an insurmountable difference between the controller and that which is controlled; control over a relationship, by contrast, means – even if only a human being who, through activity, structures a relationship, for example with nature, is the subject – that he or she must, in structured activity, treat the object of that activity *as an equal*, in order to realize his or her purpose.[6] Finally, the approach of Karl August Wittfogel should be discussed anew; among the staff of the Institute for Social Research, he formulated what was probably the most important paper for the incorporation of the topic of nature into the theory of society.

In the next step, several further considerations regarding the constitution of the object are to be presented, using the example of the discourse on "landscape," in other words on the questions:

1   What is the object of investigation of environmental science?
2   How is this object constituted?

Let me clarify the significance of the question of the constitution of the object by reference to Oswald Spengler, who postulates that the human–nature duality is not merely the product of nature, but rather that the development of human cultures, too, is subject to natural-biological laws. Human activity can thus only be seen as the destruction of the supposedly natural. If, however, the modification of the natural by human activity is analyzed from the point of view of the *reproducibility of the relationship* between society and nature, entirely new theoretical perspectives open up, which are to be sketched here using the example of the landscape. The methodologically necessary third step, the reflection of the object as the implementation of this theory of societal relationships with nature, into which the concept of nature would then be introduced in its objective and symbolic dimensions, cannot be addressed in the present context.

Again: The naturalistic formulation of the problem of society's relationship with nature – Spengler

While I do not wish to imply that the following description of the problem by Oswald Spengler is correct, I would like to use it as an argumentation strategy in order to present the ensuing considerations. It can be used to advance the interpretation of the conceptual relationships between the dimensions of the social, of activity, and of the "surroundings" or "environment," as well as the implications of the respective interpretations of these terms.

Spengler makes the following assertions and prognoses:

> The mechanization of the world [by "man, the beast of prey" – M.W.] has entered on a phase of highly dangerous over-tension. The picture of the earth, with its plants, animals, and men, has altered. In a few decades most of the great forests have gone, to be turned into news-print, and climatic changes have been thereby set afoot which imperil the land-economy of whole populations. Innumerable animal species have been extinguished, or nearly so, like the bison; whole races of humanity have been brought almost to vanishing-point, like the North American Indian and the Australian. All

things organic are dying in the grip of organization. An artificial world is permeating and poisoning the natural. The Civilization itself has become a machine that does, or tries to do, everything in mechanical fashion.

(Spengler 1932, p. 24)

The fact that people can, through their activities, exterminate plants, animals, and other people, was one that no one denied, even at that time.[7] And the fact that this activity has not only affected our organic-physical "surroundings," but, as a result, also the reproduction of societies, is something that should have become evident to all of us, by now at the latest. In other words, we can, through our activity, destroy our "surroundings," and hence alter our absolute constitutional basis (cf. Talcott Parsons) to the extent that we risk our own survival. Precisely here is the point where it becomes important to make well-grounded decisions as to where human beings and "activity systems," are to be conceptually assigned. For if they tend to fall into the category of the extra-social surroundings, in other words if they are to be understood as nature – Spengler's "man, the beast of prey" – one might say that the physical-organic milieu alters or destroys itself by way of one of its components, that being the activity, or "behavior," of human society. Social systems considered naturalistic in this way must attempt to adapt by reacting passively to changing natural environmental conditions.

If, however, humankind and the systems of activity are rather to be categorized on the cultural/social side, the alteration of the "surroundings" through activity can first of all no longer be addressed as a natural process, but rather as an organizational and formulative process of its own conditions of reproduction by the respective societal actors – albeit a negative one, at least in the descriptive framework set by Spengler. And that, at least, means (beyond Spengler), secondly, that the destruction of the physical-organic milieu is not simply the inevitable *natural* consequence of human activity, for we could, theoretically, formulate that activity in such a way that, although we would continue to modify our surroundings by changing the relationship between the environment (the conditions of reproduction of human society, including its natural component) and the natural extra-societal surroundings (to the extent that these even exist at all anymore), we would do so for our own "benefit."[8] This aspect, which particularly refers to the unintended consequences of our activities, has been very aptly described by Fernand Braudel, who, quoting Lucien Febvre, asked us to imagine how Herodotus, who had very precise knowledge about the Mediterranean area in the fifth century B.C., would react could he see it today:

How astonished he would be! He would see these bright colored fruits borne by small, dark green trees – oranges, lemons, mandarins; he would not recall ever having seen them during his lifetime. And indeed, they were introduced by the Arabs from the Far East. And these very odd prickly plants, actually pillar shaped plants bearing flowers, with such odd names as cactus, agave and aloe, and fig trees too – these too he had never seen before, for they come from America. In these large trees with their light colored leaves with the Greek name eucalyptus – they too would have been unfamiliar to him: for goodness' sake, they come from Australia.

(Braudel et al. 1990, pp. 8–9, our translation)

Tomatoes come from for Peru, eggplants from India, peaches from China by way of Iraq. In brief, everything that we today consider typical of nature in the Mediterranean realm is the – unintentional – result of human activity.[9] However, if that is true, it would seem obvious that the central statement of the program of theory of classical social science, according to which the social can only be explained on the basis of the social, collapses. It thus becomes necessary to explore *social-scientifically* for a new differentiation between "nature" and "society," and for a new connection between these two differentiated entities. For now it is also necessary to reflect social-scientifically on how certain environmental conditions enable or hamper the capacity of human beings to create, how the intermeshing of nature and society is structured and hence how the development of society is affected, and also, conversely, how the development of society modifies the natural surroundings of that society, to its benefit or to its detriment.

Spengler's "tragic worldview" only remains plausible[10] as long as humankind is seen exclusively as the product of nature which, like all other living things, has been brought into existence and given some permanence by adaptation to the surroundings in which it has emerged.[11] This model is fundamental for such diverse theoreticians as Karl Friedrichs and his concept of ecology as the biological exploration of space (Friedrichs 1937), or the above-mentioned concept of the naturally defined home of Raoul H. Francé (orig. 1923; reprint 1982); contemporary representatives of such ideas include Edward O. Wilson (1999) and Jared Diamond (1999; 2005). On the other hand, particularly the statements by Braudel, quoted above, on the landscape of the Mediterranean, and many other studies from this French school of history,[12] show that naturalistic conceptions in the Spenglerian tradition, or in that of the early ecologists, do not necessarily imply any inevitability for the determination of the relationships of human beings to their natural "surroundings." Rather, what we see here is an interactive relationship of processes of creation, formation, and structuring, in which on the one hand, human beings shaped their surroundings through their activity so as to create landscapes and to reproduce them as such, while on the other, the thus shaped landscape have impacted back upon people, their activities, and their forms of life. This implies that the reproduction of a structure which is carried out within an activity does not necessarily always simply preserve that identically, but rather changes it in its reproduction (continued reproduction) or, under certain circumstances, develops it (which is not identical with continued reproduction). In order to clarify this interactive relationship, the key factor is that the activity of human beings become the object of conceptual efforts, particularly with regard to the fact that it is not the capacity to act that is defined as the outset of an activity, with respect to which actual activity then needs to be viewed as secondary and derivative (which would immediately lead to the question as to how human beings could have acquired such obviously pre-societal dispositions toward activity other than through natural processes), but rather, that the actual activity carried out by a number of actors in the context of social cooperation constitutes the point of departure, and that on the bases of that, possible points of departure, including dispositions to activity as well as the goals and purposes governing that activity, can be ascertained by means of reconstruction. I would like to outline that in the following.

The origins of a theory of spatial structuring

This activity, as opposed to the intentionalist understanding, which uses disposition as the point of departure, must be seen as doubly reflexive:[13] reflexive on the one hand in the definition of the means of work as a means both reproduced and reproducing (and precisely thus to be described as a tool; cf. Gutmann 1999); and on the other as a result of the purpose realized through the work process upon the object. However, this "object" of activity is never a thing which is simply found in nature – or is itself nature – but rather is always an object which has already been separated from its immediate natural context: the *caught* fish, the *felled* wood, etc., as Marx repeatedly stressed. The same is true of the means of work, which, as objective means, have necessarily already been separated from their extant contexts, and which only become tools by virtue of the fact that they are not simply worn away (consumed) in the process of use, but are rather reproduced for further utilization. Both considerations, that regarding the objects upon which work is performed and that regarding the objective means with which it is performed, indicate that we are dealing here not with things which we find as various objects external to and independent of our activity, but rather with analytically discernible forces within relationships. That indicates an additional shift: production is not simply the manufacture of an object as a result of an ideally assumed purpose, but rather the reproduction of a working relationship by means of production. On the plane instituted by the analysis of reproduction, production is not the production of things; it is the production and conservation of social relations (Althusser & Balibar 1970, vol. 3, p. 269). However, the reproduction of societal relations through production leads not only to their conservation, but also to their transformation, to illustrate which we need only recall Braudel's description of the Mediterranean landscape. We can therefore state:

> . . . reproduction appears to be the general form of permanence of the general conditions of production, which in the last analysis englobe the whole social structure, and therefore it is indeed essential that *it should be the form of their change and restructuration, too.*
>
> (ibid., p. 250, my emphasis)

With this determination, reproduction is understood as a non-identical extended reproduction in which the original condition cannot be simply restored, but rather is *developed*; this conceptually important step taken by Marx beyond both the physiocrats and Adam Smith has to this day failed to receive the attention it deserves.

Societal production is always also the reproduction of the conditions of production; the conditions of reproduction, as a relationship, at the same time also determine the conditions of production.

> . . . at the same time they are the conditions which reproduction reproduces: in this sense the "first" process of production (in a determinate form) is *always-already* a process of reproduction. There is no "first" process of production for production as a concept. All the definitions concerning the production of things must therefore be transformed: in the production of the social relations, what appeared as the conditions of the first production really *determines identically all the other productions*.
>
> (ibid., p. 271, my emphasis)

The intention of such a reproduction-theoretical version of the relationship between reproduction and production in the labor process is to create a connection between societal space (the coexistence of the spatial compossible) and time (the sequence of the temporally compossible), in which spatial components dominate, inasmuch as they are what is meant by the reproductive dimension of the relations reproduced as a societal relationship in the labor process. However, if the factor production is assumed to be absolute (the productivist reduction upon which Fordism is based), then the following applies:

> . . . to take the expression [production – M.W.] literally is precisely to reproduce the *appearance* which makes the production process an isolated act enclosed in the determinations of the *preceding* and the *succeeding*. An isolated act, insofar as its only connections with the other acts of production are supported by the structure of linear temporal continuity in which there *can be no* interruption (whereas in the conceptual analysis of reproduction, these connections are, as we have seen, supported by the structure of a *space*). Only the "production of things" can be thought as an activity of this kind – it already almost contains the concept of it in its determination of the "raw" material and the "finished" product; but the "production of the social relations" is far rather a production of things and individuals *by the social relations*, a production in which the individuals are defined so as to produce and the things so as to be produced in a specific form by the social relations.
>
> (ibid., p. 271)[14]

The reproduced societal relationship encompasses not only human beings as the subjects of the labor process, but also "natural conditions," inasmuch as aspects of labor are integrated into a societal relationship, for example in the form of a – possibly new – means or objects of work. Such an integration must be conceptually more precisely defined in the reconstruction of such an integrative process, as the transfer of the possibility of activity resulting from the current relationship of reproduction to production, and/or structure to structuration, to the reality of societal relations. "Favorable natural conditions alone, give us only the possibility, never the reality, of surplus labor, nor, consequently, of surplus value and a surplus-product" (Marx 1992, p. 253).

Marx therefore saw clearly that it was not a "bountiful nature," capable of providing people with food more or less without labor, that gave them opportunities for development, but rather a differentiated nature, the differentiation of which could in turn only be understood as a result of the achievements of differentiation realized by people in the context of labor processes.

> It is not the mere fertility of the soil, but the differentiation of the soil, the variety of its natural products, the changes of the seasons, which form the physical basis for the social division of labor, and which, by changes in the natural surroundings, spur man on to the multiplication of his wants, his capabilities, his means and modes of labor. It is the necessity of bringing a natural force under the control of society, of economizing, of appropriating or subduing it on a large scale by the work of man's hand, that first plays the decisive part in the history of industry.
>
> (ibid.)

It should always be noted in this respect that Marx's statements regarding nature referred to possibilities which can only by inference, i.e. after integration into a societal context of reproduction, be discussed coherently as possibilities within nature.

Lothar Kühne has provided a systematic continuation of such considerations, which Marx always only raised *en passant*.

> The spatial environment as the fundamental aspect of material conditions of life is not provided to human beings by nature in and of itself, but rather in the context of a societal relationship objectified in nature. It is not only the foundation and the passive transmission of the societal mode of living of human beings, but rather an essential factor in their formation. In the societally relevant structures of the environment passed down to us, structures of societal modes of living are ingrained and hence solidified. Although incorporated in practice by societal interests, the environment and its motion appears to naïve perception to be determined more by natural-historical than socio-historical contexts.
>
> (Kühne 1985, p. 9)[15]

He attempts to unfold these thoughts through comparative considerations regarding the different natural-spatial/landscape-related integration processes pertaining in a village and in the city. His guiding concept is:

> In the landscape, an individual is not only connected with a certain community, by way of a house, which crowns the landscape, he or she also has, in

that landscape, the incipient spatial form of a community with humankind, because the landscape may *be* by means of the house, but is fundamentally nature, earth.

(ibid., pp. 39–40)[16]

Thus, a link between the natural and the societal, similar to that between the object and the means of work in the labor process, takes place: here too, what is at issue is the transformation of potentials in nature into realized shapes by people in their societal context.

What causes these natural conditions to become elements of the landscape is not simply the presence of people, but rather their mode of living, their practical and esthetic horizons, and the substance of their fulfillment. Only the practical and esthetic sorting of terrestrial space by people brings forth the landscape. The link by means of which the human being living in nature realizes the landscape, is the building, the structure. Nature, architecture, the human being – these are the constituent of elements of the landscape. Their harmonization as a landscape is not yet provided merely by their existence.

(ibid., p. 41)[17]

If in the conceptual analysis of the labor process the means of work assumes the position of mediation, then it is the building, and architecture, which assume that role in an analysis of the landscape. "Architecture combines nature, and technological, practical and artistic objectivity together. . . . Architecture is the shaping of the spatial conditions of the life of people" (ibid., p. 88).[18] And this shaping of the spatial conditions of life of people by people is of course historically variable, understood not only in terms of horizontal variation, but also as the development of landscapes by shaping them.

The landscape is always historical space which has come into being, but is only real for individuals by means of their own coming into being. They must develop their own wealth in order to appropriate the wealth which has become landscape; they come upon no boundaries which direct them back into their own space, for they can only form the boundaries of their space as landscape by transcending them, by unfolding their individuality as world-historical universality.

(ibid., p. 42; emphasis added)[19]

I believe that the concept of landscape, which is precisely not to be understood as a pre-existing space in which human beings live and work, but rather as a structure created through activity and reproduced through activity, can reveal why it may have appeared that the relationship between nature and society was seemingly ignored in the disciplinary constitutional process of modern social science. I would like to present the following thoughts as a hypothesis which will undeniably require further and more precise verification; here, it is particularly a comparative reconstruction of the conceptual and disciplinary genesis of ecology, social geography, and the study of history that would seem to be most urgently needed (cf. Werlen 2000; Eisel 1980; Trepl 1985).

The landscape begins to be addressed in writing and in pictures during the late Middle Ages, starting in the thirteenth century; especially art historians agree that this is the case (cf. Schneider 1999; Bätschmann 1989). If we now compare depictions of the landscape with depictions of gardens, they both certainly share the common feature of addressing the creative achievements of people. However, they differ fundamentally in that pictures of gardens have as their central emphasis the difference between the garden on the one hand and "wild" nature on the other, the latter not having been structured by people; it is separated from the garden by a wall. Hence, the garden represents a closed entity separated off from these surroundings, so that any distributions which may occur within it do not transcend its boundaries into the realm of the unstructured, the free. Pictures of landscapes, by contrast, imagine, by way of delimitation between the worked and shaped landscape on the one hand and the unworked, naturally shaped nature (which can, however, yet be shaped by people) on the other, a limitlessness, a lack of enclosure, and an openness. Patterns and sequences of fields and villages extend to the horizon and beyond, meaning that the delimitation of shaped and unshaped nature can also be symbolically charged very differently, e.g. either as a space yet to be shaped, or, esthetically, as "exalted," as the experience of untouched nature.

The function of the boundary in landscape pictures is thus also fundamentally different from the enclosure of a garden: it can and is constantly being transgressed and redefined by means of exchange, so that, through cross-border exchange, an ever newly shaped realm of circulation is obtained. The dichotomous differentiation of closed gardens and open landscapes refers to at least two further dichotomous juxtapositions, for which the attributes "closed" and "open" are constituent: on the one hand, the village and the community (*Gemeinschaft*) as closed entities; on the other, the city and society (*Gesellschaft*) as open entities, which – as Marx and Engels emphasized in the *Communist Manifesto* – burst all existing boundaries. One motif, for instance, which is used again and again in various epochs of landscape depiction, is the bridge. Martin Warnke explains:

> Evidently, in landscape painting, motifs the objective meetings of which had increasingly gained in political importance, become prominent: Roads and paths as media of conquest, of trade, and of connecting and exploring activity appear as striking motifs before the eye of the landscape painter.
>
> (Warnke 1992, p. 20)

From a reproduction-theoretical point of view, closed entities such as the garden, the village or the community can be described as identical-extended re-production entities, with the "extension" referring to forms of provision (for times of need) and/or (unproductive) accumulation of treasure; the production must/should preserve the initially existing conditions of production. Lewis Mumford describes the closed world of the village as follows:

> Before water transport was well developed, each village was, in effect, a world in itself: cut off as much by sleepy self-absorption and narcissism, perhaps, as by mere physical barriers. Even under primitive conditions, that conformity was never absolute, that efficiency never complete, those limitations never unbreakable. One might have to go elsewhere to fetch a tool or "capture" a bride. Yet the villagers' ideal remained that pictured much later by Lao-Tse: "to delight in their food, to be proud of their clothes, to be content with their home, to rejoice in their customs." Then "they might be in sight of a neighboring village, within hearing of the cocks and dogs, yet grow old and die before they visited one another." Such villages might reproduce and multiply without any impulse to change their pattern of life: as long as nutrition and reproduction, the pleasures of the belly and the genitals, were the chief ends of life, Neolithic village culture met every requirement.
>
> (Mumford 1961/1989, pp. 18–19)[20]

By contrast, open entities, such as the landscape, the city, and society, can be described as *non-identically extendable* re-production entities, in which capital accumulation has the goal not only of obtaining the means for the conservation of the conditions of production, but rather the means for increased production activities which may be changed with respect to those hitherto prevailing, or may even be entirely new. Briefly and to the point, Mumford notes the fact that society (*Gesellschaft*), as opposed to community (*Gemeinschaft*), implies completely different relations with nature: ". . . the shaping of the earth [*and precisely not the shaping of a closed segment of space* – M.W.] was an integral part of the shaping of the city – and preceded it" (ibid., p. 17).[21]

Continuing these thoughts, two more essential aspects can be elucidated which have repeatedly proven central to the debate around ecology, the environment, and society. First of all, it will be necessary to reconstruct the significance which the *Gemeinschaft/Gesellschaft* discussion has had in the disciplinary justification context of social sciences for the issue of society's relationship to nature, particularly for Tönnies. I would simply like to point out that the foil before which Tönnies established this distinction consisted of the socio-theoretical efforts to comprehend the constitution of society by way of nature and its dynamics of development, particularly, of course, motivated by biological theories of evolution. Tönnies, Durkheim, and Weber had to push through their concepts against the programs of biological/evolutionist or organicistic theory as advanced by the social Darwinists, or such authors as Riehl, Schäffle, and Gumplowicz. Secondly, and in my view very importantly, the metaphorical horizon of the formation of the word "ecology" deserves examination. For the intention of the reference to a house provided by the word *oikos* means the village/community house, the closed nature of the reproductive entity referred to as "the house." The novel *Der Nachsommer*, by Adalbert Stifter, published in 1857, which appeared in English under the title *Indian Summer – A*

Tale, is a veritable gold mine of metaphors describing the idyllic house and garden enclosure which is threatened, in the conservative view, by the open entities of society, the city, and the landscape.[22] The two forces of mediation, the means of work and the landscape, which appear to only have been touched upon by way of example, should nonetheless have shown that the activity of human beings merges society and nature, in that the potentials of nature – discovered by way of the utility potentials of tools beyond their initial context of purpose – become forces of reproduction, and even the conditions of reproduction of society. And precisely because the means of work and the landscape are organs of mediation, they can, in their analysis of the conditions into which they are tied, unfold in either of two ways: on the one hand, with regard to their position in the societal reproduction process, which is what is meant by society's relationship with nature; translated into the terminology of Parsons, this refers to the relationship between the social system and the environment. And on the other, with regard to our term "nature"; this refers to the relationship of the reality of an element of nature separated out from its original context, which, prior to being thus separated, constituted a potential within nature, which has then been transformed into reality by people. *Note that this statement can only be made in the context of a reconstruction perspective*, in other words, when we speak of nature, we can also do so with reference to the means we use and reproduce, and that our concept of nature changes in accordance with the means at our disposal. Lothar Kühne attempted to grasp this with a dialectics of double determination of the mediating object.

> It is in this dialectic that the double determination of the object is based. The dependence of the object from itself, in other words, from the laws and properties which characterize it, and which are special with regard to the societal nature of people, and the dependence of the object on people, their essential power, the laws of their societal nature, determine the complex character of the shaping qualities of the object created by people. The fact that the interaction of technological, practical and esthetic formation determinants can result in a holistically and harmoniously, technologically, practically and esthetically functioning object, shows in a very special way that nature and human beings are really interlinked, and that the laws of nature, of society and of thought share a comprehensive aspect.
>
> (Kühne 1981, pp. 40–41)[23]

Thus, "landscape" proves to be a fabric materially structured by activity, and, in the reflection upon that activity and its results, as the symbolic entity, which is then in turn reproduced within that activity due to its symbolic representation, and changed in reproduction (which in turn leads to changes in the symbolic representation at the level of reflection). The further elucidation of these thoughts not only permits an expectation that the concept of nature can be redefined in a manner extending far beyond the classical subject–object conceptions associated with the philosophy of consciousness; the interface between societal activity, the symbolic representation of that activity and its products, the sciences and policy, can be defined more precisely, moving beyond a mere critique of ideology. We can thus juxtapose a conceptual and conservationist concept to the resignation-tinged perspective of a Martin Warnke without falling back into a crude natural-ism or a social constructivism which no longer sees any points of reference.

> The leveling human valuation of nature has erased her argumentative power and her independent authority. Shot through with alien substances and doomed to decline, she may still be able to evoke sympathy and spark rescue efforts, but she is no longer capable of any argumentative, legitimating sup-porting activity. The rich reservoir of motives and experience which guided activity, and which we have tried to archive here, has been exhausted.
>
> (Warnke 1992, p. 173)

The reflection upon the structuration and reproduction of relations which has emerged in activity, as well as the reflection upon symbolic representation of this activity, permit a precise determination as to whether only certain representa-tions of, in this case, society's relationship with nature *as tangible nature* have been exhausted with regard to their function as a guide to activity; and whether the definition of *relations* with nature as objective societal relations with nature leads – or can lead – not only to different, or even new, symbolic forms of repre-sentation, but rather, in unity with that, also to different, or even new, orienta-tions for activity.

Notes

1 "Alle Naturanlagen eines Geschöpfes sind bestimmt, sich einmal vollständig und zweckmäßig auszuwickeln. Bei allen Tieren bestätigt dieses die äußere sowohl, als innere oder zergliedernde, Beobachtung. Ein Organ, das nicht gebraucht werden soll, eine Anordnung, die ihren Zweck nicht erreicht, ist ein Widerspruch in der teleolo-gischen Naturlehre. Denn, wenn wir von jenem Grundsatze abgehen, so haben wir nicht mehr eine gesetzmäßige, sondern eine zwecklos spielende Natur; und das trostlose Ungefähr tritt an die Stelle des Leitfadens der Vernunft." (Kant, 1968 Bd. XI, p. 35)
  Translator's note: Idee zu einer allgemeinen Geschichte in weltbürgerlicher Absicht; this is the translation of the title in Wikipedia (cf. Engl. and Ger. versions); another trans-lation, that of the online text referenced next, translates the title as ". . . from a cos-mopolitan point of view." The first is better; indeed, "intent" would be best. Kant's term *"weltbürgerlich,"* rendered here as "cosmopolitan," means literally "of the world citizenry."
2 In terms of economic and social theory, as indicated, the transition from cyclical and preservation models to development concepts can be found with such physiocrats as Quesnay and Turgot; cf. Turgot 1990. The physiographic model is based on the delimi-tation of natural cycles and historical developments. For the resiliency of the cyclical model in natural history, see Gould 1988.
3 For the context of this terminological differentiation, see König 1969 and 1994. See also Gutmann & Weingarten 2001.
4 See too the programmatic essays by Böhme 1999 and Görg 1999.
5 See Wehling 1992. In a critical continuation of Adorno, Jürgen Ritsert has attempted to define the concept of "nature" more precisely; see Ritsert 1996. However, the fun-damental problems of Adorno's approach seem to me not to have really been resolved.

For this, a systematic discussion of Schmidt 1971 would be necessary; for approaches in this direction, see Ruben 1969; 1978; 1995.

6 See also Görg 2003.

7 It would be very worthwhile to precisely reconstruct how the concept of the extinction of species, and, connected with it, the understanding of the finality of resources, has been established; cf. as the first efforts in this direction Sieferle 1989 and 1990. The fact that the problem of extinction has in no sense been satisfactorily solved from a bio-scientific point of view, is shown by such works as those of Gould 1991, Eldredge 1994, or Stanley 1988. At least during its initial phase, the Fordist production system was unimpressed by the biological debate regarding the possibility of the extinction of species, and clung to the idea of the unlimited availability of resources.

8 This should not be understood in a utilitarian manner, as if we might intervene into our surroundings freely and exclusively in accordance with our purposes. Although such an understanding may be factually true, whether and to what extent such a formulation would be to our "benefit" could only be determined by the reproducibility of the forms resulting from our activity, which can only succeed if the formulation undertaken for our purposes also and at the same time corresponds to an ability to create on the part of the natural surroundings.

9 Taking his thoughts further, Braudel takes us on to the symbolic level of the conceptualization of nature: "Both in terms of its landscape and of its human physiognomy, the picture of the Mediterranean is that of a world composed of dissimilar elements, which are only brought together into a coherent picture in our imagination, as in a system in which differentiated elements are first of all mixed together and then woven into an original unity." And then he poses the central question: "However, how is this obvious unity, which is the essential aspect of Mediterranean culture, to be explained?" (Braudel et al. 1990, pp. 9–10).

10 It is from the interaction of the hand and the tool as the material dimension of the struggle for survival on the one hand, and the symbolic level of the view of the world and/or of nature as the environment dominated by the eye, on the other, that, in Spengler's view, the natural peculiarity of "man, the beast of prey" emerges: humans control the world, their surroundings, theoretically by means of the eye, and practically by means of the hand. And both capabilities, as well as the structures which support these capabilities, emerged in a single step, a catastrophe (here, Spengler refers to de Vries's mutation theory).

Certainly, any people, any race, can dominate the environment with this combination of "the thinking hand and the thinking eye," and overcome boundaries, as when it proves, in a struggle against another people or race, to be the stronger. However, it will not thus have overcome the natural limits placed upon it, the compulsion to adapt imposed by nature; on the contrary: "This is the beginning of man's *tragedy* – for Nature is the stronger of the two. Man remains dependent on her, for in spite of everything she embraces him, like all else, within herself. All the great Cultures are *defeats*. Whole races remain, inwardly destroyed and broken, fallen into barrenness and spiritual decay, as corpses on the field. The fight against Nature is hopeless and yet – it will be fought out to the bitter end." Nonetheless, in spite of the fact that humankind has become a creator by means of the eye and the hand, it remains, as a creature of nature, subjected to nature (all quotes from Spengler 1932).

11 The Darwinist – as opposed to Darwinian! – concept of adjustment and adaptation necessarily implies the concept of space as a given structure of order, within which living things exhibit certain behavior. A comparison of this concept with the mechanistic understanding of classical mechanics would be important and elucidating here.

12 The interdisciplinary historical research existing there, in which various social sciences and disciplines, including geography, climate research, and animal and plant breeding have been integrated, has, to my knowledge, never yet been methodologically investigated.

13 The significance of the work of Luhmann and Giddens, among others, is based on this recognition. Both recognized the systematic weakness of the intentionalistic conception of activity, and attempted to develop alternative proposals – but both failed, in that they were unsuccessful in formulating any adequate concept of the means of work, or else passed the issue over entirely. Considerations which may be used comparatively/reconstructively in order to provide conceptual clarification for this complex of issues include those of Norbert Elias on "figuration," of Pierre Bourdieu on "habitus," and also socio-phenomenological works on the concept of structure and type formation.

14 The question of whether Althusser and Balibar have, as a mirror image of productivism, made the aspect of reproduction independent with respect to production, and have hence – in spite of criticism in that respect from Liepietz on the one hand and Giddens on the other – rendered themselves unable to conceive of the change, and possibly the development, of societal relations, should be re-examined closely.

15 "Die räumliche Umwelt als das grundlegende Moment der materiellen Lebensbedingungen ist für die Menschen nicht einfach durch die Natur an sich gesetzt, sondern in Natur objektiviertes gesellschaftliches Verhältnis. Sie ist nicht nur die Grundlage und die passive Vermittlung der gesellschaftlichen Lebensweise der Menschen, sondern ein wesentlicher Faktor ihrer Formierung. In den uns überkommenen gesellschaftlich relevanten Strukturen der Umwelt sind Strukturen gesellschaftlicher Lebensweise eingeprägt und so verfestigt. Obgleich durch gesellschaftliche Interessen in der Praxis gesetzt, erscheint dem naiven Auffassen die Umwelt und ihre Bewegung eher durch einen natur- als durch einen sozialgeschichtlichen Zusammenhang bestimmt" (Kühne 1985, p. 9).

16 "In der Landschaft ist das Individuum nicht nur mit einer bestimmten Gemeinschaft zusammengeschlossen, durch das Haus, das die Landschaft krönt, es hat in der Landschaft auch die einsetzende räumliche Form seines Zusammenschlusses mit der Menschheit, weil die Landschaft wohl durch das Haus ist, aber in ihrem Grunde Natur, Erde" (Kühne 1985, pp. 39–40).

17 "Was diese natürlichen Bedingungen zu Elementen der Landschaft werden lässt, ist nicht einfach die Anwesenheit von Menschen, sondern deren Lebensweise, ihr praktischer und ästhetischer Horizont und die Inhalte seiner Erfüllung. Erst die praktische und ästhetische Sonderung von Erdraum durch Menschen gebiert die Landschaft. Das Mittelglied, durch welches der in der Natur lebende Mensch Landschaft verwirklicht, ist das Bauwerk. Natur, Architektur, Mensch – das sind die konstitutiven Elemente der Landschaft. Ihr Zusammenstimmen als Landschaft ist durch ihr Dasein noch nicht gewährt" (Kühne 1985, p. 41).

18 "Die Architektur schließt Natur, technische, praktische und künstlerische Gegenständlichkeit räumlich zusammen. (. . .) Architektur ist Gestaltung räumlicher Lebensbedingungen der Menschen" (Kühne 1981, p. 88).

19 "*Landschaft ist stets geschichtlich gewordener Raum*, aber für das Individuum nur durch sein eigenes Werden wirklich. Es muss den eigenen Reichtum herausarbeiten, um den Landschaft gewordenen Reichtum sich anzueignen, es findet keine Grenze, die es in den eigenen Raum zurückweist, weil es die Grenze seines Raumes als Landschaft nur durch sein Übergehen, durch die Entfaltung seiner Individualität als welthistorische Universalität bilden kann" (Kühne 1985, p. 42; emphasis added).

20 On the reproductive stability of societies, see also Crone 1993. Moreover, on these themes, see Henri Lefébvre (1991). Cf. the investigations by Wittfogel (1931) on "hydraulic societies." There, the problem of stability/instability of social organizational forms is linked to the conditions of the maintenance of a specific societal relationship to nature: the water supply.

21 On "the city" from the aspect of reproduction theory, see too, Lefébvre 1974; 1990.

22 From a more conservative philosophical view, see Bollnow 1994. Regarding open and close metaphors in the spatial context, see also Bachelard 1958.

23 "In dieser Dialektik gründet sich die doppelte Determination des Gegenstandes. Die Abhängigkeit des Gegenstandes von sich selbst, also von den ihn charakterisierenden Gesetzen und Eigenschaften, die gegenüber denen der Gesellschaftlichkeit des Menschen besondere sind, und die Abhängigkeit des Gegenstandes vom Menschen, seinen Wesenskräften, den Gesetzen seiner Gesellschaftlichkeit, bedingen den komplexen Charakter der Gestaltqualitäten der von den Menschen geschaffenen Gegenstände. Die Tatsache, dass das Zusammenwirken technischer, praktischer und ästhetischer Gestaltungsdeterminanten zu einem ganzheitlichen und harmonischen, technisch, praktisch und ästhetisch funktionierenden Gegenstand führen kann, zeigt auf besondere Weise, daß Natur und Mensch real zusammenhängen und den Gesetzen der Natur, der Gesellschaft und des Denkens ein sie zusammenfassendes Moment eigen ist" (Kühne 1981, pp. 40–41).

Bibliography

(All online sources accessed Oct. 20, 2012)

Althusser, Louis, Etienne Balibar (1970). *Reading Capital.* 3 vol. London: NLB. (Republ. 1997 by Verso, London). Accessed via: www.marx2mao.com/Other/RC68NB.html

Bachelard, Gaston (1958). *The Poetics of Space.* Boston: Beacon Press.

Bätschmann, Oskar. (1989). *Entfernung der Natur. Landschaftsmalerei 1750–1920.* Cologne: Dumont.

Baumann, Claus (2011). *Was tun wir, wenn wir arbeiten?* Stuttgart: Schmetterling Verlag.

Beck, Ulrich (1986). *Risikogesellschaft.* Frankfurt: Suhrkamp.

Benjamin, Walter (2009). *One-Way Street and Other Writings.* New York/London: Penguin Classics.

Böhme, Gernot (1999). Kritische Theorie der Natur. *Zeitschrift für Kritische Theorie* 9, 59–71.

Bollnow, Otto F. (1994). *Mensch und Raum.* Stuttgart/Berlin/Cologne: Kohlhammer.

Braudel, Fernand, Georges Duby, Maurice Aymard (1990). *Die Welt des Mittelmeers. Zur Geschichte und Geographie kultureller Lebensformen.* Frankfurt: Fischer (German translation of *La Méditerranée. Arts et métiers graphiques,* 1977–1978).

Crone, Patricia (2003). *Pre-Industrial Societies: Anatomy of the Pre-Modern World.* Chino Valley, AZ: One World.

Diamond, Jared (1999). *The Wealth and Poverty of Nations: Why Some Are So Rich and Some So Poor.* New York: Norton & Co.

Diamond, Jared (2005). *Collapse: How Societies Choose to Fail or Succeed.* New York: Penguin Books.

Eisel, Ulrich (1980). *Die Entwicklung der Anthropogeographie von einer "Raumwissenschaft" zur Gesellschaftswissenschaft.* Kassel: Gesamthochschul-Bibliothek.

Eisel, Ulrich (2009). *Landschaft und Gesellschaft.* Münster: Westfälisches Dampfboot.

Eldredge, Niels (1994). *Wendezeiten des Lebens.* Heidelberg/Berlin/Oxford: Spektrum.

Fischer-Kowalski, Marina et al. (1997). *Gesellschaftlicher Stoffwechsel und Kolonisierung von Natur.* Amsterdam: Fakultas.

Francé, Raoul H. (1982). *Die Entdeckung der Heimat.* Asendorf: Mut. (Orig. 1923)

Friedrichs, Karl (1937). *Ökologie als Wissenschaft von der Natur oder Biologische Raumforschung.* Leipzig: Barth.

Gäbler, Karsten (2011). *Das ökologische Feld. Ein sozialgeographischer Analyserahmen ökologischer Praxis in Zeiten des Klimawandels.* Dissertation, University of Jena, Germany.

Görg, Christoph (1999). Kritik der Naturbeherrschung. *Zeitschrift für Kritische Theorie* 9, 73–87.

Görg, Christoph (2003). *Regulation der Naturverhältnisse. Zu einer kritischen Theorie der ökologischen Krise*. Münster: Westfälisches Dampfboot.

Görg, Christoph, Christine Hertler, Engelbert Schramm, Michael Weingarten (eds.) (1999). *Zugänge zur Biodiversität*. Marburg: Metropolis.

Gould, Stephen J. (1988). *Time's Arrow, Time's Cycle: Myth and Metaphor in the Discovery of Geological Time*. Cambridge, MA: Harvard University Press.

Gould, Stephen J. (1991). *Wonderful Life: The Burgess Shale and the Nature of History*. New York: Norton & Co.

Gutmann, Mathias (1998). Methodologische und normative Aspekte der Umweltbewertung – Elemente einer rationalen Ökologie. In: W. Theobald (ed.). *Integrierte Umweltbewertung. Theorie und Beispiele aus der Praxis*. Berlin: Springer, 65–92.

Gutmann, Mathias (1999). Kultur und Vermittlung. Systematische Überlegungen zu den Vermittlungsformen von Werkzeug und Sprache. In: P. Janich (ed.). *Wechselwirkungen*. Würzburg: Verlag Königshausen und Neumann, 143–168.

Gutmann, Mathias, Michael Weingarten (2001). Die Bedeutung von Metaphern für die biologische Theorienbildung. *Deutsche Zeitschrift für Philosophie*, no. 4, 549–566.

Hansjürgens, Bernd and Gertrude Lübbe-Wolff (eds.) (2000). *Symbolische Umweltpolitik*. Frankfurt: Suhrkamp.

Harvey, David (2006). *Spaces of Global Capitalism: A Theory of Uneven Geographical Development*. London: Verso.

Herder, Johann G. (1911). *Kulturphilosophie*. Leipzig: Insel Verlag.

Herder, Johann G. (1966). *Ideen zur Philosophie der Geschichte der Menschheit*. 2 vols. Berlin/Weimar: Aufbau-Verlag. (Orig. 1784–1791)

Herder, Johann G. (2004). *Another Philosophy of History and Selected Political Writings*. Ed. by Ioannis D. Evrigenis & Daniel Pellerin. Indianapolis: Hackett Pub.

Humboldt, Alexander von (2010). *Essay on the Geography of Plants*. University of Chicago Press.

Jahn, Thomas, Peter Wehling (1991). *Ökologie von rechts*. Frankfurt: Campus.

Janich, Peter, Michael Weingarten (1999). *Wissenschaftstheorie der Biologie*. Munich: UTB.

Kant, Immanuel (1968). *Works*. 12 vols. (in German). Ed. by W. Weischedel. Frankfurt: Insel. For the English translation see: http://www.marxists.org/reference/subject/ethics/kant/universal-history.htm.

Kant, Immanuel (1784). *Universal History from a Cosmopolitan Point of View*. Accessed via: www.marxists.org/reference/subject/ethics/kant/universal-history.htm

König, Josef (1969). *Sein und Denken*. Tübingen: Niemeyer.

König, Josef (1994). *Der logische Unterschied theoretischer und praktischer Sätze und seine philosophische Bedeutung*. Freiburg/Munich: Alber.

Kühne, Lothar (1981). *Gegenstand und Raum*. Dresden: Fundus.

Kühne, Lothar (1985). *Haus und Landschaft*. Dresden: Fundus.

Latour, Bruno (1998). Über technische Vermittlung. In: W. Rammert (ed.). *Technik und Sozialtheorie*. Frankfurt: Campus, 29–81.

Latour, Bruno (2005). *Von der Realpolitik zur Dingpolitik*. Berlin: Merve.

Latour, Bruno (2010). *Eine neue Soziologie für eine neue Gesellschaft*. Frankfurt: Suhrkamp.

Lefèbvre, Henri (1970). *La révolution urbaine*. Paris: Gallimard.

Lefèbvre, Henri (1976). *The Survival of Capitalism*. London: Allison and Busby.

Lefèbvre, Henri (1991). *Production of Space*. New York: Wiley.

Luhmann, Niklas (1989). *Ecological Communication*. Cambridge: Polity Press.

Luhmann, Niklas (1997). *Die Gesellschaft der Gesellschaft*. Frankfurt: Suhrkamp.

Marx, Karl (1992). *Capital*. London/New York: Penguin Classics. (Online edition 2008, orig. by Progress Publishers, Moscow). Accessed via: http://libcom.org/files/Capital-Volume-I.pdf

Mittelstraß, Jürgen (2001). *Wissen und Grenzen*. Frankfurt: Suhrkamp.

Müller, Jan (2010). *Arbeiten, Handeln, Wissen: Tätigkeitstheoretische Untersuchungen zu einem dialektischen Arbeitsbegriff*. Dissertation, University of Stuttgart, Germany.

Mumford, Lewis (1961/1989). *The City in History*. San Diego/New York/London: Harcourt.

Meusburger, Peter (ed.) (1999). *Handlungszentrierte Sozialgeographie*. Stuttgart: Steiner.

Ritsert, Jürgen (1996). *Ästhetische Theorie als Gesellschaftskritik*. Social science study texts, vol. 4. 2nd revised edition. Frankfurt: Universitätsdruck.

Rohbeck, Johannes (1990). Turgot als Geschichtsphilosoph. In: A.R.J. Turgot. *Über die Fortschritte des menschlichen Geistes*. Frankfurt: Suhrkamp, 7–87.

Ruben, Peter (1969). Problem und Begriff der Naturdialektik. In: A. Griese, H. Laitko (eds.). *Weltanschauung und Methode*. Berlin: Akademie.

Ruben, Peter (1978). *Dialektik und Arbeit der Philosophie*. Cologne: Pahl-Rugenstein.

Ruben, Peter (1995). *Widerspruch und Naturdialektik*. Preprint of the Max Planck Institute for the History of Science, No. 20. Berlin.

Schmidt, Alfred (1971). *Der Begriff der Natur in der Lehre von Marx*. Frankfurt: Europäische Verlagsanstalt.

Schneider, Norbert (1999). *Geschichte der Landschaftsmalerei*. Darmstadt: Wissenschaftliche Buchgesellschaft.

Sieferle, Rolf P. (1989). *Die Krise der menschlichen Natur*. Frankfurt: Suhrkamp.

Sieferle, Rolf P. (1990). *Bevölkerungswachstum und Naturhaushalt*. Frankfurt: Suhrkamp.

Spengler, Oswald (1931). *Man and Technics: A Contribution to a Philosophy of Life*. New York: Alfred Knopf. Accessed via (page nos. refer to the online version and do not correspond to the original): http://archive.org/details/ManTechnics-AContributionToAPhilosophyOfLife193253

Stanley, Steven M. (1986) *Earth and Life through time*. New York: Freeman.

Stanley, Steven M. (1988). *Krisen der Evolution*. Heidelberg: Spektrum.

Tenschert, Gerhard (1982). Forscher, Warner und Prophet. Über Raoul H. Francé und sein Werk. In: R. H. Francé. *Die Entdeckung der Heimat*. Asendorf: Mut.

Trepl, Ludwig (1985). *Geschichte der Ökologie*. Frankfurt: Athenäum.

Turgot, Anne Robert Jacques (1990). *Über die Fortschritte des menschlichen Geistes*. Frankfurt.

Wahsner, Renate (1981). *Das Aktive und das Passive*. Berlin: VWB.

Warnke, Martin (1992). *Politische Landschaft. Zur Kunstgeschichte der Natur*. Munich: Hanser.

Wehling, Peter (1992). *Die Moderne als Sozialmythos*. Frankfurt/New York: Campus.

Weingarten, Michael (1998). *Wissenschaftstheorie als Wissenschaftskritik*. Bonn: Pahl-Rugenstein.

Weingarten, Michael (1999). Wahrnehmen und Erfahren. Zum Verhältnis von Philosophie des Leibes und Handlungstheorie. In: P. Janich (ed.). *Wechselwirkungen*. Würzburg: Verlag Königshausen und Neumann, 169–186.

Weingarten, Michael (2000). *Entwicklung und Innovation*. Graue Reihe, vol. 21. Bad Neuenahr: Europäische Akademie.

Weingarten, Michael (ed.) (2005a). *Strukturierung von Raum und Landschaft*. Münster: Westfälisches Dampfboot.

Weingarten, Michael (2005b). Qualitative Modellierungen und quantitative Modelle des Zusammenhangs von Bevölkerungswissenschaft und Versorgungssystemen. In:

D. Hummel, et al. (eds.). *Bevölkerungsdynamik und Versorgungssysteme – Modelle für Wechselwirkungen*. Demons working paper 5. Frankfurt: Institute for Social-Ecological Research, 9–45.

Werlen, Benno (1997). *Globalisierung, Region und Regionalisierung. Sozialgeographie alltäglicher Regionalisierungen*, vol. 2. Stuttgart: Steiner.

Werlen, Benno (2000). *Sozialgeographie*. Bern/Stuttgart/Vienna: UTB.

Werlen, Benno (2010a). *Gesellschaftliche Räumlichkeit 1: Orte der Geographie*. Stuttgart: Steiner.

Werlen, Benno (2010b). *Gesellschaftliche Räumlichkeit 2: Konstruktion geographischer Wirklichkeiten*. Stuttgart: Steiner.

Wilson, Edward O. (1998). *Consilience: The Unity of Knowledge*. New York: Vintage.

Wittfogel, Karl August (1931), *Wirtschaft und Gesellschaft Chinas*. Leipzig: C.L. Hirschfeld.

12 The missing aspect of culture in sustainability concepts

Oliver Parodi

Introduction

Non-sustainability, sustainability and the debates and efforts for sustainable development are, like the barriers to their implementation, highly cultural phenomena. However, this fact has received too little elucidation and reflection in the academic discourse: that is the initial diagnosis of this article, meant more as input and invitation to further reflection than as a fully coherent hypothesis. An increased incorporation of cultural-scientific and cultural-theoretical considerations into the theories and concepts of sustainable development would provide a more comprehensive view, and move into the focus of discussion important issues which have hitherto been too little examined. Hence, it would provide a contribution to the success of sustainable development, while also lending it a new quality.

The cultural aspects of "sustainability"

Sustainability and sustainable development, which, by way of emphasizing the processual nature of the terms, I will use synonymously, have long since ceased to be merely a matter of concern for a small circle in the academic community, a political subculture or an elite; rather, they have diffused worldwide, into many areas of everyday life. Concern for, and discussion of, sustainability have become normal in many areas – indeed, a cultural asset. Let me emphasize that this is true for the term, but not necessarily for "sustainability" in the strict and substantively significant sense that has taken root in the scientific/ethical and societal debates as a result of the Brundtland goals (WCED 1987). Hence, we are still a long way from a global, institutionalized culture of sustainability rooted in everyday life.

The breadth which the debates around sustainability have assumed, and the wide variety of aspects of life in which they have been implemented and contextualized, can be seen from the following compilation:

"Sustainability" is:

- A policy strategy at the global, national and local levels
- A model for a form of globalization

- A new or rediscovered alternative economic paradigm[1]
- A corporate strategy, a label and a product-marketing gimmick
- An ethical "theory of everything"
- An implicit cultural and societal critique – as it were, a "Critical Theory 2.0"
- A secular expression and field of activity for the world's religions
- A theory and an interdisciplinary scientifically based concept
- A scientific paradigm (a transdisciplinary paradigm which guides the process of cognition and the shaping of knowledge).

At least as a concept and an idea, sustainability has become a solidly established cultural phenomenon in the political, economic, academic and everyday spheres of many different cultures.

However, cultural aspects and the cultural perspective in my view continue to be neglected in theoretical/scientific debates over sustainability, or, to put it more positively: a thoroughgoing and comprehensive addressing of the cultural perspective in scientific theories and concepts regarding sustainability would open up better – more forceful, more accurate – theories, and other, further-reaching and better, options for implementation, as well as new qualities for sustainable development.

Certainly, "culture" has over the past forty years repeatedly and increasingly been addressed as a concept, a perspective and a factor in the numerous debates around sustainability. A succinct chronology, albeit largely limited to the English-language realm, is provided by Duxbury and Gillette (2007, pp. 20–22). However, "culture" has remained attached to specific contexts, particularly:

- The local implementation and recognition of regional difference: culture is an important factor for action and activation, and for the development of small collectives (e.g. communities, cities), e.g. in the context of the Agenda 21 for Culture (cf. Culture 21, 2011)
- Art: as a bridge to the arts and to the cultural elite, and for the incorporation of the arts as a transformative force for sustainable development (cf. Kurt 2002; Agenda Transfer 2003)
- Education: the cultural concept also comes into focus by way of the concept of education – education for sustainable development, or sustainable development as an educational process (e.g. Holz/Stoltenberg 2011; Stoltenberg 2010)
- Lifestyles and sustainable consumption: culture is involved here in the form of norms and of orientation for action[2] (e.g. Scherhorn 2003).

Even if real, separate scientific discourses have developed around particular issues, and theory formation has to a limited degree occurred in such cases, these thematic approaches to culture have nonetheless largely remained isolated from one another. Possibly due to a significant degree to the heterogeneity of the issues, no synthesis or independent cultural dimension of sustainability has so far succeeded in being broadly established. It has not, at any rate, attained a depth and breadth in the international sustainability debate comparable, for example, to that of the ecological or economic dimensions.

But the above points nonetheless have in common the fact that culture is primarily seen as a factor, a condition or a means for achieving sustainable development. Culture has been functionalized, which in some contexts can be both inadequate and dangerous.[3] Certainly, there are also approaches which go further and posit culture as the goal and core of sustainable development, as that which would characterize a successfully achieved sustainability. In the German-language area, such approaches have been raised, e.g. by Krainer/Trattnigg 2007, DUK 2007, Grober 2010, and Parodi et al. 2010, although here too, the question of their reception and connectability remains open.

In spite of all these attempts, it is in my view still possible to identify a massive lack of cultural-theoretical and cultural-scientific component in the conceptual debate around sustainability. In addressing this issue, I would like to focus in the following on the German-language debate. In that context, I would like to elucidate and concretize this paucity of cultural reference in existing sustainability theories and concepts by way of four different poorly elucidated aspects of "culture," which can all be subsumed under a modern, synthesized cultural context:

1   A lack of interculturality and transculturality in sustainability considerations; a lack of sensitivity for other cultures, and for one's own.

2   Sustainability is primarily handled as a collective interest, which only addresses the individual – for instance the individual sphere – in certain contexts. Most importantly, the linkage between the individual and collective spheres has been neglected in sustainability debates and concepts.

3   Often, sustainability is formulated as an ethical, but not as an esthetic concept and project. Missing is any theory of the esthetics of sustainability, and of practice with reference to esthetic practitioners.

4   The neglect of the non-material aspect of sustainability: sustainability as a materialistically grounded concept thus ignores a large and effective segment of the reality of human life, particularly in cultural contexts beyond the modern/Western realm.

All of these deficits have ultimately made the implementation of sustainable developments more difficult. At the same time, contemporary cultural theory is able to consistently incorporate all these various facets in its overall perspective. On the other hand, the insufficiencies diagnosed here are not absolute. The issues raised certainly do crop up in the debate around sustainability; in my view however, in a manner both too little and too isolated.

The conception of culture

Since "culture" is both a very broad and a somewhat soft term, the understanding of the term used here must first of all be defined and elucidated. Basically, I am using the theory of culture of Hansen (2000; 2011), which represents the compilation and synthesis of the familiar cultural theories of the past two centuries (cf. also Hauser/Banse 2010).

The first key point to its use in the context of sustainable development is that "culture" is no longer to be defined as delimited from "nature," but is rather is to be described by means of the simultaneous presence of the fundamental cultural elements, *collectivity, communication* and *convention*. Thus, culture can refer to any event or phenomenon which is not exclusively caused by nature, and which has emerged from the conditions of convention, communication and collectivity.[4]

Culture, as used herein, does not mean a delimitation from other collectives, nor does it refer to the mode of communication or the conventions of, say, Austrians or Chinese. It also does not refer to that realm of "high culture" which encompasses the arts, theater, film etc., but rather generally, and much more basically, culture is something which every established collective has; it is that element of cohesion which also involves ourselves and with which our everyday life is imbued – usually unnoticed.

The term "convention" refers to the similar behavior of the members of a collective which is neither coincidental nor necessary for immediate survival. Conventions exist in all areas of human life: in behavior, in thought, in action, in communication and even in feelings. Culture is kept alive by means of living according to conventions. Institutions thus guarantee the cohesion and stability of a community. Cultural transformation occurs in the breaking up and rebuilding of conventions.

Communication has a key position in the implementation of culture. It is always tied to a collective, and only through that collective can cultural community be created at all. In the cultural context, the signs bear a number of layers of a significance which is conveyed, often subliminally or suggestively. Even technical artifacts or natural objects may function as such signs.

Culture can only occur within a collective, more precisely: in the interaction between the collective and the individual, with the "collective" inconceivable without the "individual," and vice versa. "The relationship between the individual on the one hand and culture, or the collective, on the other is hence a dialectical one" (Hansen 2000, p. 158).

The individuals form the collective, which in turn "forms" those individuals, who obtain their identities in reaction to collective stipulations, and these identities in turn stock the collective arsenal of interpretations through their deviation from those stipulations. The size, the binding commonality, and the resulting cultural characteristics of such collectives may of course be very different: cultures and culturally specific factors can be found in nations, in companies, in associations etc.

Box 12.1 Central elements of culture[5]

- Culture can be ascertained through the presence of *collectivity, communication* and *convention*
- Culture occurs in the interaction between the collective and the individual

- Culture is first of all the usual, the normal, the material, institutional and non-material glue that holds the collective together over time
- Culture is implemented over time
- Culture incorporates both the material and the non-material
- "Culture" is not (or is no longer) to be defined as the antithesis of "nature."

In the following discussion, moreover, the fact that culture encompasses a material, an institutional and also a non-material dimension is of significance. Buildings and monuments are just as much part of culture as traditional festivals or political institutions. And non-material elements too, such as foundation myths, community knowledge, manners of thinking, values or emotions are part of culture. These explanations should be sufficient to describe the conception of culture used herein.

In this context, however, yet another question emerges and deserves a response: Why is it "culture" and not "society" which is at the center of our considerations? Why should a deeper cultural-scientific and not a sociological perspective be demanded? The answer is not easy, especially since both the range of objects and the methods and perspectives of sociology and cultural science are similar in many areas, and overlap. Has the bouquet of social-scientific efforts for sustainability not been sufficient? The answer in this case is: no, an answer based not only on the above stated properties of "culture," for which the concept of "society" does not provide the requisite consistency and coherence, but also on the four deficiencies mentioned at the outset: questions of interculturality and transculturality, the interaction of the individual and the collective, the esthetic and the immaterial, and also the permanence of collectives: these are central issues for cultural science and cultural theory – and marginal ones for sociology.

Without here raising the entire disciplinary discourse of the delimitation between the themselves heterogeneous cultural sciences on the one hand and the social-scientific research tangents on the other, I would like to in addition briefly note three special aspects of cultural science which constitute differences of degree with regard to sociology, since these have proven to be of significance with reference to sustainability debates. The first of these is the in-depth concern with the foreign, i.e. with other cultures, which in turn opens up two essential cosmologies of cognition: (a) the recognition of the foreign, and hence, reflexively along with it, (b) the recognition of the foreign as different, and the deepened appreciation of the own, particularly the implicit own.[6] The second is the consistent orientation of cultural sciences as disciplines which ascertain the objects of their study from the interior, or participants', perspective, and without any inappropriately strict separation of subject and object. This constitutes at least a difference of degree from many sociological research tangents. And third, unlike the concept of "sociology," which focuses strongly on the functional contexts of a collective, the concept of "culture" focuses of the common and that which binds individuals together.[7] Thus, sustainable development can, in the context of the concept of culture, be construed and addressed as our communal and common mission.

Neglected cultural references

In the following, I would like to present and elucidate, if only provisionally, incompletely and by way of example, the cultural references mentioned above, which have been neglected both in German and international sustainability conceptions.

The lack of interculturality and transculturality of sustainability concepts – A lack of sensitivity for other cultures and for one's own

Those sustainability theories and concepts which claim global relevance, and thus expose themselves to the risk that such a claim implies,[8] often leave much to be desired in the area of cultural preconditions and intercultural differences. In the conceptual debates over sustainability, I perceive the following four deficits:

1   Reflection on one's own cultural constitution, and the conditional nature of concepts
2   The ability of theoretical/conceptual considerations to make connections across cultural boundaries
3   Respect for the boundaries of validity, and/or dealing with the claim to global validity of concepts
4   Incorporation of the possibilities and opportunities of other cultural contexts.

Sustainability, as a concept, idea and discourse, originated in a modern world which had been shaped by the West. Certainly, even with a view toward humankind as a whole, it can nonetheless be seen that sustainability is fundamentally a concept which bears a deep cultural imprint: it is "our Western concept." This is especially true for contemporary conceptions from the German or English speaking areas, but it is likewise true of the entire UN-initiated international process of environmental conferences that began during the 1970s, through the emergence of the "environment and development" concept, and all the way to the Declaration of the Earth Summit in 1992 in Rio de Janeiro, and beyond. The problem definitions and deficit analyses – prominent among them the Club of Rome reports (Meadows et al. 1972; Meadows et al. 2004) – were undertaken from a modern, Western, scientific perspective. The entire process of problem definition via the efforts of the United Nations all the way to the concretization and formulation of sustainability concepts (cf. e.g. WCED 1987; German Bundestag 1998; Kopf-müller et al. 2001; Ott/Döring 2004; Ekardt 2005; Grunwald/Kopfmüller 2006; Bread for the World et al. 2008; Vogt 2010) has grown in the soil of the West, and is imbued with Christian/secular values and perspectives. Even the globally communicated concepts and action programs of sustainable development (e.g. Agenda 21, or the Millennium Development Goals), are built on the foundations of Western culture and philosophy (e.g. anthropocentrism, utility, care and precaution, exclusive logic, a specific concept of justice, materialism, and specific conceptions of time in the future). Moreover, "sustainable development" is fed by, and dependent for its implementation upon, scientific knowledge and discovery – itself a success model of the modern West – and is with respect to its realization adapted to and fitted into modern conceptions of society, politics and statecraft; not, however, of culture. And the negotiation, the discussion and the decision-making processes regarding sustainability also occurs in a political space of interests and of power which has been strongly culturally pre-shaped. Even if we conceive sustainability as a counter-model to the excesses of the Western/modern way of dealing with the world and of the manner of living in it, it is impossible to escape the cultural dependence of sustainability concepts.

These culturally marked and pre-shaped concepts of sustainability are now to be propagated and applied worldwide, across cultural boundaries of all kinds – those between national collectives, those between cultural regions, and those between societies characterized and constituted by different religions. This raises at least two questions: first, that as to the validity and/or claim to validity of sustainability concepts in other cultural realms ("universality"); and second that as to the appropriateness of theories and concepts, and/or their abilities to connect with other cultural regions ("contextuality"). It will only be possible to avoid such issues by either completely denying the cultural dependence of constructs and concepts of sustainability, or by declaring them to be normative, and postulating sustainable development in its global implementation as something that *should* be marked by the West. The explication and fixation of such a hegemonic or cultural imperialistic premise would bring forth not only intercultural resentment and incomprehension, but also considerable intrinsically theoretical problems of justification. Moreover, global sustainable development would thereby lose the nourishment potentially provided by other cultural regions, which is needed to make one's respective own cultural background fruitful in view of the looming global questions of the future.

In order to present the cultural character of sustainability conceptions, I have in the following demonstratively overdrawn several key pillars of sustainability in terms of their cultural aspects. For example, the fundamental sustainability concept of "intergenerational justice" presupposes a distinct conception of what generations mean, including that of the sequence of generations and the passing on of assets, values, knowledge etc. However, such conceptions vary greatly between cultures, depending, for example, on whether a culture is marked by a strong sense of other-worldliness, or rather has a greater this-worldly orientation. And the nature of the conception of the other world is of significance for how the question of generations is addressed.

The key concept of "justice" has many different interpretations, even in Western philosophy (including free modern civic society), but these often differ fundamentally in both form and scope from the concepts of justice pertaining in caste societies, theocracies or tribal cultures. For example, justice may *de facto* end at the boundaries of gender, or of ethnic or religious affiliation, or it may extend to non-human life, or be interpreted as in accordance with and/or as an incorporated part of a divine plan.

The "preservation of finite resources," too, or even the material environment generally, only makes sense in the context of a material, this-worldly focus. In a culture which sees the material world and the ego as illusions (e.g. in Hindu-ism, Indian Philosophy), preservation of resources is largely unnecessary. Even such ultimate questions of sustainability as the "concern" of Hans Jonas, or the "unconditional duty for mankind to exist" might be matters which a Hindu or a Buddhist, while not rejecting, might answer completely differently.

Even if these examples are demonstrative, they do allow fundamental prob-lems of the validity and connectability of a culturally characterized concept with the claim to global validity to be identified. This theoretical problem complex attains relevance first of all, too, from global practice, since it is particularly the most heavily populated cultural regions which are less secular and (still) much more strongly characterized by religious concepts than the modern West.[9]

What is to be done? What might help? Talking to one another. The important thing is to strengthen intercultural exchange and the understanding of theories, conceptions and practices of sustainability, especially in the scientific area, and thus to promote an intercultural rationality. Moreover, approaches toward an intercultural ethic (e.g. Rappe 2003; 2005) could be more strongly incorporated into the sustainability debates, and developed further. In my view, it is also vitally important to root the concepts of culture and the cultural sciences as firmly as has already been done with those of "environment," "ecology" or "economy."[10]

That would mean, almost automatically, the establishment of a cognition tool-kit which, with a view of the foreign, would also promote a comprehension and an explication of the (implicit) own – which would also enhance sensitivity for the *intra*cultural preconditions and implications of sustainability theories. These "own" – i.e., Western/modern – basic assumptions of sustainability are hardly ever the object of reflection. One result is that concepts of sustainability are becoming – unchallenged – the vehicles of Western-modern culture, which, in other cultural regions, can lead to irritation, rejection or the failure of interna-tional sustainability efforts. If sustainable development were instead also seen as a process of cognition and of transformation of consciousness, the potential of the concept of culture for promoting self-reflection and self-realization could not be overestimated. In addition, recalling Albert Einstein's wise statement, "No problem can be solved from the same level of consciousness that created it," it may be necessary, when addressing our own fundamental cultural assumptions, to fundamentally re-examine this or that statement regarding sustainability strategy. First of all, in my view, the much-praised strategy of efficiency might be subjected to such a re-examination (cf. e.g. Luks 2010, pp. 155ff). One indication worth mentioning is the "rebound effect," widely seen as something that will just magi-cally occur.

Sustainability as an individual matter, sustainable development as a cultural process, and hence as an interplay between the collective and the individual

Many sustainability concepts and theories (e.g. German Bundestag 1998; Kopf-müller et al. 2001; Ott/Döring 2004; Ekardt 2005; Grunwald/Kopfmüller 2006; Bread for the World et al. 2008; Vogt 2010) are oriented toward large, overall societal, often global contexts, and operate at the level of collectives – for example as proposals for laws, policy regulations, technical developments, economic controls, or social reforms etc. The prospective and significance of the individual, or the individual level, is not elucidated here – or even denied. Sustainability debates which focus on the individual are rare. Those approaches which are to some degree individual-sensitive include particularly those in the areas of education for sustainable development, research into sustainable lifestyles, and trans-disciplinary approaches of "action research." These, however, constitute closed interdisciplinary discourses which hardly penetrate into the theory or concep-tualization of "societal" sustainability at all – indeed, they even lack any point of connection there.[11] By contrast, contemporary cultural theory fundamentally views culture in the context of the collective and the individual. With reference to Hansen (2000), culture is implemented precisely in the interaction of the col-lective and the individual – in processes of enculturation and individualization.

If we lay upon the theories and concepts of sustainability the duty of successful implementation, and if we ultimately seek to arrive at a culture of sustainability, it will not be possible to avoid moving individual aspects into a – second – focus alongside the collective aspect, and especially conceptually linking these two areas more closely.

This will mean, in my view, first of all a multiplication of theoretical efforts for sustainability which will move the individual into the center of scientific atten-tion. Such efforts will, however, run up against boundaries which have less to do with the issue of sustainability than fundamentally with the existing constitution of science, which, with its orientation toward the natural-scientific ideal, neces-sarily systematically overlooks the individual as a solitary and unique being.

Thus, in this context too, the question arises as to the adequate form of sci-ence for sustainable development, as it has elsewhere been raised with regard to the normative content of sustainability and its orientation for action. Transdis-ciplinary approaches – i.e. those which rise above usual science – are therefore necessary, too, for cultural-theoretical reasons.

With a view of the individual, we could for instance ask: What does the idea or the implementation of sustainable development mean for the individual? What role does identification with sustainable development play, and how does it occur? And ultimately: Is it possible for the individual to be *sustainable?* Or, conversely: What role will the individual play in the move toward sustainable development?

Sustainability touches and moves individuals, it affects them very personally, very concretely and causes them to feel affected – either as an idea and a vision, or as victims of non-sustainable development (cf. Ott/Döring 2004, p. 343; Parodi 2010, pp. 110–112). On the other hand, we must assume numerous barriers to the implementation of sustainable development, even at the individual level. Moreover, sustainable development will simply not occur if nobody joins in the effort. A collective, a society is certainly more than the sum of its individuals – it follows different systemic "laws"; but certainly, too, a collective is nothing without its individuals, and it is dependent upon their individuality.

In my view, not only the cultural sciences, but also philosophy and ethics provide productive points of approach for thorough scientific investigation of the individual, for instance through a stronger ethic of the good life, through health research, and especially through psychology. Each of these research tangents provides links to collective occurrences, and is hence directly connectable to cultural-theoretical considerations. A psychology of sustainability yet to be developed may yet provide interesting realizations. Thus, sustainability could be interpreted as a development-psychological stage (in the context of generations), or consumption as compensation for a guilt in which one is ever more deeply stuck (cf. Hauble 2011). And understanding might be gained particularly with regard to the implementation of sustainable development. For example, how are we to deal with a socio-psychological fact that it is often impulse rather than rationalism which provides the motor for social innovation?[12] Hence, one might ask the nasty question: Are not sustainability concepts based on the concept of humankind as *homo oeconomicus* and *animal rationale* and oriented toward the collective level, which thus neglects the individual, not completely faulty designs?

In the cultural perspective, the collective and the individual belong together – to deny or to overemphasize the one or the other, or to view these poles as separate, will lead to an inadequate concept of sustainable development. Hence, a comprehensive cultural theory of sustainable development is still lacking – and needed.

A lack of connection to the esthetic, a lack of esthetics in sustainability

Culture also encompasses the realm of the arts, addresses feelings – including collective feelings – and sensitivities, meaning, signs and purpose, and is concerned with the esthetic. In order to explain the relevance of the esthetic aspects in efforts for sustainability, let me here first of all cite an example that indicates that esthetics, or esthetic sensibilities, can in fact generate an important force in our striving for sustainable development. This is shown by the discussions and conflicts emerging in many areas with regard to plans for the installation of renewable energy technologies. With respect to windmills, solar farms, power lines, storage basins for hydroelectric power plants, or the large-scale cultivation of energy crops, the realization of a regenerative electric power supply is being increasingly called into question, and is often failing due to the esthetic needs of local people.

Esthetics in this sense is neither detached nor a matter merely for the cultivated elite, but rather something very basic that is broadly rooted and capable of sparking vehement reactions. Esthetic discontent juxtaposes itself to the ecological-economic rationality of regenerative energy production – a basic pillar of sustainable development. This was not on the agenda of sustainability theory, so that practice is effectively being stymied by real – esthetic – conditions.[13] Esthetics counts – and it works.

However, the neglect of the esthetic dimension of technology threatens to defeat sustainability projects. In my view, that raises the issue of the need for esthetics in sustainability and sustainability theory even more fundamentally. Sustainability conceptions have hitherto been designed as ethical or quasi-ethical approaches,[14] or as the political, economic etc. concretization of ethics. At issue, however, are the diagnosis of deficits (of resource use, environmental damage, social inequality etc.) and the rules and instruments for overcoming them. Here, sustainability is not, as for example in ancient philosophy, a theory of the good (successful) life designed as a positive life model, but rather, in its postmodern form equipped with a measure of freedom, indicates the "guiderails" for a non-negative life. In my view, such normative designs are certainly necessary, but not sufficient, for the implementation of sustainable development. Rather, the necessary supplement to an ethics of sustainability would have to be an *esthetics of sustainability*.

But why? Here, in light of a persistent gap between knowledge of and action for sustainability – at least two hypotheses could be formulated, which could make "esthetics" fruitful in a double sense: first, in the ancient interpretation of *aisthesis* as "perception," and second, in the modern sense of the "beautiful," a purpose-less beauty sufficient unto itself. Efforts for sustainability – including theoretical-conceptual ones – should also address these two areas.

First, the "beauty" thesis: it is insufficient, in the long run, to attempt to posit a view of a world which is merely useful for human beings, seen through the glasses of sustainability concepts (e.g.: "resources"). Also necessary is a beautiful world worth preserving and passing on, worth creating/re-creating, or just worth living in contentedly (Luks 2010). Landscapes and living things, for example provide not only "ecosystem services," but also useless beauty. Esthetics as opposed to economism!

Moreover, we can ascertain that the sustainability debates, sustainability goals, concepts, visions and approaches are lacking in the beautiful. "Beauty" is quite simply a non-word in sustainability theory; indeed, the terminological universe of sustainability is fairly dismal and ugly – and it has been so since the beginnings of sustainability. The ideas and concepts of sustainable development are based fundamentally on diagnoses and prognoses of scarcity; the very idea of sustainability emerged out of the realization of threatening scarcity. Our resources have been finite and often scarce, be it in the forestry of the eighteenth century (Carl von Carlowitz; see also the chapter by Grober in this volume) or in the world economy of the Club of Rome Report, *The Limits to Growth* (Meadows et al. 1972). A further fundamental, dismal module of the sustainability concept is Concern: Concern regarding the survival of humankind, fear of environmental and social catastrophe, and, in answer to that, an emphasis on the precautionary principle and the ethical impetus of "the unconditional duty for mankind to exist" (Jonas 1985, esp. p. 80). Threatening scarcity, looming catastrophes and possible social, economic and ecological dislocation paint an ugly picture of the future – and, in their ethical version, spawn a universal "thou shalt not," a vinegary, restrictive ethics of bans and austerity. That, too, is not particularly beautiful.

As important as these ethical warning signs and guiderails for non-negative life may be, they are not really worth fighting for – or, if so, only in contrast to a threatening maximum catastrophe. However, for the implementation of sustainable development, particularly in our current, still more or less functional everyday world, we also need life-values, beauty and things worth striving for. We need an add-on to the sour universe of sustainability.

My suggestion is to supplement the ethical push with an esthetic pull, particularly:

- Supplement "should" with "want"
- Supplement "concern" with "joy"
- Supplement "utility" with "useless beauty"
- Supplement "scarcity" with "abundance" (beyond material prosperity)
- Supplement "duty" with "enjoyment."

I believe that we need to strengthen the position of place of the Good Life in the sustainability debate and de-absolutize the concepts of economy and utility; to strengthen eudemonistic values as a supplement to the hitherto overpowering functional ones. It is time to initiate a fundamental philosophical debate on this issue.

I would like to mention once again at this juncture, that culture and cultural issues are often instrumentalized in the sustainability discourse: culture, cultural diversity, identity and lifestyle are important *for* the stability or the survival of societies, or *for* the implementation of sustainable development – so the argument goes – but not *as* the goals of sustainable development. The survival of the human race – not of a humanistic or culturally different type of quality of humanity – is the ecologically overblown primary factor. Essential human qualities such as the capacity for culture or esthetics are thus called into question, as are such essential humanistic achievements as freedom, autonomy or democracy. This is not only not desirable, it is even dangerous: esthetics as opposed to naturalism and ecologism!

And now a brief word on esthetics as it was seen in ancient times, as perception: psychology, education science, cognition theory, biological systems theory, cultural theory etc., all teach this: perception opens and shapes our access to the world, and hence – and that is the decisive factor – our interaction with the world around us.[15]

Even Aristotle made the direct connection between a functioning society, good policy and successful life in the community and an adequately developed perceptive capacity (Aristotle 1996). Moreover, without esthetics, ethics, too, would wither away in the long run. Nothing about this can be found today, either in the political concepts and strategies of sustainability, nor in their fundamental socio-theoretical and ethical works. Even the discourse around education for sustainable development is concerned only marginally with perception and with beauty. Enlightenment through the conveyance of knowledge, a product of classical modernity, has a firm place at the center of the program. Initiatives such as the Tutzingen Manifesto (2011), or approaches toward the formulation of theory at the intersection of esthetics, culture and sustainability (cf. e.g. Kurt 2010) are isolated exceptions.

Friedrich Schiller, himself no opponent of the Enlightenment, radicalized the significance of esthetics and even raised it to the level of an educational program. For him, there was "no other way to make a reasonable being out of a sensuous man than by making him first aesthetic" (Schiller 1794). Although it is not necessary to pursue this program in all its strictness, if we assume sustainability to be something sensible, i.e. a rational intent, Schiller's approach becomes enormously far-reaching. Even without calling upon the ancient philosophers, intricate theories of cognition, or ambitious esthetic programs, it should be a matter of common knowledge today that perception, and the sharpening of perception, are a fundamental and essential factor in the development of such "human" skills as judgment, the ability of critique, or creativity.[16]

In this context, two questions are decisive for the establishment of sustainable development: first, are we according sufficient significance to the perception of oneself and of the world, and to the sharpening of that perception? And second, in view of the fact of a predominant collective non-sustainable dealing with our environment (*Umwelt*), our fellow-world (*Mitwelt*) and our world-to-come (*Nachwelt*), we have to ask ourselves whether our pattern of perception and our pathways to perception fit the goals and demands of sustainable development. Do we need a different, separate and special type of training to sharpen our perception for sustainable development? In view of the fundamental significance of perception for living our lives, these are also fundamental questions of sustainability – which have, however, so far been theoretically neglected.

Both from the realm of perception and from that of beauty, the cry is hence being raised for theory – a "view" – of the esthetic. And returning again to the level of culture (of sustainability), we might say, recalling Kant and Hölderlin: a culture without beauty would be poor and drab. A culture without perception, however, would be dumb, literally blind and deaf, and incapable of maintaining itself. The theories and concepts of sustainability should take that into account.

Of the lack of the non-material in sustainability

Closely connected with the complex of the issues around esthetics, there is a final deficit which can however, in this context, only be alluded to: the lack of the non-material, or more precisely, the lack of reflection upon, of consideration and respect for the non-material dimension in the debates around sustainable development. Non-material aspects, in turn, can be addressed via the cultural perspective, and the non-material and the material can be consistently integrated within it conceptually (cf. Hansen 2000). Both material and non-material aspects are in my view vital for the realization of sustainable development (cf. Duxbury/ Gillette 2007, p. 20). In theoretical conceptualization, this has to date only received marginal attention.

The question immediately arises as to what we should see as the "non-material": mind, spirit, a world spirit, spirituality, "ensoulment"? To anticipate discussion as to a concept of the non-material appropriate to the sustainability discourse, let us first of all refer generally to that realm of the non-material. For that sustainable development which is a global goal and which is being scientifically addressed in sustainability concepts is – primarily – conceived as material sustainable development. Hence, the sustainability debates have been sparked and have unfolded in the context of a materialistic understanding of the world, and have largely remained tied to that understanding. Even today, arguments are based on, and focus largely on, material aspects. Such core concepts as "needs," "resources," "distribution of goods" or "prosperity" have all been materially conceived; even "justice" largely bears a materialist connotation.[17]

The question as to the non-material aspect of sustainability can be focused at two levels: a pragmatic/strategic level and a fundamental level. Strategically, one might ask: Is it enough to address, and to raise the issue of material aspects in order to achieve sustainable development? Here, at least, both advocates of education for sustainable development and environmental psychologists would answer with a clear no, and argue that education and a changed understanding of the environment constitute means for achieving sustainable development. Much further-reaching, however, is the question as to whether the currently manifest situation of material problems in the external sphere – environmental pollution, resource scarcity, national debt etc. – is not also the expression or counterpart of an internal, non-material crisis of humankind, or of collectives and cultures. And this leads directly to the question, possibly fearsome for some people, as to whether sustainable development does not necessarily – or should not – also address the non-material development of people.[18]

Let us for a moment imagine a realized culture of sustainability in a distant future. It must at least be evident that such a culture would have to be the work of other, very different kinds of people, with a changed consciousness and mental attitude. In such a culture, the Western, modern, or globalized *homo oeconomicus* would necessarily yield to a future *homo sustinens* (cf. Siebenhüner 2001).

Justifiably, in the debates around sustainability, voices are increasingly being raised which would like to see greater weight given to immaterial aspects. This is clear in the discussions around "de-growth" or "new prosperity." The goal here is to preserve and increase "satisfaction," "happiness," or "gross domestic happiness." Not only are the material restrictions and global limits to sustainability being programmatically turned around here, but rather, gradually, the potentials of the non-material are moving into our field of vision (cf. Paech 2011). This can indeed be seen as a non-material expansion of the concept of prosperity, of manners of living and of types of economy. The demand here, possibly implicitly, is for an understanding of sustainability expanded to include non-material matters: sustainable development as the material *and the non-material development* of humankind!

The inadequacy of the existing fixation on sustainable-development efforts with regard to material aspects becomes clear in their hitherto unfulfilled demand for Sufficiency. Unlike the two other major sustainable-development strategies pursued, efficiency and consistency, sufficiency refers directly to human behavior, habits and attitudes. Sufficiency as mere austerity, as only a Less, on the other hand, provides no attractive strategy for the materially oriented, egocentric *homo oeconomicus*; indeed, it fundamentally questions his legitimacy. Accordingly unpopular and unsuccessful have been all demands and attempts to date for more Sufficiency. Sufficiency can only gain attractiveness in the context of a non-materially expanded sustainability if the material Less is accompanied by an immaterial More: more quality-of-life, more joy, more happiness etc.

Final remarks

The above points indicate several vulnerabilities in today's scientific, theoretical/conceptual discourse around sustainability which, in my view, should be further cultivated. A deeper incorporation of cultural-theoretical and cultural-scientific approaches and perspectives could lead to a more comprehensive and successful view of sustainability and could move efforts for sustainable development a major step forward.

With the reinforced incorporation of the individual, the beautiful and useless, the non-material, and of the human being generally as a cultural being, the debates about sustainability would be rendered quite a bit more human. The scientific reflection and conception would approach that which was once formulated as the political guiding idea, the First Principle, twenty years ago at the 1992 UN Summit in Rio: "Human beings are at the center of concerns for sustainable development" (UNEP 2011). In the scientific investigation, attention would be diverted away from the ecological footprint and its economic relevance, and directed toward those beings and their relationships which have made these footprints. The cultural/theoretical further development of sustainability concepts would then be followed by a process of cognition which would extend from the realization of external material deficits toward a "know-thyself" of the human collective and of the individual.

With the turn toward a cultural concept, that dominant "culture of exclusion" (Shiva 2011) which continually emphasizes the delimitation from the other – collectives, people, individuals, species etc., which brings forth the egoist as the adamant prototype of this fencing-off and fencing-in process, and which, building upon that prototype, depends upon competition as the only successful strategy – would be contrasted to an emphasis on the common and on the community – with other species, individuals, people, collectives etc. Cooperation as a life strategy would be enhanced.

The conceptions of sustainable development would move into the limelight as relevant counter-concepts to the dominant, modern, globalized anti-culture of today's lifestyle and mode of economics (cf. Parodi 2011). Sustainable development would be placed on the agenda as a global task of the commonality of all people, as a project and as the realization of one humankind.

Notes

1　Albeit not yet effective, either as a scientific economic concept, or as a paradigm.
2　Albeit within the framework of a socio-scientific conception of culture, under which it often functions as a sociological residual category.
3　This is, for example, suggested by the possibility of controlling culture, and externally (systemically/technocratically) controlling collectives, for instance in order to achieve ecological sustainability. Ultimately, human beings and their lifestyles are thus turned into instruments.
4　Marginal note: Although Hansen did not mean it in this way, this definition of the term culture permits the expansion of the definition of "culture" to both human and non-human life. Even animal collectives could, to a certain degree, be seen as possessing collectivity, communication and convention, and hence culture. Such a definition of culture would even make a cultural-theoretically based concept of culture theoretically conceivable; it would thus transcend the species boundary and the isolation of anthropocentrism. Assuming an expanding "moral circle" (cf. Gorke 2000, esp. p. 86; Parodi 2008, pp. 288–291), such a sustainability concept would itself be future-capable, and might outlive the purely anthropocentric concept.
5　This preempts any possibly looming accusation of culturalism, and hence the accusation of a perspective neglect of the embedding of human life processes in ecosystemic and natural past worlds and environments (that "cultural and linguistic turn" is not to be carried out here as a total turnaround).
6　E.g. of the "normal," the pre-conscious or unconscious, unchallenged preconditions, agreements, values.
7　Here, please refer to Tönnies's (1922) distinction between *Gemeinschaft* (community) and *Gesellschaft* (society) – even if today, that *Gesellschaft* may constitute the determining factor of modern collectives.
8　Fundamentally, what is at issue is often even humankind itself, or its future (e.g.: anthropocentric + intergenerative + global = humankind).
9　Even if these concepts have, in other cultural regions, often been removed from their direct religious contexts, they still continue to operate in their respective cultures. Even our long since largely secularized West betrays the deep-seated traces of the Christian religion(s).
10　Without a doubt, there are many concrete international projects in the area of "sustainable development" which centrally and successfully take cultural and intercultural aspects into account. However, what is still too much lacking, in my view, is a reflection about cultural and intercultural aspects at the level of theoretical and conceptual debate around sustainability.
11　How separate these realms of discourse are, and how insignificant the individual aspect often appears in social-scientific designs, is shown, for example, in the article "Wider die Privatisierung der Nachhaltigkeit" (Against the privatization of sustainability; Grunwald 2010), and the discussions it sparked.
12　Contemporary indications of that are provided, for example, by the decision by the German government under Angela Merkel to phase out the use of nuclear energy after the Fukushima catastrophe; or the legal, institutional and military measures taken by the United States after the 9/11 attacks.
13　Esthetics is indeed touched upon by way of the factor of "acceptance" – e.g. of technologies or projects – but is then no longer raised as an issue.

14 Even if sustainability conceptions stem from different disciplinary backgrounds, e.g. social-scientific, socio-ecological, economic or legal, they are nonetheless similar, particularly in their normative content, and their striving for a non-negative future life for people, in their scientific rationality, and in their orientation toward practice and life, to the approaches of applied ethics.

15 The fact that perception involves not only a receptive but also an active aspect can also be seen in the use of the German word *Wahrnehmung*, from *wahrnehmen*, to perceive, but literally "to take as true," which is used not only as a passive act of reception, of sensual perception, but also as an active deed, e.g. when it means "to perform (a duty)"; there, its meaning is broader than that of the English word "perform," embodying, too, a sense of recognition of responsibility and then of actively carrying it out. Thus those "perceptions" become a fact, an object of reality.

16 "Before a person begins to think in words and categories, he perceives his environment by way of his physical senses. He literally 'grasps' and 'comprehends' [from *prehendere*, 'to grasp'] his environment, and thus takes possession of it. . . . However, the senses require stimulus and practice to prevent them from withering. . . . For this purpose, a sensual-esthetic upbringing is necessary. Perception is a holistic and active process; sense and rationality cannot be delinked – they constitute a unity" (Zimmer 2000, pp. 19–20).

17 Here, too, there are debates which are less materially focused, e.g. regarding human rights or religiously/theologically motivated sustainability approaches. However, they hardly ever connect with scientifically characterized concepts.

18 Cf. here e.g. Orr 2002, or, in greater detail, Kurt 2010.

Bibliography

Agenda Transfer (2003). *Die Kunst der Zukunftsfähigkeit. Ansätze, Beispiele, Hintergründe, Erfahrungen*. Bonn.

Aristotle (1996). Books 7–8: The Ideal State. In: *The Politics and the Constitution of Athens* (trans.: Jonathan Barnes). Cambridge, England.

Banse, G., Nelson, G., Parodi, O. (eds.) (2011). *Sustainable Development – The Cultural Perspective. Concepts – Aspects – Examples*. Berlin.

Bread for the World; Friends of the Earth Germany; Church Development Service (2008). *Sustainable Germany in a Globalized World*. Basle.

Culture 21 (2011). *Agenda 21 for Culture*. Accessed via: http://agenda21culture.net/ (Dec. 9, 2011).

DUK (German UNESCO Commission) (2007). *Cultural Diversity – Our Common Wealth*. Bonn.

German Bundestag (1998). *The Concept of Sustainability*. Final report of the Commission of Enquiry on Protection of Humankind and the Environment of the 13th German Bundestag. Bonn.

Duxbury, N., Gillette, E. (2007). *Culture as a Key Dimension of Sustainability. Exploring Concepts, Themes and Models*. Accessed via: www.cultureandcommunities.ca/down loads/WP1-Culture-Sustainability.pdf (Dec. 9, 2011).

Ekardt, F. (2005). *Das Prinzip Nachhaltigkeit. Generationengerechtigkeit und globale Gerechtigkeit*. München.

Gorke, M. (2000). Die ethische Dimension des Artensterbens. In: Ott, K., Gorke, M. (eds.). *Spektrum der Umweltethik*. Marburg, 81–99.

Grober, U. (2010). *Die Entdeckung der Nachhaltigkeit. Kulturgeschichte eines Begriffs*. München.

Grunwald, A. (2010). Wider die Privatisierung der Nachhaltigkeit. Warum ökologisch korrekter Konsum die Umwelt nicht retten kann. In: *GAIA*. No. 3/2010. 178–182.

Grunwald, A., Kopfmüller, J. (2006). *Nachhaltigkeit*. Frankfurt.

Hansen, K. P. (2000). *Kultur und Kulturwissenschaft*. 2nd revised edition. Stuttgart.

Hansen, K. P. (2011). *Kultur und Kulturwissenschaft*. 4th completely revised edition. Stuttgart.

Haubl, R. (2011). *Mut zur Angst. Auf dem Weg zu einer Psychologie der Nachhaltigkeit*. Presentation at the conference "Befreien & Befrieden – Erkundungen zu einer Psychologie der Nachhaltigkeit," Tutzing Protestant Academy, February 18, 2011.

Hauser, R., Banse, G. (2010). Kultur und Kulturalität. Annäherungen an ein vielschichtiges Konzept. In: Parodi, O., Banse, G., Schaffer, A. (eds.). *Wechselspiele: Kultur und Nachhaltigkeit. Annäherungen an ein Spannungsfeld*. Berlin, 21–42.

Holz, V., Stoltenberg, U. (2011). Mit dem kulturellen Blick auf den Weg zu einer nachhaltigen Entwicklung. In: Sorgo, G. (ed.). *Die unsichtbare Dimension. Bildung für nachhaltige Entwicklung im kulturellen Prozess*. Wien.

Jonas, H. (1985). *The Imperative of Responsibility: In Search of an Ethics for the Technological Age*. Chicago.

Kopfmüller, J., Brandl, V., Jörissen, J., Paetau, M., Banse, G., Coenen, R., Grunwald, A. (2001). *Nachhaltige Entwicklung integrativ betrachtet. Konstitutive Elemente, Regeln, Indikatoren*. Berlin.

Krainer, L., Trattnigg, R. (eds.) (2007). *Kulturelle Nachhaltigkeit. Konzepte, Perspektiven, Positionen*. München.

Kurt, H. (2002). Nachhaltigkeit – Eine Herausforderung an die Kunst? In: *Kulturpolitische Mitteilungen* No. 97, 46–49.

Kurt, H. (2010). *Wachsen! Über das Geistige in der Nachhaltigkeit*. Stuttgart.

Luks, F. (2010). *Endlich im Endlichen. Warum die Rettung der Welt Ironie und Großzügigkeit erfordert*. Marburg.

Meadows, D. H., Meadows, D. L., Randers, J., Behrens, W. W. (1972/1979): *The Limits to Growth: A Report for the Club of Rome's Project on the Predicament of Mankind*. London.

Meadows, D. H., Randers, J., Meadows, D. (2004). *Limits to Growth: The 30-Year Update*. New York.

Orr, D. W. (2002). Four Challenges of Sustainability. In: *Conservation Biology*, Vol. 16, No. 6, 1457–1460.

Ott, K., Döring, R. (2004). *Theorie und Praxis starker Nachhaltigkeit*. Marburg: Metropolis.

Paech, N. (2011). *Nachhaltiges Wirtschaften jenseits von Innovationsorientierung und Wachstum. Eine unternehmensbezogene Transformationstheorie*. Marburg.

Parodi, O. (2008). *Technik am Fluss. Philosophische und kulturwissenschaftliche Betrachtungen zum Wasserbau als kulturelle Unternehmung*. München.

Parodi, O. (2010). Drei Schritte in Richtung einer Kultur der Nachhaltigkeit. In: Parodi, O., Banse, G., Schaffer, A. (eds.). *Wechselspiele: Kultur und Nachhaltigkeit. Annäherungen an ein Spannungsfeld*. Berlin, 97–115.

Parodi, O. (2011). Personal Sustainability – Including Body and Soul: The Karlsruhe School of Sustainability. In: Banse, G., Nelson, G., Parodi, O. (eds.). *Sustainable Development – The Cultural Perspective. Concepts – Aspects – Examples*. Berlin.

Parodi, O., Banse, G., Schaffer, A. (eds.) (2010). *Wechselspiele: Kultur und Nachhaltigkeit. Annäherungen an ein Spannungsfeld*. Berlin.

Rappe, G. (2003). *Interkulturelle Ethik*. Vol. I. Berlin.

Rappe, G. (2005). *Interkulturelle Ethik*. Vol. II. Berlin.

Scherhorn, G. (2003). *Nachhaltiger Konsum – Auf dem Weg zur gesellschaftlichen Verankerung*. München.

Schiller, F. (1794). *Letters upon the Aesthetic Education of Man*, 23rd Letter. Original in Rittelmeyer, C. (2005). *Über die ästhetische Erziehung des Menschen. Eine Einführung in Friedrich Schillers pädagogische Anthropologie*. München. English: http://www.fordham. edu/halsall/mod/schiller-education.asp

Shiva, V. (2011). *Sustainability, Earth Centered and Women Centered Approach*. Presentation to the Congress "Rio+20 – local sustainability!" December 8, 2011, Hanover.

Siebenhüner, B. (2001). *Homo sustinens. Auf dem Weg zu einem Menschenbild der Nachhaltigkeit*. Marburg.

Stoltenberg, U. (2010). Kultur als Dimension eines Bildungskonzepts für eine nachhaltige Entwicklung. In: Parodi, O., Banse, G., Schaffer, A. (eds.). *Wechselspiele: Kultur und Nachhaltigkeit*. Berlin, 293–311.

Tönnies, F. (1922). *Gemeinschaft und Gesellschaft. Grundbegriffe der reinen Soziologie*. 4th/5th ed. Berlin.

Tutzingen Manifesto (2011). *Tutzingen Manifesto – To Strengthen the Cultural-Aesthetic Dimension of Sustainable Development*. Accessed via: www.kupoge.de/ifk/tutzinger-manifest/tuma_gb.html (Dec. 9, 2011)

UNEP (2011). *Rio Declaration on Environment and Development*. Adopted at the conclusion of the Conference of June 3–14, 1992, in Rio de Janeiro. Accessed via: www.unep. org/documents.multilingual/default.asp?documentid=78&articleid=1163

Vogt, M. (2010). *Prinzip Nachhaltigkeit. Ein Entwurf aus theologisch-ethischer Perspektive*. München.

WCED (World Commission on Environment and Development) (1987). *Our Common Future* ("Brundtland Commission Report"). Oxford.

Zimmer, R. (2000). *Handbuch der Sinneswahrnehmung. Grundlagen einer ganzheitlichen Erziehung*. 8th ed. Freiburg i. B.

13 Ten theses on a research agenda for sustainable development

Hans Diefenbacher

The role of science

Over the course of the past forty years or so, a number of the most important ecological problems have become known, and have increasingly become the objects of research. These include the excessive use of non-renewable resources and the destruction of important natural spaces, which is in turn leading to a reduction in biodiversity. Our realization of the effects of anthropogenic climate change likewise dates back more than two decades. A group of researchers around Johan Rockström in 2009 identified eight so-called planetary boundaries, at least four of which have already been crossed (Rockström 2009). At the same time, the fact is scientifically well-documented that the speed of change in government and society is still not enough to attain the goal of sustainability under any circumstances. A research agenda with the goal of promoting sustainable development would therefore have to include a critical self-examination – indeed, it would perhaps use such a self-examination as point of departure for its research efforts, asking such questions as: What exactly is the contribution that science can make? And: What degree of "certainty" must scientific statements have before they can become the guidelines for action in the area of sustainable development?

On the relationship between sufficiency and efficiency

At the beginning of the twenty-first century, people's everyday lives, especially in the highly developed industrialized countries, are, on average, very far removed from the models of sustainable development that have been advanced, and from the "visions of a good life" which derive from them. So deeply accustomed are we to the banality of non-sustainability that the suggestion that we address models of sufficiency – a standard scientific term – is generally perceived as a provocation or an irritating imposition. Particularly politicians tend to view such suggestions as an immediate threat to their political careers, for they seem hardly able to imagine achieving political success on the basis of a program calling for limiting growth. But in the scientific community too, research in or conscious limitation of production and consumption has more or less been put on hold. However, this question is one that sustainability research should specifically concentrate on, since gains in efficiency will probably in many cases be used up by rebound effects; so that that alone will not achieve the goal of sustainability. It would hence be worthwhile to reverse the priorities, asking not: What must yet be achieved through sufficiency after all efficiency-raising potentials have been exhausted? but rather: What reduction potentials might exist in an "economy of sufficiency," and after they have been realized, what will the remaining "efficiency gap" be?

Frontrunner and latecomers

Knowledge about ecological contexts, about the network of relationships between ecology and economy, is limited to a very small part of the elite of society. This small group is engaged in an intensive exchange among its members, is refining its knowledge, and is working on in some cases very impressive practical pilot projects. It sometimes seems, however, that this minority is increasingly moving away from the majority of the population; the gap between ecologically oriented, post-materialistic consumers and the other "consumer milieus" in German society is growing. It is too little known how a low-threshold entry into a lifestyle oriented toward the models of sustainability might be accomplished, so as not to be frozen at the level of symbolic actions, such as waste separation, but rather to guide people to a further-reaching change in their everyday consumer habits. The easy-to-achieve goals alone will simply not suffice in the long run to organize a highly developed industrial society for the goal of sustainability.

On the role of government and "windows of opportunity"

In order to support the development process addressed above, that towards an "economy of sufficiency," from the point of view of the actions of consumers, deep-seated changes in the policy framework of an eco-social market economy will very probably be required. Politicians and democratic societies whose ability to formulate policy depends in the medium term on being reelected, only dare to initiate such changes if they can be sure that the large majority of the population will support them. This can lead to a kind of imprisonment dilemma, as a result of which politicians choose ostensibly safe options, which are however often not particularly future-oriented, and have very little innovation potential; at the same time, they trust in various kinds of quantitative economic growth to soften the blow of distribution problems. A discourse about these contexts has hardly ever been carried out between the political sphere and the public; it is thus up to the scientific community to provide impulses for it to be initiated in the first place. With the Fukushima disaster in the summer of 2011, German society experienced the power of a critical political constellation to emerge and to make very far-reaching changes politically possible – in that case, the decision to terminate the German nuclear power program. However, windows of opportunity of this type seem to be fairly rare, and can evidently close again very quickly. A scientific community dedicated to implementing models of sustainability should increasingly examine the question of how societal processes of learning can be reinforced without having to depend on the occurrence of mid-level catastrophes.

Images of the "good life"

The conclusion is that the political sphere needs civil society in order to initiate change, and civil society needs the political sphere in order to not constantly be getting into situations in which ecologically oriented behavior becomes non-viable from a business point of view, or is even punished in various ways: by extreme high prices, poor quality, or stigmatization of various kinds, especially with such pejoratives as "joy-killing," "backward," "unsophisticated," etc. The question at hand is how positive models of sufficiency can even be transmitted at all: how the world of tomorrow might be qualitatively "better," and what a different quality of life might look like. Points of departure for that might be such studies as, recently, that of the Wuppertal Institute on a "sustainable Germany" (Wuppertal Institute for Climate, Environment, Energy 2008). The model of "hospitality for all" points to the demand for intragenerational and intergenerational justice; "ecological prosperity" refers to the urgently necessary expansion of the concept of prosperity beyond its material components; while "the entire economy" calls for taking into account even those aspects of value creation, such as work in the home and volunteer work, which are not mediated via the market, and are carried out beyond the purview of the money economy. From these models, it will be necessary to develop a narrative capable of connecting with the concrete everyday reality of people today – the people that these models will have to reach. Even that segment of the sustainability research community which sees itself as transdisciplinary has to date seldom dedicated itself to this task; it has some urgent catching up to do.

The dominance of GDP

A society that wishes to change in the direction of the model of sustainability will need measurement systems to show whether it is moving towards that goal or not. However, a large number of alternative policy concepts for transforming society only marginally – if at all – involve the aspect of alternative monitoring systems or measurement procedures. Especially those approaches which seek to stimulate growth by means of modern environmental technology[1] continue to use traditional macro-economic indicators as the measure of their success – primarily the gross domestic product (GDP), and secondarily, the number of jobs created through the traditional form of the commercial economy. What this boils down to is not any alternative concept of prosperity, but rather the launching of the next growth cycle, with the newest generation of technology – "green" technology. Other policy concepts do concede that it is a problem that such great importance is placed on the GDP. They even recite the basic points of criticism against the GDP and the

National Accounting System (NAS) more or less explicitly – compilations which, lest we forget, have been state-of-the-art in economic literature for some thirty-five years now![2] Unfortunately, those who level such critiques do not operationalize them in their own approaches toward the development of alternatives.

Alternative monitoring and measurement concepts

There are number of different paths one can take to avoid the constriction of using merely the GDP and other traditional indicators as measures of success. One of them involves conceiving an additional system of indicators, which then exist alongside the traditional indicators of prosperity measurement, as a supplement, without being tied to them. I would like to mention two representative examples of the many such approaches:

- an indicator system for the progress reports of the German sustainability strategy (Statistisches Bundesamt 2010), and
- the Prosperity Quartet of the group around Meinhard Miegel (Denkwerk Zukunft 2010).

The second possible path for setting a counterpoint to the GDP as a measure of prosperity is the approach of developing a composite index to aggregate the single bits of information of an indicator system with varying measurement dimensions to a single measurement figure. Here too, I would like to mention two different approaches, which can be seen as representative of a variety of basic types of this procedure:

- the Human Development Index (HDI) (United Nations Development Programme 2011), and
- the Gross National Happiness Product (GNH) of Bhutan (The Centre for Bhutan Studies 2011).

The third basic type of alternative prosperity measurement can be classified under the accounting approach; here, prosperity calculations are carried out in the form of an accounting procedure oriented toward the NAS. Here, the methodological problem of "composite indicators" is avoided by calculating the separate variables in a single dimension from the outset. Here too, I would like to mention two examples:

- the National Welfare Index (NWI) (Diefenbacher et al. 2012), which is considered a further development of such precursors as the ISEW and the GPI, and, like the GDP, is expressed in monetary units, and
- the "ecological footprint" (Global Footprint Network 2011), in which the compilation of various variables is accomplished by conversion to "hectares-of-land" equivalents.

The existing alternative monitoring and measurement systems can thus be broken down into various basic types, each of which includes different problem constellations of a methodological nature. After decades in which the issue of alternative modern monitoring and measurement systems has been relegated to the margins of scientific discourse, it has only in recent years begun to attract broad interest in the scientific community, from policy-makers and in the general public. This shows that the establishment of a certain alternative would at the same time involve the achievement of interpretive hegemony as to what constitutes "success" – a realization which has itself been broadly recognized, and has led to an extraordinary vitalization of a kind of "scientific revolution" in the form of the emergence of numerous new approaches. It is now important that we succeed in sorting out these alternative approaches, and narrowing them down to one or a few consensually established alternatives, which could then face off with the GDP on a "level playing field." This seems to be a key task facing sustainability research in the coming period.

Ecological maintainability and compromise of interests

In a publication by the German Institute of the Protestant Research Community (Fest), a group of authors of the Institute sought to ascertain the quintessence of an indicator-based analysis of the development in Germany from the perspective of sustainability.

> If the path of the transformation of society toward sustainability is to be trodden, the one thing we cannot do is nothing. The process of the economic system cannot simply continue as it has. It has been demonstrated sufficiently often that a policy of *laissez-faire* will cause our natural assets to be used up too fast and the environment to be too greatly burdened, since future generations are unable to articulate their needs on today's markets. Moreover, the separation between financial markets and the real economy has the effect that income and wealth distribution is becoming ever more unequal, so that opportunities within the currently living generation are also being ever more unequally distributed.
>
> It is just as certain that a policy of sustainability means to search the difficult path of a compromise of interests – not, however, by way of the primacy of the market, but rather within a framework not dictated by economics. A compromise of interests must stay within the bounds of the carrying capacity of the earth, and must also secure the rights of people to participation. Ecological, economic or social goals cannot be maximized within the framework of such a policy; what is always necessary is the "right balance."
>
> (Diefenbacher et al. 2011)

Hence, sustainability research always also has the task of including a view of the political implementation of its goals within the overall concept of transformation.

Policy fields of sustainable development

The above study has identified the following areas as indispensable policy fields for the transformation of society toward sustainable development (ibid., p. 163):

- a thorough-going ecological/social reform of the tax system
- the establishment of a consistent resource management system
- the introduction of a reliable, unconditional basic income system
- a massive expansion of training and further education possibilities
- a considerable expansion of local and regional economic circuits
- an expansion of ecologically oriented development contexts, in order to meet the requirements of global responsibility
- regulation and limitation of the influence of global financial markets
- a reform of societal reporting systems, as mentioned above; and
- the establishment and reinforcement of forms of democratic participation by the people in decision-making processes.

Sustainability research in the coming period will have to make intensive efforts to analyze in detail interactions and synergy effects between these fields of policy, as well as the possibilities for operationalizing them.

Sustainability in teaching

Sustainability research in Germany has not become sufficiently established in university instruction. In standard courses of study in the area of business and economics, certain courses do address some aspects of the topic, but they frequently do so purely within the framework of the discipline, and moreover concentrate on aspects of environmental economics; also, these are usually advanced courses. However, the issue of sustainability in an interdisciplinary or even transdisciplinary perspective has yet to be adopted into the established curricula, with the exception of a few universities and technical colleges which offer bachelor's or master's programs specializing in sustainability. At least two changes would appear necessary:

- The basic concepts of sustainability should become mandatory as part of the basic curriculum in standard economics study programs – that means in the first semesters. Otherwise, the study of sustainability would for many students first of all involve a phase of "unlearning" other previously taught information.
- Careers in universities and technical colleges should be supported – rather than as is currently and increasingly the case, hindered by interdisciplinary or transdisciplinary work. For this, a change in the evaluation of scientific work in the procedure for occupying tenured professorships is urgently necessary, as is a reorientation of research support in favor of interdisciplinary and transdisciplinary approaches.

194   *Hans Diefenbacher*

Notes

1 The following sections are taken from a not yet published paper prepared for an experts' workshop held in Berlin on June 21, 2011, in the context of the research project "outline of an ecologically sustainable concept of prosperity as the basis for environmental policy innovation and transformation processes."
2 For a detailed presentation, cf. e.g. Leipert 1975 or Rubik 1985; see Diefenbacher 2001.

Bibliography

Denkwerk, Zukunft (ed.) (2010). *Das Wohlstandsquartett – Zur Messung des Wohlstands in Deutschland und anderen früh industrialisierten Ländern*. Bonn: self-published. Accessed via: www.denkwerkzukunft.de/downloads/WQ-Memo-2010.pdf

Diefenbacher, Hans (2001). *Gerechtigkeit und Nachhaltigkeit – Zum Verhältnis von Ethik und Ökonomie*. Darmstadt: Wiss. Buchgesellschaft.

Diefenbacher, Hans, Foltin, Oliver, Held, Benjamin, Rodenhäuser, Dorothee, Schweizer, Rike, Teichert, Volker, Wachowiak, Marta (2011). *Richtung Nachhaltigkeit – Indikatoren, Ziele und Empfehlungen für Deutschland*. Heidelberg: FEST

Diefenbacher, Hans, Held, Benjamin, Rodenhäuser, Dorothee, Zieschank, Roland (2012). *NWI 2.0 – Weiterentwicklung und Aktualisierung des Nationalen Wohlfahrtsindex*. Heidelberg/Berlin: FEST/FFU. Accessed via: www.umweltbundesamt.de/uba-info-medien/mysql_medien.php?anfrage=Kennummer&Suchwort=3902

Global Footprint Network (ed.) (2011). *Footprint Science – Introduction*. Accessed via: www.footprintnetwork.org/en/index.php/GFN/page/footprint_science_introduction/

Leipert, Christian (1975). *Unzulänglichkeiten des Sozialprodukts in seiner Eigenschaft als Wohlfahrtsmaß*. Tübingen: J.C.B. Mohr.

Röckstrom, Johan et al. (2009). A Safe Operating Space for Humanity. In: *Nature*, vol. 461 (September), 472–475.

Rubik, Frieder (1985). Das Bruttosozialprodukt als Indikator für Lebensqualität? Kritik und Alternativen. In: Projektgruppe Ökologische Wirtschaft (ed.). *Arbeiten im Einklang mit der Natur*. Freiburg: Dreisam-Verlag, 145–176.

Statistisches Bundesamt (ed.) (2010). *Nachhaltige Entwicklung in Deutschland – Indikatorenbericht 2010*. Wiesbaden: Self-published. Accessed via: www.bundesregierung.de/nsc_true/Webs/Breg/nachhaltigkeit/Content/__Anlagen/2010-11-03-indikatorenbericht-2010,property=publicationFile.pdf/2010-11-03-indikatorenbericht-2010

The Centre for Bhutan Studies (ed.) (2011). *Gross National Happiness*. Accessed via: www.grossnationalhappiness.com/

United Nations Development Programme (ed.) (2011). *Human Development Reports 1990–2010*. Accessed via: http://hdr.undp.org/en/

Wuppertal Institute for Climate, Environment, Energy (2009). *Zukunftsfähiges Deutschland in einer globalisierten Welt – Ein Anstoß zur gesellschaftlichen Debatte*. Bonn: Federal Agency for Civic Education, vol. 755.

Contributor biographies

Hans Diefenbacher is a Professor of economics at the Alfred-Weber-Institute of the University of Heidelberg and deputy director of the Protestant Institute for Interdisciplinary Research in Heidelberg, Germany.

Felix Ekardt is a Professor of environmental law and legal philosophy at the University of Rostock, Germany. He is also Director of the Research Unit Sustainability and Climate Policy in Leipzig and a long-term fellow at the Research Institute for Philosophy Hanover, Germany.

Judith C. Enders has been a member of the study group "Global Issues" of the German Council on Foreign Relations (DGAP) since 2002. In the past she has carried out research at Rutgers University, Germany, and for the German Advisory Council on Global Change, the German Bundestag and the Institute for Advanced Sustainability Studies.

Ulrich Grober is a publicist, broadcaster and journalist, whose work covers cultural history, future visions and sustainability. He studied German and English Literature at the Universities of Frankfurt and Bochum.

Armin Grunwald is Professor of philosophy and ethics of technology at the Karlsruhe Institute of Technology, Germany, where he is also director of the Institute for Technology Assessment and Systems Analysis (ITAS).

Thomas Jahn is spokesperson of the executive board and co-founder of ISOE – Institute for Social-Ecological Research, Germany. He is also spokesperson of the Project Area F "Knowledge transfer & social-ecological dimensions" at the Biodiversity and Climate Research Centre BiK-F, Germany.

Jürgen Kopfmüller is a senior scientist at the Institute for Technology Assessment and Systems Analysis (ITAS) within the Karlsruhe Institute of Technology, Germany, where he is head of the research area "Sustainable Development and Environment."

Reinhard Loske is Professor of politics, sustainability and transformation dynamics at Witten/Herdecke University, Germany, and Senior Associate Fellow at the German Council on Foreign Relations. He was a long-standing MP in the

German Bundestag and Minister for Environment and European Affairs in the Free Hanseatic City of Bremen.

Fred Luks is head of the Competence Center for Sustainability at the Vienna University of Economics and Business, Austria. He has been working on sustainability issues in different positions in research, teaching and management.

Konrad Ott is a Professor of philosophy and ethics of the environment at Kiel University, Germany. His current research interests are climate ethics, nuclear waste deposal, energy policies and ethical foundations of nature conservation.

Oliver Parodi is a researcher at the Institute for Technology Assessment and Systems Analysis (ITAS) and the administrative manager of the Research Centre "Humans and Technology" at the Karlsruhe Institute of Technology, Germany. He is currently head of the Karlsruhe School of Sustainability and project leader of "District Future – Urban Lab."

Moritz Remig is a researcher on economic and sustainable development at the Institute for Advanced Sustainability Studies in Potsdam, Germany. He is currently studying for his PhD in ecological economics at the University of Kassel, Germany.

Joachim H. Spangenberg is an economist at the Helmholtz Centre for Environment Research, Germany. He researches ecosystem analysis and the valuation of ecosystem services.

Jörg Chet Tremmel is a Professor of intergenerationally just policies at the Eberhard Karls University Tübingen, Germany. His background is in philosophy, political science and economics, and he has studied at numerous institutions in Germany and the UK.

Michael Weingarten is a Lecturer in Philosophy at the Universities of Stuttgart and Marburg, Germany. His main interests include political and social philosophy, dialectics and social geography.

Rafael Ziegler is Deputy Professor of environmental ethics at Greifswald University, Germany. He founded the social-ecological research platform GETIDOS (Getting things done sustainably) with a specific focus on social entrepreneurship in the water sector.

Index

Note: Page numbers in *italics* indicate illustrations.